Published in cooperation with the
Hoover Institution,
Stanford University, Stanford, California

The UNITED STATES and BRAZIL

Limits of Influence

ROBERT WESSON

Studies of Influence in International Relations
Alvin Z. Rubinstein, General Editor

PRAEGER

PRAEGER SPECIAL STUDIES • PRAEGER SCIENTIFIC

Library of Congress Cataloging in Publication Data

Wesson, Robert G
    The United States and Brazil.

    (Studies of influence in international relations)
    Bibliography: p.
    Includes index.
    1. United States—Foreign relations—Brazil.
2. Brazil—Foreign relations—United States.
I. Title. II. Series.
E183.8.B7W47   327.7308   80-27514
ISBN 0-03-049106-1
ISBN 0-03-049111-8 (pbk.)

Published in 1981 by Praeger Publishers
CBS Educational and Professional Publishing
A Division of CBS, Inc.
521 Fifth Avenue, New York, New York 10175 U.S.A.

© Praeger Publishers, 1981

123456789 038 987654321
Printed in the United States of America

EDITOR'S PREFACE

This volume inaugurates the policy-oriented series *Studies of Influence in International Relations*. The series will illuminate as precisely as possible the actual relationship between a superpower and a putative Third World client-state; the phenomenon of influence as it materializes in the concrete and changing issues that are at the heart of government-to-government interactions; the reasons and the means whereby the powerful seek to affect the behavior and attitudes of the weak; and the great paradox of the second half of the twentieth century, namely, the great difficulty encountered by the powerful in imposing their preferences (short of the outright use of force) on the weak, the vulnerable, the dependent—in a word, the limited ability of a superpower to exercise influence at a time when it possesses awesome military and economic power. Indeed, so complex has the relationship become between major powers and lesser powers that the question of who influences whom on what issues, and why, goes to the heart of understanding the operation of the international system.

The U.S.-Brazilian influence relationship is a fitting beginning for an analysis of complex and changing nation-state relationships. For more than 100 years, the United States was the dominant power in the Western Hemisphere. It developed a cohesive political system and the sinews of industrial and military power before any Latin American country, and that brought disproportionate influence. Robert Wesson examines in this volume the heyday of U.S. authority and its discernible erosion in the late 1960s. He traces the evolution of U.S.-Brazilian ties and the unexpected directions that military, economic, political, and cultural relationships took in the late 1960s and the 1970s. With a knowledge based on extensive research and professional experience in Brazil, he shows how internal forces and attitudes altered the country's foreign policy and, inevitably, ties with, and the influence of, the United States. The discussion of the military's central role is especially germane and informed. For two countries that have enjoyed generally good relations, despite the dramatically troubled years of the Carter presidency, the agenda of difficulties affecting their relationship has been extensive: the multinational corporations and investment policy; Communism, Cuba, Angola, and the Soviet invasion of Afghanistan; the New International Economic Order and clashes in international organizations between the developed and developing countries; nuclear power; human rights; divergent conceptions of

v

hemispheric solidarity; and disagreements on Middle East issues as an adjunct of differing approaches to energy problems.

Brazil is a huge, booming, abundantly endowed country (except, so far, for fossil fuels). The world's second largest exporter of food, it has already emerged as an agricultural superpower, and its potential in this crucial sphere is still enormous, giving it a potential trump that may yet enable Brazil to play the oil game successfully. Possessed of a rapidly growing, young, vigorous, very much future-oriented population, the world's fifth largest nation is intent on achieving full superpower status by the end of the century. The era when Brazil was internationally passive and satisfied to follow in America's wake is over. The mood now is one of determination to plot an independent course in hemispheric and world affairs, with or without U.S. cooperation. The United States and Brazil have arrived at a watershed in their history, and this significant bilateral relationship is the focus of this study.

ALVIN A. RUBINSTEIN

PREFACE

It is the essence of diplomacy and the interactions of sovereign states that some seek to induce others to pursue or desist from certain courses of action, to join agreements, make concessions, or otherwise subordinate their policies. That is, states seek in a multitude of ways to exert influence; and most discussion of international affairs may be interpreted as a commentary on the influence of some states on others, through diplomatic, economic, or sometimes military means.

Yet, while much has been written about power and exercises of influence, there has been little effort to analyze the influence itself. The work of Alvin Z. Rubinstein in this regard has pioneered in a nearly virgin field. There has been little study of how and why one power may or may not be prepared to accede to the desires of another, or why efforts to exert influence have varying results. Possibly the political, economic, and cultural factors relevant to diplomatic or political results are excessively complicated, yet it seems necessary to confront them.

The character of relations between two powers may be extremely varied, from the antagonistic semiequal standoff of the United States and the Soviet Union to the close dependence of Mongolia on the Soviets or the strong but more distant dependence of South Korea on the United States, or from the friendly cooperation of allies such as Britain and the United States to the distant relations of the Soviet Union courting a Third World power such as Sri Lanka. Among the large number of such relationships, however, that between Brazil and the United States especially invites examination for several reasons. One is the intrinsic importance of Brazil, which may well be a major power in the next generation. Another is Brazil's representativeness of the Third World. If Brazil can find a way to a satisfactory future, very likely many or most of the poorer majority of mankind will do likewise; if Brazil cannot, the outlook is bleak.

Moreover, U.S. influence on Brazil has operated in relatively simple conditions, uncomplicated by more or less extraneous quarrels. There have been no important conflicts of interest, no common borders to cause friction, and little power rivalry. Strategic and economic interests of the two have dovetailed as well as might be expected of independent powers. Brazilian anti-Americanism, unlike that of Mexico or Colombia, lacks roots in a major grievance. Yet Brazil has been big and strong enough to have a will of its own.

The study of U.S. influence on Brazil is broadly instructive concerning relations of the United States with Latin America in general. This region was long considered a sphere of influence of the United States, over which it seemed at times practically sovereign; although spheres of influence (except the Soviet) have become blurred nowadays, Latin America remains an area of special and complex problems for the United States. It has also been an area of failure in the past two decades, as the kind of government favored by the United States has lost out in many countries and the prodemocratic tide of the first half of this century has been reversed, especially in the more advanced countries of the extreme south—Chile, Uruguay, and Argentina. What once was something like hegemony has melted away, and anti-Americanism has been nourished by social discontents and economic frustrations.

It must be hoped that the United States can find its way to a more mature relationship with Brazil and Latin America, in the framework of which the Latins can achieve more effective, better political and economic structures, and fuller nationhood. In some ways, Latin America is the most promising sector of the Third World. Almost all of it became independent over a century and a half ago, far ahead of nearly all states of Africa and southern Asia. Most Latin American states (like Brazil) are relatively well-endowed by nature, and culturally they are relatively close to Europe and the United States. Yet political and economic development have been mostly disappointing.

For relevance to modern problems, this volume concentrates on the recent period. It summarizes the development of the close relationships between the United States and Brazil, and their fraying in the 1950s and early 1960s. The military coup, or revolution, of 1964 must be considered not only because it set the scene for subsequent relations but because the United States has been given considerable credit for it. Most attention, however, goes to relations between the United States and the post-1964 military-dominated government. For a few years after 1964, Brazil was exceptionally favorable to U.S. policy; since 1967 it has increasingly gone its own way, although usually in a friendly spirit. Two major controversies have arisen, over Brazilian nuclear energy plans and over human rights, and these are treated in some detail. It seems necessary, however, to give separate attention to economic influence, trade matters, and the role of U.S. investment in Brazil, which is regarded as a form of control by Brazilian critics of U.S. policy. Something should also be said of the more subtle and diffuse influence of the United States and its culture, the most important manifestation of which is the prestige in Brazil of the democratic model and the widespread, although not unanimous feeling that government should rest in freely contested elections. Influence in this regard does not directly shape the policies but the character of the government.

Influence is like a whip that is most successful if it does not have to be applied, and it is most satisfactory if desired results can be secured without positive action.[1] The U.S. government engaged political and economic resources most amply toward determining events in Brazil in 1963 and early 1964 when fears of unpleasant developments were highest. For the period 1964 to 1967, when the Brazilian government faithfully aligned itself with that of the United States, there is not much to report; Washington felt little need to push or pull. Both sides assumed that their aims coincided, and it was easy to come to understandings without a sense of compulsion. The question of influence, or lack of it, came to the fore when the United States objected to Brazilian policies and the Brazilian government modified them or, usually, declined to change its course.

Thus, this study covers Brazil's growth into much more independent nationhood and the somewhat laggard American adaptation to the growing self-will of a once rather dependent ally. It may give some ideas how influence can be exerted by the United States, or how it may be useful to refrain from attempting to exert influence in the short run in hopes of securing solid relations in the long run. It should tell something of the problems of good order in a world where the poorer and weaker powers far outnumber the richer and stronger, and where many nations, like Brazil, aspire to feel themselves masters in their own house and equals on the world stage.

NOTE

1. As observed by J. David Singer, "Inter-Nation Influence: A Formal Model," *American Political Science Review* 57 (June 1963):21.

CONTENTS

————————Introduction:
THE MEANING AND ASSESSMENT
OF INFLUENCE

Influence is the successful use of power, and power is to international relations what energy is to physics, or money to the economy—the mediator of interactions. It is the political expression of the state; hence actors on the world stage are called powers, from super to mini. Intuitively it seems fairly evident what national power and influence are by analogy with interpersonal relations; no analysis is required to show the office boy that the boss is more powerful and exerts more influence. Yet political writers have been unable to agree on an adequate definition of power, and it is even more difficult to form useful estimates of how much a nation may possess and how much can be usefully applied, that is, utilized as influence in a given situation. Statements about military capacity (itself hard to estimate), national wealth, industrial capacity, and mobilizable manpower give only a vague idea as to the likelihood that the views or wishes of a given state are likely to prevail in conflict with those of other states. Data regarding material resources must be supplemented by considerations of quality of leadership and national will, and a hundred other imponderables may intervene between desire and outcome. No one would have contended that the Vietnamese Communist state was stronger than France in the 1950s or than the United States in 1965–73, yet both France and the United States withdrew, their purposes militarily frustrated.

Military power is decisive when called into play, but it rests to a large extent on economic power, which is continuously operative. Economic power may be largely divorced from military power; the ability of the oil-rich nations to work their will in the financial world is striking. There is also cultural power; at least there has been much impassioned denunciation of "cultural imperialism."

1

Power is a strictly relative commodity; one state is powerful only in relation to weaker or stronger states. Influence derives from inequality of power; it implies not exchange but compulsion, not quid pro quo but more quid for less quo. It is ordinarily undesirable to be influenced, as this represents some loss of autonomy, the ultimate of which is slavery. If two states are equal, neither influences the other in a political way (although they may copy styles from each other) except by way of mutual restraint or mutual support. For example, a militarily stronger state may expect more or less deference in strategic matters from weaker states. The economically more powerful states to some extent make the rules of the economic world through their control of markets and credits. The technologically weaker nation is dependent upon and influenced by the more advanced nation, while if two nations are approximately equal overall in technology, there will probably be flows—influence—in both directions because of inequality in different areas.

We consequently think in terms of U.S. influence over Brazil rather than the reverse because of the large superiority of the former by most measures. Although the two countries are of approximately the same area, the population of the United States is nearly double that of Brazil; more important, the U.S. GNP is about 10 times that of Brazil. U.S.-Brazilian trade is only 2 percent of U.S. total foreign trade, but 20 percent of that of Brazil. Brazilian investment in the United States is trivial; that of the United States dominates leading sectors of Brazilian industry. Brazilian movies rarely appear on U.S. screens, while U.S. movies outnumber and outdraw Brazilian movies several times over in Brazil. The whole atmosphere of relations between the two countries is conditioned by the fact that one looms so much larger in the eyes of the other. It would not appear that Brazilians have thought of halting a drift to irrational politics in the United States or trying to curb the production of nuclear weaponry. It should be noted nonetheless that this asymmetry has diminished markedly over the past 30 years, especially in the last 15 years, as the U.S. share in the world economy has shrunk while the Brazilian share has expanded. Brazil is no inconsiderable power. It has the largest economy of the Third World and is, after the United States, the second largest exporter of agricultural products. It is a proud nation that looks confidently to playing a larger role on the stage of the future.

Whatever the superiority of U.S. resources, it is an error to assume that this country can readily influence Brazilian conduct on any issue of importance to Brazil, as will become apparent in the course of this volume. Influence is at best limited and qualified. Military power is hardly applicable, barring some extreme turn of events. It has never been applied to U.S.-Brazilian relations (although there were contingency plans for helping one side if the coup of 1964 had turned into civil war), partly because of lack of will to take drastic measures against anything less than a clear-cut threat to national security. No matter what the strategic superiority of the United States, Brazilians know that they are in no danger of being destroyed by a peeved American administration. Even a threatening demonstration of naval vessels would be counterproductive, and the Brazilians are aware of this; anti-Americans would be charmed by such a show of bad temper. U.S. economic leverage is inhibited partly because U.S. assets under Brazilian jurisdiction far exceed Brazilian assets under U.S. jurisdiction, and Brazil owes American institutions huge amounts of money, which might be lost if Brazil were led to conclude that the trade and goodwill of the United States were valueless.

Influence of a foreign power rests to a large extent on parties or groups sympathetic to it. In accordance with this principle, the Soviet Union goes to great lengths to support Communist parties everywhere possible, sacrificing much goodwill for the sake of allies within the gates; and where the Communist party is strong, the Soviet state has powerful leverage, as in Italy and France, despite the anti-Communism of the rulers. If the United States had an influence in connection with the Brazilian army's taking power in 1964 and holding it thereafter, this was because powerful Brazilians saw their interests parallel to those of the United States. If support for human rights had some success in 1977–78, this was because many Brazilians shared the concerns of the American administration.

Moreover, influence flows not only from the stronger to the weaker but in the reverse direction. The mere fact that the nation to be influenced compels the influencer to expend resources represents a sort of influence, like the physical law of the equality of action and reaction. Parents have all the advantages of strength and resources, yet their ability to manipulate their offspring is very limited, and they may at times feel that they are more servants than masters. Something of this relationship has developed in recent years between the wealthier industrial countries and the developing nations of the Third World, whose poverty has become a claim for special treatment and economic assistance, or "reparations," as some demand. Wealth in this respect has ceased to be a means of power and become the basis of obligations toward the needier. Any economic bargaining between the United States and Brazil is a little weighted in favor of the latter by the assumption that the United States has a duty to assist its poorer neighbors. For example, as a developing country, Brazil feels entitled to ask for free access to the U.S. market while maintaining high barriers around its own market.

The bargaining position of the weaker power is also likely to be reinforced by the fact that it is strongly, perhaps passionately, concerned with issues that are of secondary importance for the greater power. Brazil has thus prevailed in several minor confrontations with the United States, such as the extension of the Brazilian territorial waters to 200 miles. Few Americans except shrimp fishers had heard of the issue, and the State Department was not prepared to take a strong line lest the fabric of U.S.-Brazilian relations be damaged over a minor matter for the United States. Usually the United States, a very pluralistic state, has lacked overriding interests in dealing with Brazil, and has consequently pressed few policies very strongly. For example, while U.S. shoe manufacturers have wanted to restrict imports of Brazilian shoes, they have not been able to secure the wholehearted backing of an administration also concerned with American exports, fighting inflation, helping the consumer, and securing Brazilian goodwill.

The United States is likely to have strong feelings about Brazilian affairs only if there is a major security issue. Thus in the 1940s, Washington was much alarmed that the Axis powers might leap the Atlantic to gain a hemispheric bridgehead in Brazil's Northeast bulge and was prepared to act vigorously to preempt the threat. Likewise in 1963–64, the American administration had visions of a radical, perhaps Castro-like movement seizing power in Brazil, and more attention was devoted to that country than before or since, although there was not a great deal effectively to do about it. Rather commonly in the past weak allies have more or less manipulated the United States because of desire for their strategic cooperation; even such dependent clients as South Korea and Nationalist China could extract much from U.S. concern that they remain dedicated to anti-Communism,[1] and the United States was very sensitive to the wants of the South Vietnamese government as long as its cooperation was wanted in the war fought primarily for the survival of an independent South Vietnam. It is conceivable that the U.S. might at some future time become very attentive to Brazilian needs if it appeared that a hostile party was about to come to power and present a major threat to hemispheric security. Yet the feebler ally cannot really lead or pressure, only plead, or better, take advantage of the concerns of the superior partner.

The inequality of capacities is basic; the very existence, or awareness of the existence of potentially overwhelming power is one form of influence. The United States has loomed overshadowingly in this hemisphere and to some extent still does, despite the substantial recession of its dominance. Latin Americans expect the United States to be influential, attribute influence to it, and credit it with far more of a role in shaping events than it has actually exercised. Latin American actions are necessarily circumscribed by fears or expectations of U.S. reactions, even though the United States may neither threaten nor promise. Any group contemplating a new policy in areas of interest to the United States will have an eye on the possible U.S. response. The political Left, in particular, has been inclined to attribute very large and often subtle powers to the leader of the "capitalist-imperialist" world, frequently crediting the CIA with capabilities that agency would dearly like to possess. The Left—and many nationalists—have also tended to equate the obvious presence of U.S.-owned corporate interests with the power of intervention of the U.S. government and to perceive a subservience of Brazilian to U.S. capitalistic interests. Negative feelings toward the stronger power thus lead radicals and nationalists to downgrade the capacities and autonomy of their own country. The relationship of inequality, moreover, has indirect, intangible long-term effects on the outlook and psychology, ultimately the politics of the weaker, judgment of which must remain intuitive.

Such diffuse influence, the generalized presence of power in various aspects, merges into a second category, the shaping of international rules and expectations, in various ways channeling the behavior of weaker members of the system. Thus Brazil has adapted itself fairly well to the world political lineup much shaped by U.S. policy after World War II, although since 1968 Brazil has reacted less to U.S. desires than to changes in the American world outlook from cold war to détente and deideologization. The prevalent postwar world economic order has been largely of U.S. making (although it has been breaking down since the early 1970s); and Brazil has adhered, more or less, to the rules set by the United States and U.S.-dominated agencies such as the World Bank and the International Monetary Fund (IMF). It should be noted, however, that the economic system largely built up by U.S. efforts was determined more by general principles than special interests; and it has not operated particularly to the benefit of the United States. This country's share of world production and trade has declined steadily over the past 35 years and in toto drastically, while the shares of Japan and West Germany, which were entirely impotent in originally shaping the structures, have grown magnificently. Brazil also has done well under the rules more or less written by the United States, at least in terms of overall growth of the national product.

A third aspect of influence, the clearest and most obvious, is direct and intentional modification of the behavior of the other power. For example, in the late 1960s, the United States pressed the Brazilian government to curtail exports of instant coffee. More importantly, in 1977 the Carter administration undertook to persuade the Brazilian government to end the arbitrary arrest and torture of political opponents and also to renounce its plans for setting up a complete nuclear cycle, including reprocessing of spent fuel, with the assistance of German technology. In the first of the latter two instances, there may have been effective influence, inasmuch as rights violations have been curbed, although Brazilian authorities would certainly not admit that they have yielded in any way to the desires of the U.S. government. In the second, the arm-twisting seems to have been counterproductive, having only strengthened nationalistic determination to proceed with the program. If influence is the ability to determine outcomes, in this case it was negative. This may almost be a rule; if the United States pushes for a certain policy, Brazilians infer that this policy is beneficial for the United States, hence supposedly contrary to the interests of Brazil. Moreover, influence in one case does not guarantee influence in another. The contrary may occur. Influence can be consumed; those who yield in one case may feel freer to resist in another.

A fourth broad category of influence, less tangible and more difficult to estimate, is the penetration of the society of the weaker state. This is the kind of influence held by the Soviet Union through Communist parties affiliated with Moscow, bringing Soviet ideas and policies into trade unions, electoral policies, the press, and so forth in such countries as France and Italy. It is also the kind of influence exercised by American religious missionaries and educators abroad in a less politically directed way. There are many official, semiofficial, private, commercial, and noncommercial American organizations in Brazil, with various purposes and programs, mostly (it may be assumed) favorable to fundamental U.S. purposes if not to the policies of the administration.

More importantly, U.S. corporations operating in Brazil, frequently in partnership with Brazilian interests, produce a substantial proportion of the industrial output of that country. They certainly affect the values and policies of the host country, intentionally or unintentionally, although their influence is impossible to disentangle and much less than it would be if they were as crafty and purposeful as many Brazilians believe. They may sway affairs in many modes: personal contacts with political, economic, and opinion leaders, through the need of the press for their advertising, through support for various causes, and so forth. It may also be possible for the United States to indirectly control outcomes by shifting power within the penetrated state. It is widely believed in Brazil that the United States has strengthened sectors of society favorable to its own ends, especially business ("bourgeois") groups and military elites, while weakening organizations of the urban and rural masses lest these acquire the ability to oppose U.S. political and economic interests. Another form of penetration is cultural. Brazilian life has always been impregnated with imported ideas and styles, which since World War II have come predominantly from the United States. Fondness for blue jeans, American soft drinks, jazz, and the like certainly has large although nebulous effects. In the opinion of many Brazilian intellectuals, the United States is mostly responsible for the atmosphere of consumerism fostered by both U.S. cultural exports and corporations. This is less significant, however, than the predilection for constitutional forms and the legitimization of government by free elections, for which the United States may accept or claim large responsibility.

The United States, in other words, has been a teacher, usually unintentionally and often contrary to the desires of the United States as a state, that is, the purposes of Washington. This aspect of influence is of less interest to decision makers than their ability to secure an immediate result by approaching the Brazilian government; and here we devote most space to policy-oriented matters. However, it is worth noting that the government, concerned less with a slowly formed atmosphere and long-term receptivity than with the problems of the day, tends to neglect the former. The Soviet Union is more purposeful in this regard, working constantly to build attitudes favorable to its system and to undermine its opponents. The United States invests little attention or resources in promoting the ideas and images favorable to itself and its spirit, although it has been much more effective as teacher than captain.

Influence may also be categorized according to who exerts it. Government officials form the top level of influence-wielders, from the president, the secretary of state, and ambassadors down through all those who deal with the foreign state. They all supposedly work together for common purposes decided by the president with his advisers; in practice, they are often somewhat at odds in their differing interpretations of their duty. For example, military attachés in Brasília have seemed to be pulling in a different direction from the representatives of the State Department. But for the most part, and certainly in regard to essentials, the agents of the U.S. government speak in harmonious tones. Frequently allied to them are the spokesmen of various international financial agencies, not only because of the U.S. share in their directorship but also because their interest in the open and stable international order coincides with that of the United States.

Business leaders, primarily of corporations, working in Brazil comprise another category of influence-wielders. Their purposes are their own profit, but they share with the U.S. government an interest in a legal, stable Brazilian state hospitable to foreign, particularly U.S., enterprises and favorable to maximum participation in the world economy. If they encounter difficulties, they may call upon their government for support; and the American embassy tries to assist them in many small ways—as all governments seek to help their business interests abroad. The very large corporations especially consult and collaborate with official agencies, the Departments of State and Commerce, perhaps the CIA and others, for mutual benefit; but for the most part they carry on their business, making drugs or tires, without much consideration for policies of Washington.

How far the U.S. government acts for corporate interests is a highly controversial question.

A third category of carriers of influence includes persons not associated with official policies even to the extent of the multinational corporations. They are the tourists, journalists, academics, writers, artists, and the like, whose voices are not at all attuned to the needs of the government. For example, countless Americans, newspaper writers, religious figures, and sundry intellectuals condemned human rights violations in Brazil for many years; their feelings were echoed in Congress, but the administration only wanted the issue to go away. Often, of course, unofficial America has spoken quite at odds with both official America and U.S. corporate interests. American intellectuals, for example, have given much nourishment to dependency theory, whereby Latin America's woes are laid to political and/or economic domination by the United States. Most of the factual material for anti-U.S. writing is supplied by Americans. It may be assumed that the unofficial representatives of the United States abroad mostly win respect or friendly feelings for it, but this is by no means certain; not infrequently Americans abroad are irritating or patronizing.

Influence may be further categorized according to the means employed, from military force to political or economic pressure to gentle suasion and indirect persuasion. Some means are, of course, considered more morally acceptable or legitimate than others. In the modern world, there has been a generally growing distaste for military action or threats, inherently unsuitable for a highly civilized society and a potential danger for all in the nuclear age; and an intervention such as landing Marines in the Dominican Republic in 1965 was probably counterproductive. But the continuing applicability of force in international affairs has been demonstrated by wars in Africa and South Asia, the Vietnamese occupation of Cambodia, and the Soviet occupation of Afghanistan. There has been a considerable effort, especially on the part of Third World nations, to repudiate all forms of intervention, especially by the United States, as a violation of sovereignty. Even expressions of concern for violations of human rights in Brazil, Argentina, and other nations have been seen as undue interference. Similarly, the United States has been widely blamed for contributing to the troubles and downfall of the Allende government in Chile (1970-73) by declining to furnish or support loans to it as well as by more direct intervention in Chilean politics. So far as force or the threat or fear of force disappears between two nations, their relations tend to become disaggregated into what has been called "complex interdependence."[2]

Although they are not much afraid of a military attack, Latin American countries have been inclined to interpret U.S. actions rather sensitively, partly because of the imbalance of power; and Brazil has been no exception. For example, in 1961 President Jânio Quadros was angered by the U.S. ambassador's request for Brazilian support for anti-Cuban measures, an American exhortation to fiscal restraint, and criticism of his government by a retired former U.S. ambassador,[3] all of which were quite legitimate by conventional standards. Quadros no doubt resented the implied rebuke for his friendliness toward Cuba and the calling of attention to Brazilian financial difficulties, about which he could do little. The American consultations, advice, and criticism were probably counterproductive, in effect, negative influence.

This raises the question of how influence is to be assessed.[4] The most convincing way is to find instances in which the conduct of one side has corresponded not to its own interests or inclinations but to those of the other, especially concessions made by one to the other without due compensation, or inhibitions on the conduct of one side in compliance with the wishes of the other. Public statements often indicate deference, implying at least potential influence. The analyst may also look to declarations of participants in policymaking or others with insights into events. However, these must be evaluated critically. Political leaders may overestimate the factor with which they are most familiar, that is, their own role. For example, it is possible that Henry Kissinger has given himself undue credit for the overthrow of the Marxist government of Salvador Allende to the neglect of factors outside his control or perhaps knowledge. On the other hand, Lincoln Gordon, ambassador to Brazil at the time of the 1964 coup, may have been at pains to play down his own role where awareness of his intervention (if it was important) would tend to defeat his objectives.

A major problem in the estimation of influence is that the less conspicuous it is, the more likely to be influential. Open and overt influence is quite generally resented in a world in which states are supposed to be morally as well as legally equal. It is humiliating to appear to be doing something because of the wishes of the stranger; influence implies inferiority, which is not cheerfully accepted. Relations of marked unequals are seldom very easy and always susceptible to misinterpretations. This is true not only in the political but the economic sphere. It is sin enough on the part of the multinational corporations that they are large, rich, conspicuous, and alien, making and doing things in Brazil that Brazilians feel they should be able to make or do for themselves. The immediate explanation for the role of the foreigners is that they are powerful and ruthless and are backed by a great power. Hence in the economic realm as well as the political the fundamental relationship between the United States and Brazil has been practically by definition imperialism. Brazilian writers, even those friendly to the United States, ordinarily use that term.

Relations of the United States with Brazil, however, have been less distorted than those with other Latin American countries. Brazil derives some self-confidence because of its sheer size. It has been obvious for many generations that Brazil is potentially a giant among nations, and Brazil has not felt so threatened by U.S. power as its smaller neighbors. The saying "God is a Brazilian" is more of a genuine conviction than a joke; and if God is with them, the Brazilians can relax.

NOTES

1. Robert Keohane, "The Big Influence of Small Allies," *Foreign Policy*, no. 2 (1971):161–82.

2. Robert O. Keohane and Joseph S. Nye, *Power and Interdependence: World Politics in Transition* (Boston: Little, Brown, 1977), p. 99.

3. Álvaro Valle, *As novas estructuras políticas do Brasil* (Rio de Janeiro: Nordica, 1977), p. 217.

4. Several criteria for measurement of influence are suggested by Alvin Z. Rubinstein, "Introduction," in *Soviet and Chinese Influence in the Third World*, ed. Alvin Z. Rubinstein (New York: Praeger, 1975), pp. 11–12.

1
TRADITIONAL FRIENDSHIP

SPECIAL RELATIONSHIP

In a world where powers find countless differences, hardly any two major states have seen such generally smooth relations over a long period as the giants of North and South America, which have never seriously quarreled during the entire period of their existence. Their association has occasionally been ruffled, but they have usually assumed that they had much in common; and they have long felt, as they feel today, that they have more to gain from harmony than enmity. Some causes of their friendship have remained constant, especially the fact that each has been inclined to respect the continental weight of the other. An enduring factor has also been Brazilian receptivity toward the United States because of some sense of antagonism toward or at least differences with South America, especially the traditional rival, Argentina. The fact that Argentina emerged in the first decades of this century as the leading critic of the United States in South America and rival for leadership in Latin America was reason enough for Brazil to assume a pro-U.S. stance. The United States for its part has always respected Brazil for its size—respect at times lacking for smaller Spanish American countries—while Brazil has never felt really threatened by the United States and has regarded itself as entitled to preferential treatment over its neighbors. Contrariwise, the abatement of Argentine-Brazilian rivalry in the past decade has been accompanied by more independent attitudes of Brazil toward the United States.

The beginnings of U.S.-Brazilian relations were auspicious. The United States welcomed the transfer to Brazil of the Portuguese court fleeing Napoleon's armies in 1808, and in 1824 became the first state to recognize Brazilian independence. At this time Brazil was the only Latin American country to welcome the Monroe Doctrine, intended for the protection of all the independent countries of the hemisphere. Several times up to the First World War Brazil endorsed applications of that doctrine, although Spanish America has generally been skeptical to hostile.

The United States was quite well disposed toward the Brazilian empire, although some ardent republicans felt that its monarchy was contrary to the principles of the New World. There were a few minor misunderstandings during the nineteenth century, perhaps the most serious arising from Brazilian fears that the interest of some Americans in the Amazon area was a threat to their sovereignty of that huge unsettled area,[1] a reflection of a sensitivity that is still much alive, as shown by suspicious reactions to the Jari project of D. Ludwig. Meanwhile, commerical relations slowly grew; from the middle of the nineteenth century, the United States has always been the largest buyer of Brazilian coffee. However, through the decades of the empire, up to 1889, the United States gave rather little attention to Brazil. The British, who ferried the Portuguese court to Brazil in 1808, were the most important foreign influence for over a century. In 1810 Britain, having dominated the foreign trade of the colony since the latter part of the eighteenth century, secured a favorable trade treaty, and through the nineteenth century supplied Brazil with most of its manufactured needs. British capital was more dominant than American was ever to become, and Brazilian irritation with British investors was like recent resentment of multinational corporations. One cause of friction with Britain, which was greater than ever with the United States, was the British role in securing (in 1828) the independence of Uruguay on territory that Brazilians thought ought to be theirs. Another was the British role in forcibly ending the slave trade, in part by invading Brazilian territorial waters and rivers—an interference in pursuit of humanitarian goals parallel to the American advocacy of human rights but far more violent and provocative. Culturally, the Brazilian upper classes looked to France. But Britain was, like the United States in later times, the foreign power most admired and against which there were the most complaints.

While Britain was the model for the parliamentary monarchy of the Brazilian empire, the republicans always looked to the United States. Even before independence they had done so; an uprising headed by the Brazilian national hero, Tiradentes, in 1788 sought to establish a republic on the U.S. model. In the latter part of the nineteenth century, the feeling grew that the Brazilian monarchy was out of place in the New World, and in 1889 the emperor was deposed in the name of freedom by a military coup. Early in 1890, the United States became the first power to recognize the new republic; and the country gave itself a federal constitution following that of the United States even more closely than the constitutions of other Latin American nations.

With the fundamental difference of political institutions swept away (and slavery abolished in Brazil in 1888), relations between the United States and Brazil became and long remained notably cordial. On several occasions, the United States supported the young republic in its dealings with its neighbors, and Brazil returned the favor. Notably, it stood by the United States in the confrontation that nearly led to war between the United States and Chile in 1892. There was then what there has sometimes seemed to be in recent years, an unwritten understanding of Brazilian subleadership in South America (recently called "subimperialism"): in return for Brazilian deference and support, the United States assisted Brazil against Spanish South America.

Brazilian-American friendship was most promoted by Foreign Minister Baron of Rio Branco (1902-12). Rio Branco made this "special relationship" the keystone of his foreign policy, not because he was especially enamored of the United States but because he wished to offset British domination and he needed U.S. support in border controversies and in rivalry in the Plate region. Brazil in this period applauded U.S. gunboat diplomacy in the Caribbean and opposed the Argentine Drago Doctrine of nonintervention. However, Rio Branco wanted to multilateralize the Monroe Doctrine in order to preempt unilateral U.S. intervention.

In the first part of this century, Brazil was the only close friend of the United States in Latin America. U.S.-Brazilian commerce reached a high point in 1904, when the United States took 50 percent of Brazilian exports. In the same year, Brazil was the first (and long the only) South American country to exchange ambassadors (instead of the ministers formerly sent to the less important countries) with the United States.[2] Brazil was several times helpful to American diplomacy, as in the quarrel with Mexico in 1914. In 1917, when the United States went to war against Germany, Brazil followed, the only Latin American country to do so. The decade after the war was uneventful and almost untroubled, with friendship supported by growing prosperity and trade.

ALLIANCE

For Brazil, as for most countries, the 1930s were a time of political upheaval, economic strain, ideological politics, and foreign entanglements. Brazil came under a semidictatorship, flirted briefly with Nazi Germany, and then became the only real wartime ally of the United

States in Latin America. It thereby laid the foundations for close economic and political involvement with the United States in the postwar period.

The old order in Brazil, dominated by the oligarchies of the several states with their own armies, came to an end in 1930, when a disappointed contender in the presidential elections, Getúlio Vargas, raised the standard of revolt. Partly because of weariness with the corrupt system, partly because of economic discontent, the armed forces rallied to Vargas against the state of São Paulo, and Vargas became an extraconstitutional president. The Paulistas tried to reassert their leadership in 1932 but were again defeated. Since then, no state has been able to stand against federal forces. One of the major achievements of Vargas, who governed for 19 years, was the forging of a centralized state and the fortification of Brazilian nationalism.

Questions arising from the collapse of international trade and debt default caused irritation in the early 1930s, but Franklin Roosevelt opened a new era of inter-American relations with his Good Neighbor Policy and the end of U.S. military intervention in the Caribbean. Brazil was the first nation to enter a Reciprocal Trade Agreement (1935) in accordance with Roosevelt's program of chipping at tariff walls through reciprocal concessions and Most Favored Nation conventions. U.S.-Brazilian commerce prospered, and a few American firms dominated the market for coffee, Brazil's dominant export. Brazil was the more inclined to seek U.S. backing because of the Chaco War between Paraguay and Bolivia (1932–35) and because Argentina was building up military forces beyond obvious defensive needs.

From the mid-1930s, however, Nazi Germany, hopeful of finding a ideological partner in the authoritarian Vargas regime, moved energetically to penetrate the Brazilian economy. The United States wanted to promote trade on an open market basis and was rightly apprehensive of the political connotations of the Nazi trade offensive; however, it did little to assist imports from Brazil to offset the U.S. export surplus. The Brazilians were hospitable to German overtures because they wanted both to get rid of hard-to-sell coffee, cacao, cotton, and the like, and to reduce dependence on the United States, which seemed on the way to replacing Britain in domination of the Brazilian economy. Nazi Germany, on the other hand, wanted to procure raw materials, agricultural and mineral, and to bind Brazil to itself through government-controlled trade; for this purpose it was prepared to take Brazilian surpluses on blocked accounts and to offer German goods very cheaply in return. Although the Brazilians partly deferred to U.S. economic philosophy because they saw the need for U.S. capital, they were much tempted by the German compensation agreements. The German share of Brazilian foreign trade rose rapidly from 14 percent in 1935 to 25 percent in 1938, in that year slightly surpassing the 24 percent of the United States. In 1938, moreover, Brazil purchased large quantities of arms from Germany. In 1937 Vargas had proposed military cooperation with the United States, offering the use of a base in Brazil in return for the arming of Brazilian forces; but the United States was not yet sufficiently concerned with Nazi expansionism to be much interested.

The efforts of the Vargas government to play the United States and Germany against one another and the German economic offensive were cut off in September 1939 by the war and the Allied blockade. But Brazil also represented an ideological-political problem. On November 10, 1937, Vargas preempted presidential elections by a coup and established an outright dictatorship, in more or less fascist style, the "New State" (Estado Novo). He suspended the Congress, which did not meet again until after World War II, dissolved state assemblies, and gave himself power to intervene in states and to decree laws. The worldwide prestige of fascism was high, and Vargas was more or less inspired by the examples of Hitler, Mussolini, and Salazar, the Portuguese dictator. He was also under some pressure from a Brazilian hypernationalist or fascist movement, the green-shirted followers of Plínio Salgado, the "Integralistas." Vargas gave Salgado to understand that he would incorporate Integralista ideas in the New State and perhaps join the Nazi-led Anti-Comintern Pact.

Vargas, however, was no Hitler. He neither established a totalitarian party nor adopted any particular ideology; and he assured the United States that the old friendship was unchanged, even that Brazil would continue a "very liberal policy with respect to foreign capital."[3] Most Brazilians accepted the New State as the alternative to disorder, as did the United States, which saw Vargas as a modernizer and unifier of Brazil; good relations with Brazil were the cornerstcne of the Good Neighbor Policy. Moreover, Argentine anti-Americanism made it more necessary to remain on good terms with Brazil (although in mid-1937 the United States in deference to Argentine feelings halted the sale of several destroyers to Brazil, thereby offending the Brazilians; military leaders saw this as a breach of the old U.S.-Brazilian understanding).

The U.S. press, however, sounded the alarm over fascism in Brazil. Vargas derided liberalism and praised fascist virtues and leaders; although nominally in favor of democracy, he equated democracy with disorder. Many officers, especially in the navy, were Integralista sympathizers and they even attempted a coup in May 1938. The armed forces, by default of the United States, obtained German arms; and Rio became a German propaganda and espionage center. Vargas' inner circle was divided. Some, notably Minister of Justice Francisco Campos (who was to play a role in the military regime of 1964) wanted to cooperate closely with Germany and to set up the mainstays of a fascist state, including a mass party. On the other side, Oswaldo Aranha, ambassador to Washington and from March 1938 until August 1944 foreign minister, adhered to the tradition of Rio Branco and gave priority to friendship with the United States. The great ability of Aranha and his adherence to firm democratic convictions while serving an authoritarian government were crucial for the wartime course of Brazil. Thanks to Aranha, Brazil supported the U.S. call for hemispheric unity at the December 1938 Lima conference; and more than any other single person, he was responsible for the policies that ultimately made Brazil a fighting ally.

The Nazis had an advantage in the large number of Brazilians of German origin. The German-born, concentrated in southern Brazil, were only about $\frac{1}{2}$ percent of the total population in 1938, but many more were of German background. The dominant language in many areas was German; many Black Brazilians spoke no Portuguese but only German. Eight percent of Brazilian agricultural production was in German hands; 10 percent of industry, 12 percent of commerce.[4] The Nazis were quite successful in organizing the German community and for a time operated an extension of the Nazi party in Brazil. This effort to exert German influence backfired, however. While the United States looked on as an interested spectator, the Vargas government counterattacked, outlawed all foreign political organizations, required schools to be Brazilianized, and insisted that ethnic Germans become Brazilians. The Nazis were for a time rather arrogant, and they blamed the anti-German measures on nefarious U.S. influence; but even pro-Axis elements in the Vargas administration, led by Campos, were determined to preserve Brazilian sovereignty. The German government, faute de mieux, backed down; and Brazilian-German relations improved substantially in 1939.

The United States, although still unprepared to furnish arms to Brazil, in 1939 agreed to extend credits and furnish technical assistance for the development of mineral production. In return, Vargas promised to treat U.S. investors equally with Brazilian and offered cooperation in the production of strategic materials.[5] After private American interests declined a proposal to build Brazil's first steel plant, the U.S. government to forestall the Germans undertaking the project, in 1940, stepped in and provided financing and gave the Brazilians priority in procurements. Through most of 1940, however, the Brazilian government held to a fairly neutral position and resisted American efforts, seconded by Aranha, to take a stance against the Axis. Some arms were still being received from Germany by transshipment through the blockade.

In August 1940 Congress was finally persuaded to provide arms for Brazil, which became exposed by the fall of France. If Britain were beaten, possibly even if it were not, a logical next step would be for the Axis powers to leap the South Atlantic to the undefended Brazilian coast.

Meanwhile, the Brazilian government, seeking to cover itself for the case of a Nazi victory, was dickering with Germany about postwar trade. Moreover, there was much hostility toward Britain, partly from old grudges, partly because of anger at the interference of the naval blockade with Brazilian trade. However, late in 1940, the German armies having failed to cross the Channel and the United States having moved toward entry into the war, Vargas cast his lot with the United States. The pragmatic dictator preferred security and economic advantages to ideology and chose the democratic cause—which was ultimately to bring his dictatorship to an end.

U.S.-Brazilian cooperation was nominally close from late 1940 onward, but little was done for over a year, mostly because U.S. armaments were very slow to appear. The first U.S. objective was to garrison the Northeast of Brazil against a possible Axis incursion, but the Brazilians were unwilling to have U.S. forces on their territory unless their own army was sufficiently strengthened to assure the national sovereignty. Well aware of the strategic importance of their country, they drove hard bargains for military and economic aid. Although the popular reaction to Pearl Harbor was emotional, the government did not move rapidly. At this time, in contrast to recent years, the Brazilian people were considerably more pro-United States than their leaders.

Only after the Rio Conference of hemispheric countries in January 1942 recommended breaking relations with Axis powers, did Brazil do so. This action, which was contrary to the wishes of many military men and the advice of War Minister (later President) Dutra, was taken on the basis of a promise that U.S. war materials were finally on the way. Thereafter, collaboration progressed more rapidly. In February there was a new agreement for arms deliveries, cooperation regarding strategic minerals, and the enlargement of bases in Brazil, which were very useful for controlling shipping lanes. Naval cooperation followed, and in August 1942, after more than a dozen Brazilian ships had been torpedoed, Brazil declared war on Germany.

Entry into the big war on the side of the democracies stimulated national feeling and unity and strengthened the government. Vargas personally was happy to play a part on the world stage and was flattered by Roosevelt's assurance that they would sit together at the peace table. Probably the biggest Brazilian contribution to victory was furnishing strategic materials; most important to Brazilian feelings, however, was the dispatch of an expeditionary force of somewhat over 20,000 men to the Italian campaign of 1944, a force that led to a close and enduring relationship between the U.S. and Brazilian military establishments and was perhaps the strongest single factor of U.S. influence in Brazil in the 1960s.

The United States turned down a Mexican proposal for sending a unit to the European war on grounds that it would cost more than it would be worth, but the Brazilian request could not well be denied. The Brazilian Expeditionary Force (FEB in Portuguese) required almost everything from the United States, transportation, weapons, rations, even uniforms; and the training and condition of the troops at first were poor. They rapidly improved, however; and, under U.S. command, gave an accounting of themselves of which Brazilians could rightly be proud. To this day, in Brazilian history books the central battles of World War II were those in Italy, as a result of which a German division surrendered to the Brazilians.

The alliance brought the United States and Brazil closer in many ways. Brazil became more than ever the favored Latin American country; three-fourths of all U.S. military aid to Latin America during the war went to Brazil.[6] Not only did Brazilians and Americans fight together; the respective economies were more than ever meshed. The steel plant built at Volta Redonda with U.S. aid became the symbol and bellwether of Brazilian industrialization, followed by many lesser projects. American corporations undertook production of strategic minerals, a monopoly of which was given to the United States. A great variety of missions, military and economic, brought numerous Americans to Brazil. Pan-American replaced the German airlines that had covered Brazil, despite some reluctance to permit a new foreign monopoly. American detachments took over airfields, American bases were established, and American forces acted in the strategic Northeast area almost as though at home. The Brazilian navy was placed under an American admiral.[7] Cooperation was closer because of the old Brazilian rivalry with Argentina. That country maintained as pro-Axis a stance as it feasibly could, and at times there were unrealistic fears that Argentina might invade the southern German-influenced part of Brazil.

The very high degree of noncoercive U.S. influence in this period rested on both sides' views of their own interests. U.S. policy was rather of cooperation than domination, especially under the perceptive guidance of Sumner Welles, Undersecretary of State until August 1943; it sought not only military advantages but postwar friendship.[8] On the other hand, Brazilians accepted the role of the United States because they saw it as well-intentioned and not menacing to Brazilian independence, while it furnished military strength and built up their economy.

FRAYING BONDS

The wartime alliance raised admiration and sympathy for the United States to its zenith. But these feelings and the discredit of fascist authoritarianism, defeated and stained with the shame of unprecedented atrocities, were disastrous for the man who presided over Brazil's participation in the war. The officers of the FEB, who used American material and worked with American personnel and who came home via the United States, got a poor opinion of the fascism Vargas once admired and were not inclined to look favorably on dictatorship at home after having fought against dictatorship in Europe. Wary of them, Vargas brought the force back quietly and demobilized it rapidly. But the expectation of democratization—raised by the American ambassador's public praise of Vargas for a vague promise to hold free elections—was overwhelming. Vargas moved to organize elections; but the military feared he was actually maneuvering to keep himself in office and forced him from the presidency in October 1945. Brazil in this regard was following a general mode; about this time dictatorships fell also in Cuba, Guatemala, Venezuela, and Peru.

A democratic constitution was adopted in 1946, and Vargas' minister of war, Eurico Dutra, won the presidency in a free election. During his administration, the close relations between Brazil and the United States apparently continued with little change. The United States endeavored to secure Brazil a permanent membership on the Security Council of the United Nations, an effort that failed because of British and Soviet opposition. Brazil remained the chief ally in Latin America and a faithful supporter of the anti-Communist cause. The United States continued to be Brazil's dominant customer and supplier. However, after Vargas returned to the presidency in 1950 by victory in a free election, the bonds began visibly loosening.

A primary reason was that the United States became deeply concerned with Communist expansionism in Europe and Asia. From 1947, the dream of cooperation with the Soviet Union had been shattered and the cold war was the order of the day. Western Europe had to be rebuilt under the Marshall Plan, and Communist pressure was to be countered militarily in Greece, Turkey, and elsewhere under the Truman Doctrine and the philosophy of containment. Latin America seemed to present no threat; after all, it, including Brazil, had prospered greatly during the war. Little attention or money was directed south; Brazil received only $125 million in loans from 1946 to 1950.[9] Brazilians saw their industrial development suffering from the emphasis on the recovery of Europe. At the same time, the military were disappointed that the United States, instead of continuing to help them, sharply reduced arms sales to Brazil, on the basis that Latin American countries should spend on armaments only what was necessary for internal security. It was further irritating to the Brazilians that the United States put on an equal basis formerly pro-Axis Argentina and formerly allied Brazil. Not surprisingly, Brazil in 1951 refused repeated requests to send at least a token force to the Korean war.

There were more basic reasons for change, however. Vargas rode back to the presidency in 1951 on the growing urban lower-class vote; the increasing mobilization of the masses by populist parties threatened a new brand of politics with anti-American implications as the economic situation deteriorated. The United States had encouraged the idea that the victory of the United Nations would bring industrialization, modernization, progress, and wealth; and the first postwar years were prosperous, thanks to large reserves of foreign exchange built up during years when Brazilian exports were in great demand and there was not much to buy abroad. But the reserves were rapidly depleted and replaced by debts as the country went on an import splurge without pushing exports correspondingly in an increasingly competitive world market. The Korean war was helpful for Brazilian trade, as raw materials prices zoomed, but in its wake difficulties began piling up.

During the Vargas administration, the feeling grew that the United States was neglecting its special friend and failing its duty to help narrow the development gap and assist Brazil to its proper place in the world. Large loans were proposed, but only a small fraction were realized, and these were to tide Brazil over foreign exchange shortages, not to improve production.[10] The Eisenhower administration felt that economic development should be the responsibility of private enterprise following the imperatives of the market; it liquidated a Mixed Commission for Economic Development from Truman years, to the chagrin of the Brazilians. Class tensions rose, and agitation against foreign capital became the cutting edge of anticapitalist politics. The nationalists, with whom Vargas as politician associated himself, began seeing American corporations as more burdensome than beneficial; and the government undertook a number of restrictive measures to control foreign investment and the remittance of profits. In 1953–54 the Vargas administration, as urged especially by the Communist Party,[11] ended efforts of U.S. corporations to exploit Brazilian oil resources (then assumed to be very large) by setting up a Brazilian state corporation, Petrobras, with a monopoly of the production of petroleum.

The military command was increasingly divided between the nationalist-leftist wing and those, chiefly former members of the FEB, who remained faithful to the pro-U.S. orientation and who feared that Varguista demagoguery, as they saw it, played into the hands of Communist and near-Communist groups. In 1950, a Varguista slate headed by Gen. Newton Estillac Leal won an election for the directorate of the Military Club in Rio, an important barometer of sentiment among the officers; among the defeated was Gen. Humberto Castelo Branco, who was to become a leader of the 1964 coup and subsequently president. Estillac Leal was made war minister by Vargas. But feeling shifted rapidly as Vargas alienated many officers, and in March 1952 anti-leftist sentiment forced Estillac Leal from office. In May 1952 the anti-Communist faction, organized as the Democratic Crusade, was victorious in Military Club elections. In February 1954 Gen. Golbery do Couto e Silva drew up a manifesto, to which many second-ranking officers subscribed, complaining of corruption in government, poor conditions for the army, and labor agitation; this led to the resignation of Vargas' minister of labor João Goulart. A few months later, the generals, angered because the chief of Vargas' bodyguard had organized an attempted assassination of a right-wing publisher-politician, Carlos Lacerda (in the course of which an airforce officer was murdered), demanded that Vargas himself withdraw.

Unwilling to retire a second time to his ranch, Vargas killed himself, leaving behind a melodramatic note of self-justification and blame for the "forces and interests," domestic and foreign, that had caused his downfall. According to his testament:

> Once more the forces and interests which work against the people have organized themselves afresh and break out against me . . . underground campaign of international groups. . . . These people whose slave I was will no longer be the slaves of anyone. My sacrifice will remain forever on their souls and my blood will be the price of their ransom.[12]

This was less than completely logical, since Vargas' immediate troubles arose from the violent action of his personal guard; but it evoked an outburst of more or less spontaneous anti-U.S. riots, and Vargas' martyrdom by the foreign corporations loomed large over Brazilian politics for the following decade. After 1954, anti-Spanish, anti-Portuguese, anti-British, and anti-German feelings seemed all transferred to the United States, the great enemy for Brazilian nationalists.[13] The Brazilian Left, hostile toward the U.S. presence, brought into question the commitment to a basic free enterprise economy and the U.S.-dominated anti-Communist alliance.

In the political vacuum after Vargas' suicide, one provisional president followed another in an atmosphere of uncertainty. In 1955, however, a moderate of the Vargas following, Juscelino Kubitschek, was elected president, with Vargas' former labor minister, João Goulart, as vice-president. Anti-Varguistas in the Armed Forces, bitterly opposed to Vargas adherents in principle, made some moves toward annulling the elections on grounds of corruption, which was certainly present although probably not decisive. But the Minister of War, Marshal Henrique Teixeira Lott, carried out a sort of legalistic countercoup, deposed the acting president, and assured the investiture of Kubitschek and Goulart in January 1956.

During the Kubitschek administration, the economy expanded satisfactorily under policies of import substitution by industrialization, and the government managed to keep on top of increasing inflation and shortage of foreign exchange, thanks partly to some $845 million of American loans.[14] But tensions grew; several minirebellions by armed forces officers testified to restiveness and extremism. Although Brazil continued to rely on American aid and a special relationship was still taken for granted, there were various strains. In 1956 the United States, because of Argentine objections, refused to sell Brazil an aircraft carrier, in a replay of the destroyer incident of 1937. The Brazilian government, decidedly annoyed, ordered a carrier from Britain. The Kubitschek government moved toward better relations with Spanish America, thereby reducing its reliance on the United States; Brazilian leadership in Latin America implied opposition to the United States. Kubitschek criticized the United States for neglecting its former ally and questioned the value of loyalty. He began looking around at possibilities of trade with Communist countries—relations with the Soviet Union and its allies, established at American insistence in the world war, had been broken at the beginning of the cold war. Somewhat to the embarrassment of the United States, Kubitschek in 1958 proposed "Operation Pan America," a big development program for Latin America—a challenge taken up by President Kennedy a few years later in the Alliance for Progress. The Eisenhower administration continued to think in terms of security for investors and monetary stabilization. To the contrary, in June 1959, Kubitschek dramatically rejected the fiscal austerity imposed by the International Monetary Fund as condition for a loan, thereby establishing his nationalist credentials.[15] Eisenhower made a state visit to Brazil in 1960, but nothing was done to halt the erosion of the U.S. position.

LEFT TURN

The estrangement of the United States and Brazil became conspicuous under a president elected as a candidate of a relatively conservative and pro-American party. Jânio Quadros carried around a broom and promised to sweep out corruption, to the delight of the anti-Vargas coalition. But he also courted votes of nationalists and leftists by promising an independent foreign policy and recognition of Communist states. Before becoming president, he made a trip to revolutionary Cuba in defiance of the boycott of that country by the United States and the Organization of American States.

Quadros boasted a spectacular electoral victory, and his inauguration was the most hopeful in Brazilian history. It represented the evident vindication of democracy, virtually the first and only time in Brazilian history that power had been transferred to an opposition party by legal process. It seemed to be the opening of a new political era. It ushered in a time of troubles and breakdown of constitutional government.

Quadros began trying to straighten out the economic confusion into which the free-spending Kubitschek had led the country, and he moved toward what the United States regarded as financial sanity. But his seven months in office were marked mostly by his new foreign policy. He placed priority on economic development and wanted to stand with the Third World movement, for which development was the major issue. He wanted Brazil to take a nonaligned position in the cold war to improve its bargaining position, and to open diplomatic and commercial relations with all states. He favored receiving Cuba back into the American family of nations; and, without consulting his ministers, he ostentatiously pinned a high decoration on "Ché" Guevara, Castro's revolutionary right hand, when he was passing through Brazil. He did not get around to actually establishing diplomatic ties with the Soviet Union, but he sent commercial missions to various Communist countries. During most of his tenure he declined to see the U.S. ambassador.[16] All this might have become alarming to the United States in time; but the Kennedy administration, seeing Quadros a little like one of its New Frontiersmen, badly wanted to see him succeed. Approving his conservative economic policies, it put through a favorable debt renegotiation to give him more room to maneuver[17] and closed eyes to his foreign policy deviations.

It can only be guessed how leftish foreign policy might have harmonized with efforts toward fiscal soundness, because Quadros in August 1961, entirely without warning, submitted his resignation to the Congress. His stated reason was the refusal of Congress to grant him extraordinary powers; but he spoke in his message, in imitation of Vargas' highly successful suicide note, of "forces of reaction," selfish groups "including foreign ones," and the like.[18] He seems to have hoped that an aroused nation would demand that he return with carte blanche to save it.

The constitutional successor was João Goulart, whom the military had forced from ministerial office in 1954 and had consistently disliked as a rabble-rouser. Although candidate of the Labor Party, Goulart had been elected vice president at the same time that Quadros was elected president as candidate of the conservatives. When Quadros resigned, Goulart was appropriately far away in China on a commercial mission; and Quadros seems to have assumed that the military would bar him from office. The generals would have to take charge temporarily and would have to choose between swallowing their dislike for Goulart or compelling the Congress to take him, Quadros, back on his own terms.

The Congress, however, did not even debate declining the abdication; and the few small demonstrations in Quadros' favor petered out.

Brazilians were shocked, but they quickly forgot Quadros and went on to discussing what to do next. Quadros had alienated many of his conservative following by his neutralist initiatives—the fiery Carlos Lacerda had even talked of a possible military move against him. At the same time, Quadros, who made much of his independence of traditional politics but whom many considered simply eccentric, had failed to build party support or a solid following of his own. The Communist leader, Luis Carlos Prestes had applauded the shift from alignment with the United States, but no one mobilized radicals or any other group to back Quadros in his need.

The letdown from the euphoria of Quadros' new-broom inauguration to his futile resignation generated a sense of crisis and instability, a feeling that Brazil was perhaps ungovernable, as Quadros claimed it was, and that basic change might be necessary. Quadros had to some extent united radicals and conservatives; his departure left the nation deeply divided, near civil conflict.

As Quadros anticipated, the military establishment in general was most reluctant to see Vice-President Goulart become their commander in chief, as dictated by the constitution; and the three military ministers took power in a semicoup, set controls over the media, and proclaimed the ineligibility of Goulart as a menace to public order. But the fact that he was in China postponed a decision about the succession, and sentiment built up strongly for legality. The Congress refused to declare him unqualified, and the press generally favored him; he had, after all, demonstrated sufficient popular support to win the vice presidency (by a small plurality in a three-cornered race) in the face of the Quadros landslide, and he was a longtime familiar figure on the political scene whom the politicians knew as one of their own. Moreover, the commanding general in Goulart's home state of Rio Grande do Sul threatened to fight for him; and the governor of that southern state, the leftist Leonel Brizola, brother-in-law of Goulart, proclaimed his state on a war footing.

Faced with a threat of civil war, the anti-Goulart generals accepted a compromise whereby he became president with reduced powers under a parliamentary system somewhat like the government of the empire. The military remained distrustful, but the country favored a constitutional succession, he had done nothing very reprehensible, and the generals felt unable to bar him for what he *might* do.

Goulart, who was hardly charismatic but was a skilled politician, was rather successful in disarming his enemies in the Armed Forces by moderation and restraint for more than a year. He made some effort to check inflation. Most markedly, he backed away from the anti-American slant of Quadros' foreign policy. He made no flamboyant neutralist gestures but conferred frequently with the U.S. ambassador, Lincoln

Gordon, who freely gave advice on economic matters and new cabinet nominees.[19] In April 1962 Goulart went to Washington for talks with President Kennedy. Discussions were not entirely harmonious, since Kennedy and other Americans wanted to keep the alleged danger of Communism to the fore, while Goulart and his aides were unimpressed by that alleged menace but wanted to talk about economic aid and the "deep urge of the Brazilian people to assert their personality in world affairs."[20] Goulart was prepared to reaffirm solidarity with the United States in regard to Cuba, but his expectations of rich rewards were disappointed. However, Goulart was pleased by his cordial reception and rapport with Kennedy; and his ambassador to the United States, Roberto Campos (until February 1964), worked strongly for good relations. Despite misgivings, the American administration was evidently prepared to give Goulart the benefit of the doubt; and Brazil welcomed Kennedy's Alliance for Progress, under which the United States pledged a billion dollars yearly for Latin American nations moving toward economic growth and social justice.

Doubts on both sides were increased by the visit of Attorney General Robert Kennedy to Brazil in December 1962. This was an effort gently to twist arms in view of growing radicalism in Brazil. Kennedy warned against extremism and Communist infiltration in various largely government-controlled unions; Goulart did not like being told, in effect, that he was a poor judge of character. He was not worried by the growing power of some Communist leaders who, after all, supported him, while he complained of low prices for Brazilian exports, concerning which Kennedy could promise nothing. And it seemed to Braxilians that Kennedy tried to influence nominations to the cabinet.[21]

Meanwhile waters had been muddied by controversies over the old issue of foreign investment. A law was passed in 1961 limiting remittance of profits to 10 percent of the investment, without consideration for reinvestment or the rapid depreciation of the cruzeiro; this was not put into effect until shortly before Goulart's downfall, but it chilled the atmosphere for foreign corporations. In February 1962 Brizola, as governor of Rio Grande do Sul, expropriated with trifling compensation a U.S.-owned utility for the evident purpose of sabotaging Goulart's efforts to win U.S. confidence. Negotiations, in which Goulart could take no firm position for or against his radical brother-in-law, dragged on irritatingly and led Congress to enact the Hickenlooper Amendment to the effect that economic aid must be denied to countries taking property of U.S. citizens without adequate prompt compensation. In a related issue, President Kennedy was satisfied with a Brazilian offer of $135 million compensation for ten American utility interests, three-fourths being held for reinvestment in enterprises approved by the Brazilian government. From the

American point of view, this was a rather generous bargain; Congress certainly would respond to uncompensated expropriation by halting Alliance for Progress funds. The nearly unanimous Brazilian reaction, however, was that it represented a sellout.

Thanks to Goulart's conciliatory policies, sentiment grew for vesting in him the traditional powers of the Brazilian presidency. Although he was far from a figurehead, he seems to have been determined from the beginning to prove the parliamentary system unworkable; and he demanded an early plebiscite on the issue. The Congress, enjoying its enlarged powers, was somewhat reluctant; but it gave way after the commanding general in Rio Grande do Sul threatened civil war if the Congress refused to allow the vote.[22] Held in January 1963, it favored Goulart by five to one. However, this represented much less a testimonial to Goulart than an expression of dissatisfaction with deteriorating economic conditions amid political uncertainty.

Thereafter, Goulart undertook to push his own policies. His moderate leftist ministers, San Tiago Dantas and Celso Furtado, promoted a three-year plan for stabilization with a large amount of aid; they proposed to reduce the balance of payments imbalance, and curtail the government deficit by an austerity program including removal of subsidies holding down prices of certain essentials and the more effective collection of taxes. This was designed to fit Brazil into the program of the Alliance for Progress; approved by the United States and the IMF, it might in time have brought good results. A loan, contingent on the stabilization program, was approved in April. But Goulart was not really interested in economics or administration but in immediate popularity, and he was not prepared to take painful measures for the sake of a distant tomorrow. He may even have been satisfied to let things get worse in order to justify his contention that more or less dictatorial powers were needed to save the country. The Three-Year Plan was allowed to wither; and in June 1963 Goulart dismissed the entire cabinet, including its proponents, and plunged from the moderate to the radical Left.

Up to mid-1963, the U.S. policy had been in cautious cooperation with Goulart while warning of growing Communist or allegedly Communist penetration in unions and various state agencies (especially Petrobras) and encouraging moderate reform while harping on the need to check inflation, which was getting ever worse. But after July, the American authorities concluded that further aid to the Goulart government would be wasted, and no new commitments were made except for the supply of some surplus wheat and some projects for the impoverished Northeast.[23] It was resolved to furnish aid directly to anti-Goulart state governments, most of the important states being controlled by more conservative leaders—with, of course, the formal consent in each case of the federal authorities. Aid would then go to "islands of sanity" in the Brazilian confusion, a policy that became celebrated as much because of the striking phrase as because of its actual importance.

U.S.-Brazilian relations were increasingly strained during the second half of 1963. Brazil became the foremost Latin American opponent of the anti-Cuban measures that the State Department wanted to make hemispheric policy, and Goulart tried to make Brazil leader of Latin America and the Third World against the richer nations. The old issue of compensation for expropriated utilities was still dragging, because the leftist forces would permit no settlement that the United States found reasonable. The assassination of Kennedy in November caused an outpouring of sympathetic sentiment but removed a link; Goulart had been well impressed with the young American president and had admired his handling of the missile crisis. There was no personal bond to Lyndon Johnson, and the Johnson administration was less committed to democracy in Latin America and to the ideals of the Alliance for Progress with the assumed accompaniment of a flow of U.S. funds to the area. U.S. support for the Goulart government sank steadily as Goulart seemed to be half pushing, half permitting, the slide toward radicalism.

It can hardly be said that Goulart took a strong leftist position, because he was weak and indecisive, a vacillating extremist on whom no one could rely. He repeatedly changed ministers and adopted policies only to abandon them, leaving supporters frustrated and demoralized. Even as he appealed to leftist-nationalist passions, the dynamic leaders of that wing, such as Leonel Brizola, Communist party chief Luis Carlos Prestes, governor of the Northeastern state of Pernambuco Miguel Arraes, and Peasant League leader Francisco Julião, regarded him as unreliable.[24] However, Goulart laid his stakes increasingly on the radicals and the mobilized masses, especially workers in the government-patronized and manipulated unions. Giving up on efforts at stabilization as less rewarding than promising social change, he evidently saw "basic reforms" as the way to win the people and write his name in history.

Goulart's following included the Moscow-line Communists, with whom he had been allegedly collaborating when ejected from the Ministry of Labor in 1954 and who strongly supported his election in 1960. The Communists' major theme was always opposition to U.S. influence,[25] and as long as Goulart was cooperative with the United States, they denounced his policies and the "bourgeois" in his cabinet. But they embraced him so far as he adopted their philosophy, and he found them useful as organizers in such bodies as the General Command of Labor and the National Union of Students, both of which were officered by Communists and made pronouncements that could well be taken for Communist.

The Brazilian Left was not Communist in a Leninist sense, however; Communist parties have never been able to weld a mass movement in Brazil or indeed anywhere in Latin America. There were radical splinters of various kinds, Maoist, Trotskyite, Castroite, and many lacking any definite affiliation, undisciplined groups with amateur leaders. Leftist Catholics were about as anticapitalist as the Communists without ceasing to be believing Catholics. Peasants wanted land, and workers wanted raises. But anti-U.S. feeling was the chief bond of the Left, and the galvanizing idea was dislike for the big foreign corporations, half of which were U.S.-owned. Brazil's troubles, they held, were due to exploitation by the profit-making interests; and the Left wanted to prohibit remittance of profits, suspend payment on debts, and perhaps confiscate foreign holdings. The language was Marxist, and foreign capitalism was associated with native oppression, feudalistic landholding, and the unloved status quo. The foreign bourgeoisie was also held responsible for the cultural invasion, for the corruption of the press, and for militarism. Nationalism joined radicalism. The alliance with the United States was seen as hegemony, and only the mobilized masses could free Brazil from foreign domination. The most dynamic leader of this tendency, certainly the most feared, was Brizola, a crude, ambitious, arrogant man. An electrifying campaigner, he stirred hugh audiences by flaying reactionaries, foreign interests and their Brazilian flunkies, imperialists, the U.S. Embassy, the IMF, and the Brazilian Congress that refused to enact the demanded "basic reforms."

The rapid economic growth that had softened class conflicts through most of the postwar years slowed in 1961 and turned negative in 1963; and there was no apparent possibility of straightening the economy within the democratic system. Inflation, which usually strikes middle classes hardest, was 55 percent in 1962, 81 percent in 1963, and at a yearly rate of 140 percent in the first months of 1964.[26] Foreign investment had almost halted. Strikes were rampant, while unemployment was swelling in the stagnant economy with a rapidly growing labor force. There was growing agitation for land reform, and Goulart demanded a constitutional amendment permitting payment in bonds, which would rapidly lose value through inflation. The poor and backward Northeast was more or less in turmoil. The Peasant Leagues, led by a young lawyer of the landowner class, Francisco Julião, threatened to take over the estates by force, Castro boasted of revolutionizing the area, and the Goulart government collaborated with the local Communists. The wealthy were the more alarmed by peasant unrest because the strength of the Conservative parties rested on rural bossism.

Brazilian society seemed to be coming loose from its moorings. The proud old aristocracy was still there, but it was being displaced by the new wealthy professionals and entrepreneurs[27] while the urban masses formed a new unsettling political force, making demands that the system could not accommodate. The electorate (limited especially in the countryside by the requirement of literacy) was swelling rapidly and making profound readjustments necessary.

As the economy weakened, polarization and tensions grew. Some, then, were confident that revolutionary change, if not a revolution, was in the offing, as for the first time in Brazilian history a president spoke in terms of social radicalism. The Left, believing a new ideological era had dawned, greatly overestimated its strength and powers of mobilization. On the other side were growing fears.

The political system seemed to be breaking down. The chief parties lost a large fraction of their votes in the series of postwar elections, until in 1962 half the members of Congress were elected as candidates not of parties but of opportunistic alliances. It was no great scandal that Goulart made extreme use of government funds in the 1962 elections.[28] From 1961 to 1963 the federal payroll increased under Goulart, five times over,[29] and corruption reached a new high. The government could not tax effectively because of incapacity and venality of the apparatus, nor would it probably have been able, without thorough reorganization, to administer a redistributive program.

The need for a radical cure seemed evident to both the Left and Right, and extremists on both sides called for extralegal action. Conservatives perceived Goulart using the funds and authority of the state to give dangerous agitators control of unions and other organizations, and they suspected that he promoted chaos in order to make possible a coup to give himself full power. The slide toward anarchy certainly gave weight to Goulart's thesis that change was necessary. There was talk of the need for a "syndicalist republic," that is, a state run by the unions, a proposal less attractive to many because of the role of Communists and persons who talked like Communists in the unions. Goulart was prepared to employ violence; he closed by force some antileftist groups and wanted to use paratroops to abduct the rightist firebrand Lacerda.[30] There were parallels between Goulart and Argentina's Perón, who had used urban masses to make himself dictator and whom Goulart openly admired. Moreover, many feared that, Goulart although no Communist, was leading Brazil toward Communism. Many were more afraid of what might come out of disorder generated by Goulart than of Goulart himself. In the worsening times, some of the wealthy sent their families abroad and kept bags packed to escape if need be.[31]

Washington saw with dismay how a country in which the United States had been universally popular and which had assumed close friendship with the United States as the chief axiom of its foreign policy in a mere 15 years turned to such official and popular antagonism that it might be on the way into the pro-Soviet camp. This transmutation came about in the absence of any particular crisis, great grievance, or important hostile act on either side. Causes were partly to be sought in the accidents and personalities of Brazilian politics. But more fundamental were the worsening economic situation, for which the United States had no acceptable remedy, and the increasing (although still very incomplete) politicization of the masses. In the deep inequality of Brazilian society, their discontents were inevitably economic; and their demands were directed most strongly against the foreign capitalists, the conspicuous intruders in the Brazilian economy, that is, mostly the American or American-affiliated corporations and the power behind them. Intellectuals and students seemed almost automatically hostile to the United States, on which was laid responsibility for the sad condition of Brazil and the disappointments and frustrations of the educated in a nation not progressing as they believed it should.

Thus, in difficult times, the U.S. economic presence, potentially and in some ways a major source of influence, was converted by domestic politics into a cause of antagonism. This has frequently occurred in Latin America, as democratic institutions have logically led to populist politics. Anger at obvious economic injustice is directed against the alien interests that have invaded the country to profit from it, that is, to draw wealth out of it; and hostility toward the United States accompanies the rise of tensions and social polarization. Where this has occurred, in the Argentina of Perón and the Chile of Allende as in the Brazil of Goulart, the outcome has been military coup and dictatorship.

NOTES

1. Roger W. Fontaine, *Brazil and the United States: Toward a Maturing Relation* (Washington, D.C.: American Enterprise Institute, 1974), p. 13.

2. E. Bradford Burns, *Nationalism in Brazil: An Historical Survey* (New York: Praeger, 1968), p. 53.

3. Frank D. McCann, Jr., *The Brazilian-American Alliance, 1937–1945* (Princeton: Princeton University Press, 1973), p. 43.

4. Ibid., p. 79.

5. Ibid., pp. 128–30.

6. *Estado de São Paulo*, July 1, 1980, p. 8.

7. McCann, *The Brazilian-American Alliance*, p. 295.

8. As remarked by Stanley Hilton, *Estado de São Paulo*, July 1, 1979, p. 8.

9. *Estado de São Paulo*, July 1, 1979, p. 8.

10. Albert Fishlow, "Flying Down to Rio: U.S.-Brazilian Relations," *Foreign Affairs* 57 (Winter 1978–79):390.

11. Peter Flynn, *Brazil: A Political Analysis* (Boulder, Colo.: Westview Press, 1978), p. 179.

12. John W. F. Dulles, *Vargas of Brazil* (Austin, Tex.: University of Texas Press, 1967), pp. 334–35.

13. Burns, *Nationalism in Brazil*, p. 91.

14. *Estado de São Paulo*, July 1, 1979, p. 8.

15. Flynn, *Brazil*, p. 207.

16. Jan K. Black, *United States Penetration of Brazil* (Philadelphia: University of Pennsylvania Press, 1977), pp. 39–40.

17. Thomas Skidmore, *Politics in Brazil: An Experiment in Democracy 1930-1964* (New York: Oxford University Press, 1967), p. 195.

18. John W. F. Dulles, *Unrest in Brazil* (Austin, Tex.: University of Texas Press, 1970), p. 53.

19. Black, *United States Penetration*, p. 40.

20. Phyllis R. Parker, *Brazil and the Quiet Intervention, 1964* (Austin, Tex.: University of Texas Press, 1979), p. 20.

21. Ibid., p. 30.

22. Skidmore, *Politics*, p. 221.

23. Ibid., p. 323.

24. Alfred Stepan, "Brazil," in *The Breakdown of Democratic Regimes*, eds. Juan J. Linz and Alfred Stepan (Baltimore: Johns Hopkins University Press, 1978), p. 124.

25. See Ronald H. Chilcote, *The Brazilian Communist Party: Conflict and Integration, 1922-1972* (New York: Oxford University Press, 1974).

26. Mario H. Simonsen, "Inflation and the Money and Capital Markets," in *The Economy of Brazil*, ed. Howard J. Ellis, (Berkeley: University of California Press, 1969), p. 136.

27. Charles Wagley, *An Introduction to Brazil*, rev. ed. (New York: Columbia University Press, 1971), pp. 93–94.

28. Skidmore, *Politics*, p. 231.

29. F. LaMond Tullis, *Modernization in Brazil* (Provo, Utah: Brigham Young University Press, 1973), p. 20.

30. Alfred Stepan, *The Military in Politics; Changing Patterns in Brazil* (Princeton: Princeton University Press, 1971), p. 71.

31. Fritz Stern, "Between Repression and Reform," *Foreign Affairs* 56 (July 1978): 808.

2

THE MILITARY REGIME
AND THE UNITED STATES

THE COUP

The deterioration of U.S.-Brazilian relations, especially in 1963–64, was caused by political developments internal to Brazil. The Johnson administration and the State Department were impressed with the gravity of the trend, but there was not much they could do about it within the limitations of their economic and political resources. So far as Goulart leaned on those for whom anti-Americanism was valuable and a major means of influence, he was not to be influenced; the most that could be done, it seemed to American policymakers, was to endeavor to weaken him and counteract his policies.

The measures taken, however, were rather limited, as will appear subsequently. The course of Brazilian politics was turned around by a military coup in late March to early April 1964. The United States had an interest in the coup and approved it, contrary to the more common policy of disapproval when, as has occurred hundreds of times in Latin American history, the generals eject the civilians.

The military have always represented a major political force in nearly all Latin American countries because of weaknesses of constitutional structures and democratic traditions, the division of society, and the inability to resolve conflicts within a legal framework. They have intervened for many purposes: to protect their own interests or their military integrity, remove corrupt authorities, control or set aside elections, or repress disliked (mostly populist) movements, if not because of leaders' hunger for power. The constitutions of most Latin American states frankly give the military the role of guarantor of the constitutional order, that is (as it is ordinarily interpreted), the military is authorized to act extralegally if the legal order is endangered, as by a president seeking to make himself dictator. All Brazilian constitutions have required the military to obey the president only "within the limits of the law" and to guarantee the regular order of government under the constitution, applying the "moderator" power inherited from the emperor, whom the military deposed in 1889.

Since the last decades of the nineteenth century, the Brazilian armed forces have had a certain messianic vocation, a mission of internal order and, since early in this century, of modernization.[1] Since World War II, they have been at the center of every crisis and have shown willingness to exercise their constitutional mandate by interventions in 1945, 1954 (twice), 1955, and 1961. From 1926 to 1964, the military were involved in ending all presidencies except those of Kubitschek and Quadros. In each case, however, the armed forces after acting on the political stage under the Brazilian motto of "Order and Progress," returned to the barracks to leave government in elected civilian hands. Democracy as a self-contained political process was (and doubtless is) incomprehensible in Brazil without the "moderator" to enforce rules of the game; indeed, the principle of absolute obedience of the military to a civilian authority would lead directly to dictatorship.[2]

Consequently as soon as Goulart began to move toward extremist positions in opposition to the majority of the Congress, questions were urgently raised about the role of the armed forces, the decision of which would be crucial. Goulart, well aware of this, hoped to assure military support for himself—not entirely without reason, because he had received military backing in the plebiscite of January 1963. He used his authority to promote nationalist or leftist officers, while those known to be pro-United States were passed over or given posts without command over troops. Generals who actively courted the Left, such as Osvino Alves, were advanced; and Goulart favored personal friends, such as Amaury Kruel, commander of the São Paulo forces.

Goulart was not free, however, to demote and, in view of military cohesiveness, had to follow more or less rules of seniority in promotions. His efforts to ensure a high command favorable to himself backfired because of resentment of those passed over and the feeling that he was infringing upon the regular order of command.[3] Even generals sympathetic to Goulart were more devoted to the military institution, while those who had pushed Goulart from the Ministry of Labor in 1954 and tried to prevent his becoming president in 1961 had ample reason to fear his achieving the full powers he was seeking. There consequently gradually developed a sort of conspiracy among anti-Goulart generals, mostly in a sense of mutual feeling out of sentiments and reaching an understanding for eventual action. They were restrained, however, by fear of division within the armed forces and the reluctance of many or most high officers to move without widespread civilian support and an overt threat to the constitution.

Goulart would probably have been allowed to finish out his term to the beginning of 1966 if he had not evoked a crisis. Leading politicians who aspired to the presidency wanted Goulart to continue, and Goulart's position as constitutional president was strong, although hardly so firm as though he had been elected president. His acute troubles began in September 1963 when a group of noncommissioned officers of the Air Force and Navy (significantly not the Army) rebelled briefly, apparently at Communist instigation,[4] for a time holding prisoner various high magistrates. Their chief demand was the right to run for political office; and Goulart, who hoped to use the lower ranks to neutralize the upper, refused to condemn them. This gravely disturbed the commissioned officers, who feared politicization of the ranks and infiltration by the leftist trade unions. On October 4 Goulart sent a message to Congress claiming that vital reforms could not be carried out by ordinary procedures and requesting emergency powers for 30 days. Nearly everyone was opposed, even labor leaders and radicals such as Brizola, fearing that Goulart might use extraordinary powers against their interests. Three days later Goulart withdrew the request, but the incident heightened distrust of the president. A general strike in São Paulo further raised the political voltage and alarmed conservatives. There was a scheme, nurtured in high circles, if not by Goulart, to remove forcibly two governors, rightist Carlos Lacerda of Guanabara and leftist Miguel Arraes of Pernambuco; and Goulart ordered the prosecution of an officer who had refused to participate and had denounced the plot.[5] In December the Congress remained in session over the Christmas season in fear lest Goulart take advantage of a recess to declare a state of siege. In January Goulart finally put into effect the remittance law, in effect shutting the door on foreign business.

In the first weeks of 1964, the prestigious army chief of staff, Marshal Humberto Castelo (or Castello) Branco, lent his weight to the discussions of the overthrow of Goulart. The president, however, was misled by his yes-man military advisors into thinking that he still had ample military support and in fact counted on the military to press Congress to adopt his program.[6] He moved boldly toward a showdown by escalating the call for reforms and special powers to bring them about and summoning the masses to move against Congress.

Goulart's followers, with the cooperation of the unions and the Ministry of Labor, organized a demonstration meeting of some 200,000 persons in Rio de Janeiro on March 13. Brizola energetically urged for replacement of the "reactionary" Congress by a constituent assembly of workers, peasants, and enlisted men and called, as he had many times, for arming guerrilla "groups of eleven."[7] Ché Guevara's handbook on revolution was their bible. Goulart, with a member of the Central Committee of the Communist Party at his side,[8] dramatically signed before the multitude illegal decrees for limited land reform without compensation and for the expropriation of privately owned oil refineries, suggesting legislation by the masses. He also called the constitution unjust and obsolete and proposed a package of changes: extreme land reform, extending the franchise to illiterates, legalization of the Communist party, amendment of the constitution to give him legislative powers, and bypassing Congress through referendums; and he urged the masses to force adoption of these changes.[9]

The president seems to have been intoxicated by the applause. But his following was a cheering section, not a coherent party; and on the other side there were many appeals in the press for military intervention. It did not seem ridiculous to suppose that Goulart was taking Castro as his model, and the restructuring of the state he called for implied staying in power beyond the end of his legal term, which would expire in less than two years. Communist infiltration of the government was by this time taken for granted,[10] and the military plotters saw themselves opposing Goulart's intent to overturn the constitutional system.

On March 19 Goulart crimped financial transactions by decreeing a halt to rediscounting operations. His purpose was to impede access of the opposition to funds, but he worsened the economic crisis and exacerbated the hostility of the business community.[11] On the same day, the opposition showed its strength in São Paulo by a "March of Family with God for Liberty," in which some half million persons shouted anti-Communist slogans. There was a smaller outpouring in Belo Horizonte; and other marches were planned, as were progovernment marches, in major cities in days ahead, promising confrontations. The multitudes who took to the streets convinced the generals that an anti-Goulart move would be popular. About this time the governors of the most important states subscribed to the anti-Goulart movement. Lacerda of Guanabara had been opposed from the first; in the latter part of March he was joined by Ademar de Barros of São Paulo and José de Magalhães Pinto of Minas Gerais, both of whom spoke of using state forces to resist presidential designs.

Goulart had undercut his title to govern and claim to the obedience of the army by attacking the constitution, while raising fears of leftist dictatorship in an approaching economic collapse.[12] Under these circumstances, Castelo Branco in effect warned the president by a memorandum to senior officers pointing to the dangers of destruction of democracy, setting aside the Congress, and fomenting division within the armed forces. It is not certain, however, whether or when the military might have struck if Goulart had not challenged their command of their troops. They had long feared that Goulart would like to convert the armed forces into party-controlled militias,[13] and Castro's destruction of the Cuban army made Communism seem a real threat to their existence.[14]

It was, then, Goulart's misfortune that on March 26 some thousand sailors mutinied in support of a sailor disciplined for organizing a labor union in the navy. They took up positions in the Communist-led metal-workers' union building, issued denunciations of U.S. interests and Brazilian reactionaries, and refused to disband. The naval minister wished to punish the mutineers; but Goulart amnestied them and replaced the naval minister by a retired admiral acceptable to the labor federation. Goulart seemed to have cast overboard the sacred principle of military discipline, and the mutiny was the more alarming because of its Communist-syndicalist association. On March 30, he capped his challenge to the military by holding a meeting in the company of radical leaders of the sergeants and sailors and made a bellicose speech on television in support of the mutineers.[15] The commanding general in the state of Minas Gerais, Olimpio Mourão Filho, was so incensed by what he heard on his radio that he immediately set about moving his forces toward Rio. Meanwhile the generals had set April 2 as the date to act,[16] and Castelo Branco tried to hold Mourão back, but the impatient Mineiros had cast the die. On March 30 Governor Magalhães Pinto of Minas Gerais, shortly before the Goulart speech, had issued a manifesto condemning the Goulart government and calling for its ouster; next day, state and federal forces were on the road, a vanguard of about 2,500 men with 200 vehicles.[17] As they crossed the Minas Gerais–Rio de Janeiro border, Mourão issued a proclamation that they were acting to preserve the discipline of the armed forces, freedom, and the constitution against a Communist menace.

The uprising seemed a doubtful gamble, because everyone overestimated the strength of the Left and because the largest force, based on the city of Rio, was under the command of Goulart loyalists. So far as there was a plan or plot, it failed to coordinate much. The issue was decided when Goulart rejected several pleas for compromise and his friend Gen. Amaury Kruel in São Paulo declared against him.[18] The governors of all major states aligned themselves with the movement. Then the troops sent to halt the invaders from Minas Gerais changed sides and joined the coup, or revolution; and Goulart's power was at an end. Goulart, making no effort to organize a desperate resistance, fled on April 1 to Brasília, later that day to his home state of Rio Grande do Sul, and shortly afterward into exile in Uruguay. On April 1 the president of the Senate declared the presidency vacant, and the president of the Chamber of Deputies, Ranieri

Mazzilli, was somewhat illegally (Goulart still being in the country) sworn in as acting president.

There was no bloodshed, although the generals (and the United States) had feared a fierce civil war. One reason was Goulart's lack of fortitude. He dashed away even when some, such as Brizola, urged him to muster his adherents for a stand. However, labor and leftist leaders never fully trusted Goulart, and his supporters were mostly lukewarm. For example, his minister of war, Dantas Ribeiro, in a hospital bed, avoided having to choose sides.[19] The noncoms, whose favor Goulart sought at the cost of alienating the generals, were discontented because their pay did not keep up with inflation; and the lower-ranking officers were generally even more hostile to what they saw as a danger of Communism than the senior generals. The unionized workers did not take to the streets, as many had expected; a call for a general strike went almost unheeded. The Left was, as usual, disunited. In the agitated, supposedly near-revolutionary Northeast, the peasant masses did nothing to defend the leaders who promised them much. An era ended quietly.

THE U.S. ROLE

The United States stood over the coup-revolution of 1964, although whether as fairy godmother, midwife, or practically mother is controversial; and so far as the military regime was a creation of the United States it may have been its creature. The question of the responsibility of the United States and the propriety of its policies will probably long remain controversial.

The United States did not have to teach Latin American soldiers to enter politics. From the beginning of the republic in 1889 and the "tenente" movement of the 1920s, the Brazilian military had felt some confidence that they were better qualified than civilians to lead the country; and they had the mission of combatting subversion since the Communist insurgency of 1935.[20] However, there were close relations between the U.S. defense establishment and the Brazilian armed forces, or at least a substantial proportion of its upper echelons; and actions and policies of the United States contributed to the outlook and attitude of many Brazilian officers. The United States in 1963–64 was much worried by the drift of Brazilian politics and hoped to check that drift, while it is reasonable to assume that many Brazilian military leaders were influenced by what they perceived of U.S. moral, perhaps material support.

Only with the alliance in World War II did the Brazilian armed forces strongly accept U.S. leadership and values. Earlier contacts were rather thin, although Brazil was favored over other Latin American countries. A

U.S. naval mission was established at Rio in 1922, the first in Latin America. The United States shared military influence in Latin America with European countries, especially France and Germany. Brazil had a French training mission from 1919 to 1940. Typically, Marshal Castelo Branco studied in France before the U.S., and his second language was French.

With the rise of the Nazi-fascist threat, the United States began paying more attention to its southern neighbors. Early in 1938 a U.S.-Brazilian military assistance program was initiated, but it moved slowly for several years because of the reluctance of the U.S. government to supply to Brazil arms that were badly needed for U.S. and Allied forces. In August 1939 and afterwards top military men were traveling between the two countries, and cooperation became closer as the war moved toward the Americas. The primary American concern was for the security of the Northeastern bulge; President Vargas was at first reluctant to admit American forces, but after 1942 Brazilian and U.S. personnel worked closely together, especially on a string of airfields and bases in the Northeast, while the Brazilian and American navies developed traditions of close cooperation that long outlasted the war.[21] Many wartime economic programs also tied the two nations.

By far the most important aspect of cooperation, however, was the Brazilian Expeditionary Force (FEB) in Italy, which Americans equipped, trained, and fought beside. Brazilian officers had been going to the United States, especially Fort Leavenworth, for training since 1938; and their number swelled by 1943–44 to fill the needs of the Force. The FEB raised the self-confidence of the military and its sense of a role in the national destiny. Brazilians tried hard to overcome their inferior and dependent position, and they proudly succeeded. The cooperation was sealed in blood; of a total of some 22,000 men, there were 11,600 casualties.[22] Organization and tactics as well as weaponry were integrated with those of the United States. Many FEB officers formed personal bonds with U.S. officers, some of which lasted for many years.[23] Young Castelo Branco was tentmate and close friend of Vernon Walters, the best of the few U.S. Portuguese-speaking officers, subsequently military attaché in Rio. Castelo Branco and others came to esteem the American system and to oppose the totalitarianism that they perceived as its opposite. Even before the FEB left Italy in 1945, its commander, Gen. João Machado, observed divergences with the Communists and foresaw a new war.[24] Upon returning to Brazil, the FEB leaders forced Vargas from office, and participation in the FEB was the clearest distinguishing mark of anti-Goulart generals in 1964.[25]

After the war, the United States had a monopoly of military missions in this hemisphere until Cuba broke away in the 1960s. Especially as the cold war chilled, there was built up an extensive program of military aid for Latin American countries and training for officers in the United States and the Canal Zone. A Mutual Defense Assistance Program was begun in 1953, and the unique Joint Brazil-United States Military Commission left over from World War II was given permanent status in 1954. Military aid (about two-thirds grants) was not munificent, however; it was around $20 million per year during the decade after 1950, usually much less. Although it was expanded in the early 1960s as the United States moved to the "flexible response" posture and saw Communism increasingly as a global danger, in 1964 it came to only $17.5 million, 3.1 percent of the Brazilian defense budget.[26] Critics saw it not so much an aid as dumping of obsolete arms.[27]

About one-third of Brazilian line generals on active duty in 1964 had received some schooling from or in the United States.[28] The political effect of such training is uncertain, however. Many Peruvian and Panamanian officers exposed to U.S. military education have adopted an anti-United States or anticapitalist stance. In 1962 Secretary of Defense McNamara opined that close contacts between U.S. and Latin American officers would foster democratic attitudes among the latter, while Senator Frank Church suggested to the contrary that U.S. officers, by promoting military programs, would contribute to the militarization of Latin American society.[29] The philosophy of U.S. military personnel is at least consonant with civilian supremacy in government; there is no good evidence that U.S. military assistance has either favored or disfavored military governments in general.[30]

Indirectly, however, it seems that U.S. training, policies, and attitudes contributed to military interventionism in Latin America and Brazil in the 1960s. After the victory of Fidel Castro at the beginning of 1959, the adherence of Cuba to the Soviet Union, and the calls for turning Cuba into a base for the liberation of Latin America from the U.S. yoke, the United States became concerned about its southern neighbors. It became a major purpose of the Eisenhower administration in its last months and of the new Kennedy administration to assure the security of the hemisphere. This meant not to beat back invaders—the U.S. Navy was unchallenged—but to undercut the threat of subversion, or guerrilla or revolutionary movements of the masses, who had cause enough to be discontented.

The potentialities of radical movements under Communist leadership were amply demonstrated in Southeast Asia and Cuba; from 1961 it became the chief purpose of the U.S. military program in Latin America to prevent their spread in this hemisphere. Antisubversion or counterinsurgency became the mode, taught in U.S. military schools and journals and carried to Latin America by trainees and U.S. advisors. This was no novelty to the Brazilians, some of whom, such as Gen. Golbery do Couto e Silva, had been thinking in such terms since the mid-1950s;[31] and their friendly disposition toward the United States made them receptive to the U.S. approach. It accorded well, moreover, with their old vocation of "Order and Progress," which was hardly fulfilled by standing guard against nonexistent dangers of invasion.

The antisubversive mission required investigation of radical movements, such as Castroism, and the means of countering them. It meant broad study of political, social, and economic problems, by virtue of which the military leaders were probably educated better, or at least more systematically, than civilian politicians promoted by the hazards of electoral victory.[32] The defense of the state required economic development and political solidification; in the default of civilian leadership, these might be undertaken by the military organization, which had always seen itself as ultimate guardian of the state. Professionalization for external security meant separation from civilian politics;[33] professionalization for internal security thrust the soldiers into the heart of civilian politics.

Counterinsurgency erased the boundary between civilian and military affairs and made ambiguous the concept of enemy. The military had to decide who represented the danger, which came not from a foreign nation but from a political tendency. It seemed up to the military not only to maintain order but to undertake, as urged by U.S. authorities, civic action programs normally in the civilian sphere. It was necessary to look out not only for overt enemies but also for covert or potential enemies. Indeed, if the political and social order was so defective as to invite subversion, it might be up to the military—who else?—to reshape it.

The successive crises and radicalization during 1961-64 made counterinsurgency relevant; Castroite agitation, supported by the clouds of rhetoric emanating from Cuba, seemed a genuine threat to many. The military, taught to combat Communist infiltration, was incensed at President Quadros' pro-Cuban policy and for this reason refused to stand up for him when he resigned. By 1964, strikes and inflation could be seen as the result of some kind of internal aggression. If this was a misjudgment, it was shared with the radical Left, which was confident of coming to power by more or less revolutionary means.[34]

Counterinsurgency was developed under a theory of total conflict in the cold war between good and evil, in which the nation was at stake and its whole forces were to be guided. The intellectual basis for this approach was furnished by the Superior War College (Escola Superior de Guerra, ESG), a remarkable institution important for the formation of the higher officers before 1964 and subsequently for the ideological direction of the military government. It was an outgrowth of wartime cooperation. In admiration of American power and efficiency, the Brazilian ministry requested a mission to assist the founding of a Brazilian counterpart of the U.S. National War College. The founders of the ESG also looked into British and French experience, but the U.S. model was decisive. The program and courses were patterned after those of the National War College with the aid of several American advisors and instructors, some of whom remained for many years—although, according to the founder of the school, Gen. Cordeiro de Farias, U.S. instructors never interfered politically.[35]

The ESG soon acquired an importance for Brazil much beyond that of the National War College for the United States because of the relative weakness of other centers of sociopolitical studies and the relative political strength of the military in Brazil. Its curriculum was (and is) comprehensive, dealing with all aspects of broadly conceived national security, not merely strictly military matters but also economics and politics, national and international.[36] Because of its breadth, the ESG brought in civilians as both instructors and and students. About half of the somewhat over a hundred students admitted yearly were drawn from civilian professions, business, banking, education, law, and so forth; labor leaders were excluded by the prerequisite of a university degree for entry. The course was only one year, but there was an extensive extracurricular program of meetings, lectures, seminars, travel, and practicums; and graduates formed an association that carried the ideas of the ESG to all major cities.[37] The result was much increased communication between civilian and military leadership and presumably increased confidence of the latter in their ability in civilian affairs. The Brazilian Command and Staff College also undertook general and political instruction.

As the leading intellectual institution of the armed forces, the ESG developed a broad ideology of National Security. Its principal propositions were: National Security derives more from the general health of the nation than from the particulars of its armed forces; Brazil had the potentials of a great power but was held back by causes that could and should be removed; Brazil needed new institutions and outlook to realize its potential.[38] The ESG wanted Brazil to cooperate with the Western Christian world and perceived Communism profiting from naive politicians, unsuitable institutions, and popular ignorance.[39] It gave military leaders an intellectual basis and technical expertise to cope with national problems.

Only a minority of the top generals were ESG graduates at the time of the 1964 coup, but the Sorbonne group, as they were called, was influential and relatively united. Its leader was Castelo Branco, who had gone as instructor to the ESG in 1956; and his close connections with the ESG were a strong factor in making him a suitable candidate for the presidency.[40] Membership in the ESG group was a principal bond of anti-

Goulart conspirators,[41] and Castelo Branco's government was dominated by them.

In such ways, the United States, through its collaboration with the Brazilian military, exercised a background influence on the genesis and course of the overturn of 1964. There were more direct influences, however, or at least various efforts to exercise influence from 1962–64 as the United States became alarmed over instability and radicalism. In some interpretations, these amounted to unwarranted intervention by a stronger power to overthrow the democratic system of a weaker one.[42] For example, as was noted earlier and will be discussed later, the United States shied away from helping the Goulart government by debt renegotiation,[43] greatly reduced economic aid to it, and tried to funnel aid to more conservative state governments.

There were also efforts of the CIA to influence politics. Among these was sponsorship (under cover of the AFL-CIO) of the American Institute for Free Labor Development to promote American ideas of labor organization and train labor leaders politically favorable to the United States, in some cases perhaps to act as CIA operatives.[44] Reportedly, 136 labor leaders were involved.[45] They had no success, however, in impeding the Communist infiltration of trade unions. An agent was sent in 1962 to the troubled Northeast to organize non-Communist or Church-related cooperatives and unions, and to gather information on the peasant movement; CIA personnel attached to the consulate at Recife increased from one in 1961 to three in 1964.[46] More important was the Brazilian Institute for Democratic Action (Instituto Brasileiro de Ação Democrática, IBAD) founded in 1959 as a conduit for funds to influence Brazilian public opinion against Communism. It was supposedly financed by Brazilian business but probably mostly by foreign corporations plus—to an unknown amount—the CIA. It is alleged to have spent $12 million on the 1962 congressional election, including perhaps $5 million of U.S. provenance;[47] it was outlawed in October 1963 on suspicion of being foreign-supported.[48] Among organizations assisted by IBAD was the Institute for Investigations and Social Studies (Instituto de Pesquisas e Estudos Sociais, IPES), a conservative organization at least nominally composed of Brazilian businessmen, with a leadership which overlapped that of the ESG group.[49] The IPES carried on multiform cultural and political activities, working with the press and in electoral campaigns. Its most signal contribution, however, may have been supporting and helping to organize the huge anti-Communist marches that shortly preceded the coup of March 31, 1964.[50] No one seems to have claimed, however, that the women were paid to march. It is very flattering to the CIA and injurious to Brazil to assume, with Philip Agee, that the agency brought about the fall of Goulart by "careful planning and consistent propaganda campaigns dating at least back to the 1962 election operation."[51]

A more important role was played by the U.S. ambassador, Lincoln Gordon, who arrived about the time Goulart took office in 1961, and his gifted military attaché, Col. Vernon Walters of the Italian campaign. On his arrival, Walters was met by 13 generals, and he was obviously able to fulfill Gordon's wish, "to be able in some measure to influence [the army] through you."[52] From the first, Walters was vehemently accused by leftists of plotting against Goulart; and in fact he and the ambassador were soon visited by officers hopeful of support against the president.

Among the first was Adm. Sílvio Heck, naval minister under Quadros and a leader in the effort to keep Goulart from the presidency. After an inquiry, however, Gordon dismissed Heck's account of a conspiracy as unfounded.[53] Such visitors became very numerous in late 1963 and early 1964, and in all probability they came away with the impression that the United States would be happy to see a change of government. That the ambassador or his military attaché in any way joined a conspiracy, however, has not appeared. Walters was extremely discreet and desirous of avoiding any appearance of plotting; he even ceased going to the house of his good friend Castelo Branco when he learned of the planning for a coup about a month before it.[54]

There was, indeed, not so much a conspiracy as a feeling out of sentiments of high officers more or less unhappy with the Goulart government to coordinate attitudes and responses if they should judge a coup necessary. It did not prove possible, in fact, to organize the action properly; the outcome depended on the undecided commanders. To prepare the generals for a coup, there was no need or reason to seek the assistance of American authorities. It was important only to know that the United States would not oppose the action, but probably would help in case of prolonged civil conflict.

The ambassador and the State Department were eager, of course, to do whatever they judiciously could. They had become convinced months before the coup that Goulart was an incompetent opportunist who might well lead Brazil into chaos and Communism—and if Brazil fell, all the South American dominoes might follow. Gordon told the Senate, "It had become clear months before his deposition that his purpose was to put an end to constitutional government in Brazil in the interest of establishing some form of personal dictatorship."[55] By March 1964 the embassy saw Goulart clearly moving toward dictatorship in cooperation with the Communist party (as Gordon told the State Department March 27) and had become convinced of the necessity of a coup.[56] Moreover, those watching from Washington, like everyone else, grossly overestimated the strength of leftist forces and anticipated possible civil war. There were consequently drawn up plans for the support of a serious struggle—against the advice of Walters.[57] They contemplated the shipment of arms by six transport planes and the dispatch of an aircraft carrier, six destroyers, and four oilers from Norfolk on April 1—the oilers because it was feared pro-Communist petroleum workers might deprive anti-Communist forces of fuel.[58] These plans were hastily put together a few days before the coup when Gordon informed Washington of the imminence of action. Operation "Brother Sam" was cancelled, of course, before the task force got far in the Atlantic, because of the success of the coup. It may have been important that the prospects of U.S. assistance helped to reduce the risks for the generals ousting the president; it has not been shown, however, that they decided the waverers.

Various Brazilian writers credit Gordon and Walters with central roles in the anti-Goulart movement, an interpretation that seems to belittle the capacity of Brazilian generals to move on their own. In the more conspiratorial interpretations, the CIA is even credited with provoking the sailors' mutiny, Goulart's handling of which triggered his downfall.[59] The leader and momentary hero of the left, José Anselmo, was allegedly a CIA agent. One fable was that the United States had introduced about 4,000 combatants into Brazil, especially in the Northeast, to leap into action in case of need.[60]

For many ideological critics, the situation has been clear enough in theory that documentation was superfluous: the Brazilian ruling class and the foreign capitalist interests, backed by the U.S. government, felt threatened by the workers and peasants mobilized by Goulart, Brizola, Julião, and their followers. The national and international capitalists plotted with and through the military leaders to crush this threat by smashing democracy and constitutional government, which they support only so far as profitable. Little is said of the faults of Goulart, who in defeat became something of a shining knight to the leftists.

Evidence of U.S. complicity includes the record of intervention in Latin America from the Mexican War through the Dominican intervention in 1965. The latter particularly lent credence to a readiness to intervene in Brazil in 1964. The conspicuous presence of American capital in Brazil put an additional burden of proof on those who might claim the United States was not responsible. The well-known relations of the Brazilian Armed Forces to the American was additional evidence; the arms used in the coup had come from the United States and many of the generals had received training in the United States. That the United States was unhappy with the Goulart government was undeniable, and the coup was greeted with obvious joy. The Johnson administration recognized the new government within hours (partly in hopes of strengthening a civilian succession) and quickly followed up with economic aid. The final proof of U.S. involvement was the preparation—divulged only years later—to furnish military support to anti-Goulart forces. It was also satisfying for Brazilian writers to see imperialism behind the establishment of the dictatorship. On the one hand, this discredited the widely disliked military rule as an alien imposition manipulated by foreigners; on the other hand, it relieved Brazilians of responsibility for the lapse from respectable, legitimate government.

However, when San Tiago Dantas on March 31 offered the theory to Goulart that the State Department was managing the coup,[61] it can only have been a visceral analysis. There is no doubt that U.S. influence in Brazil in the early 1960s was very strong, and in many ways the United States was involved with influential sectors of Brazilian society, culture, economics, and politics. Its participation was taken for granted and sought by many Brazilians although rejected by many others in one aspect or another. American influence, however, is complex and in many ways contradictory. The democratic and equalitarian ideals of Goulart and his followers were not in the native Brazilian tradition but were imported, to a large extent from the United States; likewise, the Brazilian military took up the ideas and approach of counterinsurgency less because the United States favored them than because such ideals well suited their condition and needs.

If Latin American societies were well-integrated and politically effective, there would be little room for U.S. intervention and little anxiety about it. Such militarily weak countries as Belgium or Denmark are hardly concerned about U.S. manipulation of their politics. But Brazil in the early 1960s was profoundly divided, and the central administration was hardly master of its own house. Class conflict was consciously fanned, but there was no leadership capable of channeling and directing discontent for effective political action, while a strategy of economic deterioration to make special powers necessary (if such really was the president's strategy) was extremely hazardous. The Goulart administration was not really in command of its own house; for example, it was unable to carry through an investigation of IBAD to show clearly whether it was foreign (presumably CIA) financed. A supplementary military agreement was reached with the United States early in 1964; this is cited as preparation for intervention,[62] but it was a voluntary act of the Goulart administration.

The military elite itself was by no means united; if some were pro-United States, others were nationalistic. In Military Club elections, the majority was first with one side, then with the other, and pro-Goulart forces nearly won as late as 1962. Irving Louis Horowitz wrote shortly before the coup that "a large portion and perhaps even a majority to the military elite favors a rigorous anti-U.S. and strongly nationalistic economic and political program."[63] Vernon Walters kept in touch, as his duties required, not only with Castelo Branco and the Sorbonne group but with pro-Goulart generals.[64] But the generals were united in dedication to their institution, and Goulart alienated his friends and sitrred his enemies to action by his attack on the cornerstone of their status, military discipline.

The direct intervention of American authorities—trying to help conservative state governments, contributing to anti-Communist movements, and the like, hardly seems of major importance. It was, in any case, more or less counterbalanced by the contrary intervention of Cuba, whose Fidel Castro promoted revolution in Brazil to the extent of his limited capacities. A negative American policy was possibly more important: the withdrawal by the Johnson administration of the Kennedy administration's support for democracy in this hemisphere. In the early 1960s, democratic regimes had come to power in Argentina, Peru, Venezuela, and other countries; and hopes were high that political and economic development was on the way. The Alliance for Progress (1961) assumed that democracy, economic justice, economic development, and U.S. business and political interests were all compatible, and that the United States was competent to lead the junior brother republics to the benefit of all these purposes. But the Alliance bogged down, and it became increasingly evident that in such unequal societies as those of Latin America, democracy, in the sense of mass participation in politics, is likely to open the way to radical attacks on both economic and political interests of the United States. The U.S. penchant for democracy thus conflicted with the desire for stability and pro-U.S. governments, because the United States was the obvious target of groups seeking change. It could be argued that democracy might open the gates to Communist influence; if so, it might be well for military governments to act as guardian of order until economic progress should make democracy practicable. Perhaps Kennedy would have continued his policy of discouraging military coups, but Johnson took a more pragmatic approach. A speech by Assistant Secretary of State Thomas Mann, March 20, 1964, was extensively reported by the Brazilian press as indicating that the United States was no longer opposed to military coups on principle.

In sum, the United States, because of its weight in the hemisphere and its close relations with the Brazilian military establishment, had something to do with the coup of 1964, which it strongly favored. However, as Lincoln Gordon said in 1966, "Certainly in Brazil in the last four years I have been very aware of the limitations of our influence. Brazil is a very large country with a very active political life of its own, and the American voice, although a significant one, is in no sense a controlling one."[65] He assured the Senate Committee on Foreign Relations, "Neither the American Embassy nor I played any part in the process whatsoever." Brazilian officers were prepared to cooperate with the United States for their own purposes in combatting what they perceived as a Communist danger.[66] They were above all concerned to end what they regarded as a threat to the integrity of their forces.[67] In March 1964 there was universal anticipation of a coup or civil war without reference to any U.S. actions.[68] Evidence that U.S. authorities instigated, directed, or significantly participated in planning the coup is absent.[69] Those who claim the contrary are capable of seeing the U.S. plotting, for example, to prevent Kubitschek from taking office in 1955.[70] The coup might well have occurred even if the United States had been neutral or opposed, as conceded by a critic of the United States.[71] So far as the United States was influential, it was mostly in helping to create the atmosphere in which the coup was gestated and emboldening the makers of it. The concrete actions taken seem to have been trivial in their effects. They were partly counterproductive so far as they became known at the time and subsequently as they were cited to discredit the regime that the United States favored.

THE PRO-AMERICAN GOVERNMENT

If the United States desired the coup, it did not intend a permanent military regime. Americans shared the general assumption that historical patterns would be repeated, and the military leaders spoke in terms of protecting the constitution and democracy. It was natural to expect this because the coup was broadly supported by civilian authorities, most of the Congress, and a large majority of state governors; the military acted only against the Goulart administration and consequently had little reason to fear returning power to civilians. The traditional "moderator" role of the Brazilian armed forces assumed that representative government is normal and legitimate and that the forces, having acted to protect the constitutional order, would step back as soon as practicable and return the government to elected civilian leadership. The middle and upper classes that desired a coup did not foresee loss thereby of civil liberties, of freedom of speech and the press, and of representative government with unhampered political parties. The state governors wanted the military not to preempt but to guarantee free elections in which they might contend for the presidency. The military intervened ostensibly to protect the constitutional power; and it has always, unlike Vargas' New State, presented its rule as temporary, designed to use special powers to prepare for an eventual return to full democracy.

Official instructions to Gordon on March 31, as the coup was getting under way, insisted on the need for a constitutional succession; a military junta might be acceptable "as a last resort, but that would make U.S. assistance more difficult."[72] One reason for the haste of Johnson's congratulatory message, released less than 18 hours after the installation of Mazzilli as provisional president, was to encourage adherence to a "framework of constitutional democracy."[73] It was the U.S. position that the coup should be considered a legal reaction to illegal actions and threats of actions by Goulart, should respect legitimate claims to the succession, and should be approved by the Congress and ratified by state governments,[74] all of which was apparently feasible.

When the barrier to action had been broken, however, the military authorities resolved to use their power to make much more change than was possible within the old political framework or with the consent of elected bodies. They recalled that returning the government promptly to civilians had had poor results in 1950 and 1954, and saw the old set of leaders wanting only to get back to the old political game, while they, like the radical Left, thought Brazil needed a deep change. The whole system seemed tinged with corruption and demagoguery, as well as leftist radicalism.

The first step of the new rulers was to arrest some 7,000 persons and remove 9,000 from office. The military leadership wanted Congress to pass an enabling act granting full powers; when the Congress hesitated, the generals quickly took to themselves the prerogative of constitution making and decreed an Institutional Act, later known as Institutional Act I when a number of successors had been promulgated. This Act, drawn by Francisco Campos, who had authored a sort of constitution for Vargas' New State in 1937 and had leaned toward Germany before World War II,[75] assumed de facto legitimacy by the authority of the successful revolution, sanctioned the purges, and conferred emergency powers on the president to be elected to finish the term of Goulart, after which a new elected president would govern under the old constitution.

Marshal Humberto Castelo Branco was accepted as interim president by a purged Congress on April 11. He continued the revolution by depriving over 300 persons of political rights for ten years, including everyone prominently associated with the Goulart government and some, such as ex-President Quadros, who were not. There was also a purge of military ranks; and there were extensive and frequently abusive investigations, detentions, and maltreatment of prisoners suspected of subversion or Communist connections. Castelo, however, was a moderate who reassured the country of the intended return to the democratic order. Although he held great powers as president, he permitted the Congress and courts to function more or less normally with reduced powers, tolerated the activities of the political parties, and maintained freedom of the press.

If Ambassador Gordon and his superiors were displeased by the failure of the military to return the government promptly to civilians, they were happy with the choice of Marshal Castelo Branco, an enlightened gentleman with ties to the United States—conceivably the favor he enjoyed in American eyes was a factor in his selection as president. Castelo had undergone training in the United States, as had 80 percent of the generals close to him, but only 24 percent of other generals.[76] He was also the most eminent veteran of the FEB and was leader of the group associated with the ESG.

Although the new government resisted such pressures as there may have been to return to democracy, in most respects it proved highly satisfactory to the United States. It brusquely rejected the neutralist foreign policy of previous years to restore the old special relationship It gave priority to the struggle against Communism in close cooperation with U.S. military and diplomatic personnel, holding up the United States as leader of the Western alliance and guardian of civilized values. A United Nations Third World conference was under way at the time of the revolution; the Brazilian position in its debates immediately changed from pushing the attack on the industrial nations to taking a position more favorable to the United States than any other Latin American state.[77] Diplomatic relations with Cuba were broken within weeks. The Quadros government had taken a neutral position in the conflict of Portugal with uprisings in its African colonies; Castelo Branco went back to the traditional posture of support for the motherland.

In August 1964 Castelo Branco expressed solidarity with the United States in connection with the Tonkin Gulf incident, when North Vietnamese boats allegedly attacked U.S. destroyers. There were negotiations for sending a Brazilian force to Vietnam in 1965 and 1966, in return for which the United States would furnish Brazil two destroyers and other arms.[78] Only a medical team was sent, however—no great contribution but more than that of any other Latin American nation. Castelo Branco turned away from Latin American regionalism as adverse to the United States and preferred pan-American unity, including the United States as chief force.[79] Brazil joined eagerly in the U.S. intervention in the Dominican Republic in 1965, despite the widespread unpopularity of this action. Brazil supplied troops and a nominal commander for the inter-American interventionist forces not only to cooperate with the United States but to step onto the world scene. The decision was announced before it could be discussed with U.S. representatives so that it would be plain that Brazil was acting on its own initiative.[80]

The basic idea of the Castelo Branco foreign policy was that the world was divided into hostile blocs by the cold war, in which Brazil and the United States were on the same side of an irreconcilable moral division. Brazilian security depended, then, ultimately on the United States, but it was up to Brazil to do its share in combatting subversion and indirect aggression in Brazil and in Latin America.[81] Brazil and other more developed Latin American nations would act as subleaders to protect weaker countries from infiltration, placing collective security ahead of national sovereignty. Foreign Minister Juracy Magalhães went so far as to say, "What is good for the U.S. is good for Brazil."[82]

That Castelo's foreign policy hewed close to that of the United States owed something to the new government's need for all-around support; and the new concord was equally apparent in economic affairs. Washington moved after the coup to provide aid with rapidity extraordinary for the bureaucracy; a moratorium on debt payments was proposed almost immediately, and by June a loan of $50 million was approved. Program loans totaling $625 million had been authorized during the Quadros-Goulart period, but only $100 million disbursed; the remainder was now released and supplemented by more than $600 million in 1964-68.[83] Castelo Branco's chief economic advisor, Roberto Campos, was a long-time friend of the United States; and he and the president consulted Lincoln Gordon at every turn.[84] In October 1964 the government ratified the long-pending settlement of the expropriation of U.S.-owned utilities to nationalist shouts of "sellout" and "neocolonialism;" the rightist Lacerda, hoping to be a presidential candidate in 1966, was one of the loudest.[85] The profits remittance law was repealed in August, but the nationalists still had enough strength to delay the enabling act until the following February.[86] Castelo Branco sold a state-owned motor factory, opposed making a state monopoly of the petrochemical industry, and authorized concessions to various foreign corporations, including the Hanna Mining Company, bête noire of the nationalists. Castelo Branco came close to equating economic nationalism with pro-Communism, and saw "false nationalism" in attacks on foreign investments.

It was the understanding of the Castelo Branco government that, in return for its cooperation, the United States would assist Brazil economically by opening the U.S. market not only to traditional Brazilian exports but to the products of new industries, support commodity prices, and supply investment capital and technology. To a considerable degree, these expectations were met by the economic assistance already mentioned, although the influx of U.S. capital became massive only after several years of stabilization. Military sales, $2.5 million in 1965, rose to $12 million in 1966. Economic aid totaled $2 billion from 1964 to 1970, more than to any other country except Vietnam and India.[87] The United States also collaborated with the "apprentice great power" (Alfred Stepan's phrase) by furnishing technical assistance in many areas, including surveillance and control of subversion, and administrative management. In almost any Brazilian government office there was an American advisor.[88] U.S. official personnel more than doubled, to 1,357 in 1966,[89] apart from regular embassy staff and Peace Corps.

Brazil never subordinated itself entirely to U.S. policy; for example, relations established by the Goulart government with Communist countries were not broken (except with Cuba), and the military government proceeded pragmatically to expand trade with the Soviet Union. However, it would be difficult to find another example of a major nation so amenable to the wishes of a superpower without coercion or threat. It was widely believed in Brazil during the Castelo Branco presidency (1964–67) that Ambassador Gordon was the real master of the government.[90] One writer, for example, speaks of the "protectorate of Mr. Lincoln Gordon."[91]

NOTES

1. Georges-André Fiechter, *Le régime modernisateur du Brésil* (Leiden: Sijthoff, 1972), p. 34.

2. Fernando Pedreira, *Brasil político 1964–1975* (São Paulo: Difel, 1975), pp. 42, 250.

3. John W. F. Dulles, *Castelo Branco, the Making of a Brazilian President* (College Station, Tex.: Texas A & M University Press, 1978), p. 309.

4. Ronald H. Chilcote, *The Brazilian Communist Party: Conflict and Integration 1922–1972* (New York: Oxford University Press, 1974), p. 80.

5. Thomas Skidmore, *Politics in Brazil: An Experiment in Democracy, 1930–1964* (New York: Oxford University Press, 1967), p. 299.

6. Alfred Stepan, "Brazil," in *The Breakdown of Democratic Regimes*, eds. Juan J. Linz and Alfred Stepan (Baltimore: Johns Hopkins Univeristy Press, 1978), p. 123.

7. *New York Times*, March 15, 1964, p. 24.

8. John W. F. Dulles, *Unrest in Brazil* (Austin, Tex.: University of Texas Press, 1970), p. 7.; U.S. Congress, Senate, Committee on Foreign Relations, *Nomination of Lincoln Gordon, to be Assistant Secretary of State for Inter-American Affairs*, Hearing, February 7, 1966, p. 10.

9. Ronald M. Schneider, *The Political System of Brazil: Emergence of a "Modernizing Authoritarian Regime"* (New York: Columbia University Press, 1971), p. 93.

10. Chilcote, *The Brazilian Communist Party*, p. 81.

11. Moniz Bandeira, *O governo João Goulart: As lutas sociais no Brasil, 1961–1964* (Rio de Janeiro: Editora Civilização Brasileira, 1978), pp. 166–67.

12. Hélio Jaguaribe, *Brasil: crise e alternativas* (Rio de Janeiro: Zahar Editores, 1974), p. 50.

13. Dulles, *Unrest*, p. 150.

14. Vernon A. Walters, *Silent Mission* (Garden City, N.Y.: Doubleday, 1978), p. 396.

15. *New York Times*, March 31, 1964, p. 1.

16. Skidmore, *Politics in Brazil*, p. 299.

17. Dulles, *Unrest*, p. 314.

18. Bandeira, *Goulart*, p. 180.

19. Ibid., p. 167.

20. Peter Flynn, *Brazil: A Political Analysis* (Boulder, Colo.: Westview Press, 1978), p. 321.

21. Michael Morris, *International Politics and the Sea: The Case of Brazil* (Boulder, Colo.: Westview Press, 1979), pp. 182–89.

22. Frank D. McCann, Jr., *The Brazilian-American Alliance, 1937–1945* (Princeton: Princeton University Press, 1973), p. 431.

23. Alfred Stepan, *The Military in Politics: Changing Patterns in Brazil* (Princeton: Princeton University Press, 1971), p. 128.

24. José Alfredo Amaral Gurgel, *Segurança e democracia: uma reflexão política* (Rio de Janeiro: Livraria José Olympio, 1975), p. 35.

25. Stepan, *Military*, pp. 49–50.

26. Harold A. Hovey, *United States Military Assistance* (New York: Praeger, 1965), p. 64.

27. Bandeira, *Goulart*, p. 399.

28. Stepan, *Military*, p. 131.

29. Jan K. Black, *United States Penetration of Brazil* (Philadelphia: University of Pennsylvania Press, 1977), p. 216.

30. Hovey, *United States Military Assistance*, pp. 66–67.

31. Stepan, *Military*, p. 130.

32. Alfred Stepan, "The New Professionalism," in *Authoritarian Brazil*, ed. Alfred Stepan (New Haven: Yale University Press, 1973).

33. As contended by Samuel Huntington, *The Soldier and the State: The Theory and Politics of Civil-Military Relations* (New York: Vintage Books, 1964).

34. Joseph A. Page, *The Revolution that Never Was: Northeast Brazil, 1955–1964* (New York: Grossman, 1972), p. 19.

35. *Estado de São Paulo*, July 1, 1979, p. 12.

36. Gurgel, *Segurança*, p. 30.

37. Stepan, *Military*, p. 176.

38. Gurgel, *Segurança*, pp. 30–31.

39. Eliezer Rizzo de Oliveira, *As forças armadas: política e ideologia no Brasil 1964–1969* (Petrópolis: Editora Vozes, 1976), pp. 22–23.

40. Dulles, *Unrest*, p. 345.

41. Oliveira, *As forças armadas*, p. 52.

42. See especially Black, *United States Penetration*.

43. Skidmore, *Politics in Brazil*, p. 271.

44. Winslow Peck, "The AFL-CIA," in *Uncloaking the CIA*, ed. Howard Frazier (New York: Free Press, 1978), p. 264.

45. *Veja*, August 1, 1979, p. 27.

46. Page, *Revolution*, pp. 128–29, 155.

47. Phyllis R. Parker, *Brazil and the Quiet Intervention, 1964* (Austin, Tex.: University of Texas Press, 1979), p. 27.

48. Black, *United States Penetration*, p. 255.

49. Fiechter, *Le régime*, p. 37.

50. Bandeira, *Goulart*, p. 166.

51. Philip Agee, *Inside the Company: CIA Diary* (New York: Stonehill, 1975), p. 362.

52. Walters, *Silent Mission*, p. 374.

53. Parker, *Intervention*, pp. 10–11.

54. Dulles, *Castelo*, p. 332.

55. Senate, Committee on Foreign Relations, *Nomination of Lincoln Gordon*, p. 7.

56. Ibid., p. 12.

57. Walters, *Silent Mission*, p. 388.

58. Parker, *Intervention*, pp. 68–69, 76.

59. Bandeira, *Goulart*, p. 169.

60. Oliveira, *As forças armadas*, p. 52.

61. Robinson Rojas, *Estados Unidos en Brasil*, (Santiago: Prensa Latinoamericana, 1965), p. 154.

62. Moniz Bandeira, *Prescença dos Estados Unidos no Brasil* (Rio de Janeiro: Editora Civilização Brasileira, 1973), p. 154.

63. Black, *United States Penetration*, p. 43.

64. Irving L. Horowitz, *Revolution in Brazil: Politics and Society in a Developing Nation* (New York: Dutton, 1964), p. 399.

65. Senate, Committee on Foreign Relations, *Nomination of Lincoln Gordon*, p. 7.

66. Ibid., p. 44.

67. For a view minimizing the U.S. ingredient see Max G. Manwaring, "The Military in Brazilian Politics" (Ph.D. diss., University of Illinois, 1968).

68. Black, *United States Penetration*, p. 27.

69. Parker, *Intervention*, pp. 102–3.

70. Rojas, *Estados Unidos en Brasil*, pp. 62–66.

71. Black, *United States Penetration*, p. 257.

72. Parker, *Intervention*, p. 75.

73. Schneider, *Political System*, p. 119.

74. Parker, *Intervention*, pp. 74–75.

75. McCann, *The Brazilian-American Alliance*, p. 34.

76. Stepan, *Military*, pp. 339–42.

77. Black, *United States Penetration*, p. 52.

78. *Isto É*, December 14, 1977, pp. 42–45.

79. Carlos Estevam Martins, *Capitalismo do estado e modelo político no Brasil* (Rio de Janeiro: Editiones de Braal, 1977, p. 378.

80. Álvaro Valle, *As novas estructuras políticas brasileiras* (Rio de Janeiro: Nordica, 1977), p. 219.

81. Martins, *Capitalismo do estado*, pp. 369–71.

82. Ibid., p. 373.

83. Peter D. Bell, "Brazilian-American Relations," in *Brazil in the Sixties*, ed. Riordan Roeth (Nashville, Tenn.: Vanderbilt University Press, 1972).

84. Dom Bonafede, "Blunder in Brazil," *Nation* 200, May 26, 1969, p. 663.

85. Fiechter, *Le régime*, pp. 73–74.

86. E. Bradford Burns, *Nationalism in Brazil: An Historical Survey* (New York: Praeger, 1968), p. 121.

87. Thomas E. Weil et al., *Area Handbook for Brazil* (Washington, D.C.: American University Press, 1975), p. 295.

88. John W. Tuthill, "Operation Topsy," *Foreign Policy* 8 (Fall 1972):62–85.

89. Black, *United States Penetration*, p. 62.

90. Bell, "Brazilian-American Relations," pp. 93–94.

91. Euzébio Rocha, *Brasil, pais ameaçado, e o acordo de garantias* (São Paulo: Fulgor, 1965), p. 7.

3

INDEPENDENCE

BRAZIL FIRST

Exceptional warmth and uncritical admiration for the United States soon began to wear out, as the euphoria of the revolution waned, both among the political leaders and those outside. Gratitude, a peculiarly fragile emotion, faded; and frictions returned. The nationalistic tendencies in the armed forces were not destroyed in 1964 but submerged, and presently they began to resurface. Nationalism was becoming more important than either anti-Communism or pleasing the United States. Some officers protested the "denationalization" of the Brazilian economy, and the thinking of the military was turning from respect for the sanctity of property to indignation at high profits.[1] By 1967, the country and the regime were ready for a "Brazil first" policy.

After 1967, economic expansion, with a 27 percent annual increase of exports during 1967–73, eroded the special relation by bringing Brazil more fully into the world economy and reducing particular dependence on the United States. At the same time, the discomfiture and eventual defeat of the United States in Vietnam and the climate of sharply anti-U.S. sentiments in much of the world made it impossible for the Brazilian leadership to uncritically admire and automatically applaud U.S. positions. It became evident that the great leader could not effectively combat Communism at a distance and was no longer a determined chief of the anti-Communist battalions in a waning cold war. Equally important was the ebbing of U.S. economic domination, evident in the monetary crisis of 1971 and especially following the 1973–74 rise in oil prices.[2]

In 1969 the Rockefeller Report urged a benign attitude toward anti-Communist military governments in Latin America, but the feeling had been growing that military aid was linked to military coups and that it was improper to furnish or sell arms to Latin American governments for use primarily against their own peoples. The U.S. military mission, around 200 in 1968, was down to 60 in 1971[3] and arms deliveries were sharply curtailed, although military assistance continued at a low level. Economic aid was also phased out after 1968, partly because of the decreased worldwide American commitment, partly because it seemed less needed as the Brazilian economy boomed and the American stagnated.

A sharp turn came with the inauguration on March 15, 1967, of Gen. Arthur da Costa e Silva as president. Castelo Branco did not prefer Costa e Silva, but his following in the Armed Forces was not strong enough to enable him to choose his successor. Costa e Silva was more hard-line and less intellectual than his predecessor, did not belong to the group centered on the ESG, had not participated in the FEB, and had no special love for the United States. He brought in a new corps of advisors whom American officials found less competent and less congenial.

Castelo Branco and his friends were apprehensive that Costa e Silva might turn to economic nationalism and scuttle the policy of monetary stabilization that they had imposed for several years to provide a basis for future growth. He did not do this because the Castelo Branco approach of qualified liberalism had momentum and was promising. But he redirected foreign policy, as Jânio Quadros had done six years earlier, toward independent nationalism. Although his moves were, like those of Quadros, more gesture than substance, he reaffirmed Brazilian nonacceptance of the Nuclear Non-Proliferation Treaty, withdrew support for the Inter-American Peace Force (a lost cause in any event), demanded tariff concessions from the United States, and engaged in a controversy over instant coffee.

Another change of personalities also contributed to the reduction of U.S. influence. Lincoln Gordon, who had been very close to Castelo Branco, turned over the embassy to John Tuthill not long after Costa e Silva's inauguration. Tuthill (and ambassadors who followed him) was not especially attached to Brazil and developed no intimacy with its leaders. After Tuthill ventured to meet with Carlos Lacerda, who had become almost as critical of the military government as he had been of Goulart, Costa e Silva refused to see the ambassador at all. Tuthill's contribution to U.S.-Brazilian relations was to prune severely the inflated embassy staff. He became convinced that he could not only save money but also make U.S. policy more effective by reducing the personnel in half. Against the expectable resistance of many who liked their jobs in Brazil and of their agencies in Washington, he managed to relieve about a third of the employees.[4] Some of this was cutting bureaucratic fat; for example, there were 52 persons, half U.S. citizens, manning a quite unnecessary radio communication system.[5] Various controversial programs were phased out, such as a project for joint educational planning. But slashing them represented a judgment that the involvement they represented was not productive.

The United States and Brazil also moved apart because of the growing authoritarianism of the latter. In 1964 there had been no plan to establish a military dictatorship, but it evolved step by step as a dominant sector of the officers reacted to what they perceived as threats to their revolution. In October 1965 Castelo Branco held free elections for governorships; and many, mostly younger officers were enraged when men who seemed representatives of the old order won in two important states. The hard-liners came near forcing the ouster of Castelo Branco; to placate them he was compelled (while allowing the elected governors to take office) to issue Institutional Act II. This provided, inter alia, for indirect (and hence controllable) elections for president and governors, reduction of the freedom of Congress to deal with bills, and the dissolution of the old parties. These were replaced by two new docile parties, one to support the government, the other to act as a very loyal opposition. Earlier, Castelo Branco extended his own term of office, although he disqualified himself from seeking reelection. Gordon proposed a protest against Institutional Act II in order to support Castelo Branco against the military extremists.[6] But the military command accepted that firm action and full powers were necessary to put the program of the new government into practice.

The succession of Castelo Branco not by an elected civilian but by a general chosen by the generals dismayed some in the American government. But Costa e Silva took a bigger stride toward authoritarianism at the end of 1968. When the Congress balked at lifting the immunity of a deputy who had spoken slightingly of the Armed Forces, Costa e Silva dissolved the Congress, imposed censorship, and made many arrests. Then by Institutional Act V he set up an almost unlimited dictatorship, making explicit the authoritarianism inherent in the revolution. Ambassador Tuthill wanted his government to send a strong demarche, but Secretary of State Dean Rusk declined to do so on the ground that no one had been killed and U.S. investments had not been endangered. Loans were held up for a few months, but normal relations then resumed, despite disappointment that the movement intended to protect the legal order and democracy had become arbitrary and coercive. Widespread repressions, often accompanied by torture, especially from 1969 to 1972, precluded cordiality between Washington and Brasília, although a good climate for business was maintained.

At the same time, the leadership role of America was sapped by the trauma of Vietnam, economic problems, the demoralization of Watergate, and the chronic balance of payments deficit. The American mood was to reduce commitments and engagement abroad, while Brazil was attributing less importance to the United States.[7] Besides the steps already mentioned, the Costa e Silva government tried to organize a Latin American nuclear community (excluding the United States),[8] and downgraded the Alliance for Progress, so far as this was not already moribund. Seeing the United States and the Soviet Union on the way to détente, the Brazilians began emphasizing less the cold war and more the conflict of interests of the rich and the less developed countries. Underdevelopment seemed more of a problem than Communism. Increasingly taking a Third World position, Brazil was a leader in the formation of the Group of 77 in 1968. Brazil also sought to broaden relations with the industrial world. Arms were purchased in Britain, breaking a long U.S. monopoly, and in 1970 Mirage fighters from France. The U.S. share of Brazilian foreign trade was declining, and the Brazilians were annoyed because the United States consistently bought less than it sold. A loan was negotiated with the Soviet Union for the purchase of hydropower equipment, and there were a number of other agreements to increase Soviet-Brazilian trade—not very successful, withal, because of lack of Brazilian demand for Soviet products.

Brazil was not basically hostile to the United States, however; and ordinary Brazilians were hardly aware of the cooling.[9] In 1967, Costa e Silva paid a state visit to Washington. In 1968 he vetoed a bill restricting the sale of land to foreigners.[10] Brazil came to the assistance of the United States in the dispute of the latter with Peru over the nationalization of oil properties.[11] Brazil cooperated with the International Monetary Fund and the United States on monetary matters and maintained a benign atmosphere for foreign corporations in Brazil. When American Ambassador C. Burke Elbrick was kidnapped by leftists in September 1969, it hastened to accede to their conditions, releasing 15 political prisoners to Mexico, to the disgust of the tough nationalists. Differences with the United States were of little depth; typical controversies were those arising over details of disarmament proposals, the promotion of birth control, and questions of trade barriers.

Costa e Silva was incapacitated by a stroke, August 29, 1969. A committee of generals, bypassing the vice president, selected as his successor Gen. Emilio Garrastazu Médici. To validate his presidency, the Congress was brought back; and the Congress has continued to function as part of the military-dominated but regularized government. The administration of Médici was strongly anti-Communist and fundamentally in sympathy with the United States and the Nixon administration, yet Brazil continued to assert its own interests. Encouraged by its growth, demographic as well as economic (the population passed 100 million in 1972), it began looking to change in the world order and nourishing its claim to be a future world leader, a "world power" before the end of the century.

Independence meant broadening the interests of Brazilian diplomacy from coffee and loans to questions of protectionism, the international monetary system, ownership of the seabed and territorial waters, arms sales, and so forth. As the cold war waned, the Médici administration saw the United States and the Soviet Union trying to hold world power structures fixed in their favor, to the detriment of rising Brazil. A key point of Brazilians became and remained opposition to "containment" by the superpowers, as by the U.N. charter (giving great power status to France but denying it to Brazil), the Nuclear Non-Proliferation Treaty (closing the doors of the atomic club), international control of pollution, population control policies, and international trade structures favorable to the developed countries.[12] The Médici government rejected the Kissinger idea of a pentagonal world (United States, Soviet Union, European Economic Community [EEC], China, and Japan), claiming a corner for itself. It was inclined to agree with the nationalists and leftists that capitalist structures transferred wealth from the poor nations to the rich, and it had little confidence in any special relation with the United States.[13] Capital and technology had not flowed so abundantly to Brazil and the U.S. market had not been opened so freely as Castelo Branco had hoped. As the United States became less ideological with Nixon's opening to Peking and Moscow, Brazil looked to its own interests, which inevitably diverged from those of its great friend.

The United States accepted that Brazil would act for itself, and the "low profile" approval of the Nixon years precluded serious attempts to exert influence unless rather important U.S. interests seemed endangered.[14] The Médici government did not seek to change the world or to challenge for the sake of challenge, but to improve its place, a desire quite understandable to U.S. policymakers. With the passing of the cold war and the leaders formed in it, Brazilian aspirations became primarily economic. An official goal proclaimed in 1970 was to raise Brazil to the level of the advanced states by the end of this century thanks to a 7 to 10 percent yearly increase in GNP.[15] This was to be achieved by bringing in capital and technology, with an increasing role for state capital, in the long term to make Brazil the power it always deserved to be, in the short run to legitimate the military rule based originally on force. National prosperity was by a wide margin the goal most often mentioned in speeches of Médici, seven times as often as international prestige.[16]

The character of U.S.-Brazilian conflict was exemplified by the controversy over the extension by fiat of Brazilian territorial waters to 200 miles in March 1970, at a time when only a few countries, particularly those of the west coast of South America, asserted such a claim. The issue was somewhat emotional for Brazilians because a few years earlier their pride had been injured by the French navy's successful protection of French lobster fishermen off the Brazilian coast. Public opinion was ahead of the government, which moved not because of foreign policy but for domestic and bureaucratic reasons.[17] But there was no effort to appeal to nationalism or anti-imperialism. Negotiations were limited to the issue of territorial waters, concerning which the bargaining power of the United States was slight because Brazil had little interest in fishing in U.S. waters. The United States refused in principle to recognize the validity of the claim, but agreed to limit fishing in the waters claimed by Brazil and to make a small contribution toward surveillance. A potential confrontation became a piece of quiet bargaining.[18] Perhaps because shrimp are less valuable than tuna, there was far less friction with Brazil than with Ecuador.

The Nixon administration was basically sympathetic to the Brazilian objectives of development and was happy to welcome Médici on an official visit to Washington in December 1971. On this occasion, Nixon uttered a much-quoted aphorism, "As Brazil goes, so will go the rest of the Latin American continent."[19] The Brazilians were flattered but somewhat embarrassed, because they no longer wished to be seen as U.S. agents—"subimperialists" in Latin America. As Secretary of State Rogers saw it in 1973, "We don't have any problems, really, at the moment at all between Brazil and the United States."[20] On a brief visit to Brazil in June 1973 he omitted such matters as instant coffee and Brazil's territorial waters to concentrate on amiability. Nixon hoped to visit Brazil, but Watergate intervened.

Through the 1970s, Brazil continued to move away from the old dependence. Trade with Eastern Europe multiplied fivefold to $1 billion from 1970 to 1977. Brazil tried to boost exchanges with the USSR, especially to procure Soviet agricultural machinery and hydroequipment; in 1974 it hosted a Soviet commercial fair. The government that in 1964 jailed a Communist Chinese commercial mission as spies in February 1974 established diplomatic relations with the People's Republic, more than four years ahead of the United States. The government encouraged trade and investment from many countries in order to reduce the U.S. predominance.

Brazil sought increasingly to serve its interests by collaborating with other states of the Third World. In some ways Brazil was at odds with the large majority of Third World states—in opposition to socialism, cordial relations with the United States, hostility toward Castro, hospitality for multinational corporations, and concern for markets for industrial as well as primary products—but Brazil shared and shares many Third World concerns. Alignment with the U.N. majority increases Brazilian leverage with the developed nations, while Brazil has stood in the forefront of movements to organize cartels of coffee, cacao, sugar, iron ore, and bauxite. From 1970 to 1973 Brazil sided with the struggle of the Portuguese motherland to keep its African colonies; as it became evident that the guerrillas would win independence, Brazil, desirous of keeping influence in Portuguese Africa, changed sides. It recognized the Soviet-Cuban backed Angolan government in 1976 when very few non-Communist powers had done so, to the irritation of the United States and to some annoyance of Brazilian military leaders troubled by the Cuban role in Africa.

The Médici government also took general Third World positions in the rejection of population control and saw concern about pollution as detrimental to the industrialization of developing nations. Probably more from respect for oil power (over 80 percent of petroleum is imported) than convictions, Brazil has since the early 1970s taken a pro-Arab and pro-Palestinian position. In 1975, the government of Ernesto Geisel (who became president March 15, 1974) voted along with Mexico for a U.N. resolution equating Zionism with racism, to the displeasure of the United States. Geisel, learning of the widespread negative reaction to Brazil's anti-Zionist position, contemplated changing it in the final vote; but he refrained because of irritation at U.S. pressure to do so.[21] In 1979, Brazil recognized the Palestine Liberation Organization (PLO) as representative of the Palestinians. Brazil has seemingly desired moral credits for backing Third World causes and has liked to stand publicly with fellow Latin American countries. However, Brazil is less concerned with leading the Third World than with entering the First.

In most matters of trade and security Brazil has continued to stand firmly with the United States.[22] Yet in the latter part of the Geisel administration (1974–79), U.S.-Brazilian relations became more troubled. General Geisel had been chief of Petrobras, an essentially nationalistic enterprise; and he named a somewhat tactless nationalist, Antônio Azeredo da Silveira, as foreign minister. "No more automatic alignment" was the motto, as it had already been the fact, and the motive was unabashed self-interest. The frank objective of economic growth was to gain independence of foreign, that is, U.S. influence. Geisel went to France, Britain, and Japan with the express purpose of broadening horizons but stayed away from the United States. Ideology being second to trade, relations with Communist states—except Cuba—were upgraded. Petrobras worked with countries hostile to U.S. oil interests.[23] Brazil, however, was quite willing to accept American deference. In February 1976, Secretary of State Kissinger (who was unpopular in Brazil because he cheered for the wrong side in a Netherlands-Brazil soccer match[24]) and Foreign Minister Silveira signed a "memorandum of understanding" promising that the two powers would collaborate broadly, consult on all important issues of mutual concern, and hold semiannual meetings, as suitable for major allies.[25] The Brazilians welcomed this acknowledgment of their standing, although it had no great practical consequences, and hoped that with it U.S.-Brazilian relations would be raised to a new level, as they were by the exchange of ambassadors in 1904. It seemed that the United States was rather wooing Brazil than influencing it, as Kissinger had accepted Brazil as a chief ally, "a people taking their place in the front rank of nations."[26] But Brazil was making no concessions. It was proud to have similar agreements with France, Britain, and Germany; and at the time of the Kissinger visit, a major trade agreement was signed with Poland.[27] The height of U.S.-Brazilian cordiality came in an agreement of May 1976 settling several minor trade questions.

President Carter's administration was by temper less congenial to the Brazilian government than Nixon's, and in his campaign he had pointed to the Kissinger-Silveira "memorandum of understanding" as an example of the misguidedness of the Kissinger-Ford approach to world affairs.[28] He was also more eager to bring idealism into foreign policy and less inhibited in attempting to apply the influence of the United States; he consequently brought U.S.-Brazilian relations to a crisis of sorts shortly after taking office in 1977.

In particular, President Carter undertook to check the potential proliferation of nuclear weapons and to defend human rights around the globe. Among the numerous nations capable of making atomic weapons was Brazil, which in June 1975 had contracted with West Germany for the construction not only of several nuclear plants but for facilities for the enrichment of uranium and the reprocessing of spent fuel. The Carter administration tried (as detailed later) to nullify the agreement, to the considerable ire of Brazilians, who resented what they saw as U.S. efforts to stymie their independent technological development. Carter also offended Brazilian authorities by including Brazil in his campaign against human rights violations, a campaign directed in the first instance against the Soviet Union. One result was the liquidation of long-languishing U.S.-Brazilian military cooperation and the cancellation by Brazil of the military agreement in effect since 1952. Foreign Minister Silveira criticized the United States sharply regarding these and other matters, such as U.S. tariffs on shoes and certain other Brazilian manufactures. President Geisel spoke of "obstacles to development resulting from the desire of the more advanced countries to retain the structure of privileges.[29] It looked somewhat like the twilight of a fine friendship.[30]

The Carter administration, however, seemed impressed by Brazilian reactions and endeavored to smooth feelings. Rosalynn Carter in Brasília in June 1977 had agreeable meetings with governmental leaders. Secretary of State Cyrus Vance conferred with Silveira in November 1977 in what Brazilians saw as a fulfillment of the Kissinger-Silveira memorandum, although President Carter had repudiated it because it singled out Brazil over other Latin American countries—its chief virtue in Brazilian eyes.[31] Subsequently Silveira declared that he had been reassured that the Carter administration regarded the memorandum as valid.[32]

Vice-President Walter Mondale also tripped to Brazil; and in March 1978 President and Mrs. Carter, Secretary Vance, and National Security Advisor Zbigniew Brzezinski all paid a state visit—invited by themselves, Foreign Minister Silveira told the press.[33] Carter did not press either the nuclear or the human rights issue—the former seemed fruitless, the latter decreasingly urgent—and much of the chill was removed from U.S.-Brazilian relations. However, Geisel declined an invitation to Washington. And in 1978 the Brazilian government underlined its independence by failing to send a single student to the officers' school at Fort Gulick in the Panama Canal Zone, breaking a 30-year tradition.

Mondale, at the inauguration of President João Baptista Figueiredo, March 15, 1979, secured his promise to visit the United States. It was postponed, however, to 1981. Figueiredo made such statements as "We are no longer little boys to have our ears pulled," but in August 1979, his foreign minister, Ramiro Saraiva Guerrero, said that U.S.-Brazilian relations were very good and whatever differences there might be were negotiable, echoing the statement of Assistant Secretary of State V. P. Vaky, "When differences are understood they can be settled.[34] At the same time he saw much in common with developing countries, but relations with Cuba were still seen as distant.[35]

There was some prospect of renewal of relatively close ties with the United States. Having torn up the military cooperation agreement, Brazilian authorities tried to turn to the French for training but found that Brazilian equipment and doctrine too linked with the United States. Furthermore, they recognized that in an emergency they would certainly work with this country and needed to maintain compatibility. They hence thought in terms of a renewed alliance based on the new stature of Brazil and the desirability of cooperation for stability in Latin America and against Soviet-Cuban expansionism in Africa.[36] A segment of military opinion was opposed to dealings with Communist states and favorable to more free enterprise and better ties with the United States.

The accent, however, was on Brazilian independence. When Carter fished for Brazilian support on the issue of a Soviet combat unit in Cuba in 1979, Ambassador (formerly Foreign Minister) Azeredo da Silveira pretended not to hear.[38] Brazil offered itself as an alternative for the Soviet Union in Angola and Mozambique and increased trade with those countries.[39] When President Carter proposed to chastise the Soviet Union for the invasion of Afghanistan by cutting off grain shipments and boycotting the Moscow Olympic Games, Brazil stood ostentatiously aloof, not visibly unhappy over prospects of increasing food exports to the Soviet Union.[40] The new cordiality of Brazil and Argentina in 1980 removed a basic reason for Brazil to lean especially on the United States, while some Brazilians felt that the Carter administration was less to be relied on because of its vacillations.

Yet relations between the two powers were in 1980 as smooth as they had usually been through their history. There was cool mutual respect, and the two powers shared basic goals in the world. The biggest U.S. concern was whether Brazil could come to grips with its inflation and foreign debt.[41] So far as there were differences, the United States avoided friction by not trying to impose its view.

BASES OF INDEPENDENCE

Several reasons for the cooling of U.S.-Brazilian relations from the exceptional warmth of 1964–65 have been noted, including the inevitable natural deflation of what had been extraordinarily inflated and the change of personalities and outlooks from Castelo Branco and his U.S.-oriented associates to the more nativist Costa e Silva and his followers. A deeper cause was the general decline of the U.S. share of world military and especially economic power and the withering of U.S. self-confidence since 1965. This country's loss of leadership was general and its relatively reduced resources were engaged in Vietnam, the Near East, and elsewhere. The withdrawal was especially felt in a country, like Brazil accustomed to look to the United States for guidance. In the 1960s, even if the Brazilian government was unfriendly, as under Goulart, the United States was central to Brazil's view of the world; in the 1970s, Brazil felt much more on its own.

At the same time, economic growth has given Brazil strength and confidence to carry on autonomous, even slightly hegemonic regional policies, while Brazil has assumed a political shape definitely alien, although not abhorrent to the United States. Paradoxically, these causes of distancing from the United States, economic success and authoritarian government, are the exact opposite of the cause of anti-Americanism prior to 1964, economic troubles and populist-democratic politics. Opposite causes do not produce the same result, however. Recent negativism toward the United States is of a different temper, more pragmatic, more mature and self-assured, and less emotional than the earlier hostility. The memorandum of the technocrat has replaced the outcry of the crowd. Whether or how far the foreign corporations through capital resources, technology, management, and marketing can be made to forward Brazil in the world is a matter more of calculation than rhetoric.

The basic factor in the growing independence of Brazil is productive capacity. Its economy has long expanded considerably more rapidly than the world average—from 1933 to 1974 it grew at a rate of 6.1 percent yearly,[42] a rate that hardly any country surpassed over that extended period. Because of this habit of growth, the slowdown of 1962–64 was the more painful; and the economy was slow to respond during 1964–67 to the regime's attempt to stabilize and reduce inflation. But from 1968 to 1974, the GNP grew 9 percent or more yearly, while inflation was moderated to around 20 percent. Industrial production increased 170 percent from 1963 to 1975, while electrical output nearly quadrupled.[43] Exports expanded from about $1 billion in 1967 to $12 billion a decade later. In 1973 exports increased in dollar terms by 55 percent, and the boom looked unstoppable.

In 1974, however, the fourfold increase of the cost of imported petroleum put the balance of payments into severe deficit, and a large price increase of wheat compounded the troubles. Petrobras was established in 1954 with much enthusiasm to keep Brazilian petroleum resources in Brazilian hands, but it has found very little oil; there is no comparable expanse of land anywhere with so little fossil fuel. Brazilian oil production has been virtually stationary for many years in the face of continually rising demands of an economy based on automotive transportation; and fuel is perhaps the greatest problem for Brazilian economic and foreign policy. Recently domestic oil has filled only about 15 percent of the demand, and half of export earnings have gone to pay for oil, in 1980 about $11.5 billion out of exports totaling about $20 billion.

Because of increased petroleum costs, inflation soared again and growth slowed to 4.2 percent in 1975—a rather encouraging figure by comparison with many countries that showed little or no growth. It was found necessary to impose emergency import controls, restricting credits for capital goods and virtually prohibiting the importation of nonessentials. Since then, the growth rate has recovered somewhat, but inflation rose in 1980 to the level of Goulart days, about 100 percent, while the foreign debt had risen at the beginning of 1980 to $50 billion. In 1979, industrial production increased 7 percent and real wages 5.2 percent.[44]

The Brazilian boom has not been entirely industrial, and agricultural production has grown much more rapidly than population. On a basis of 1961–65 = 100, the index was 139 in 1970 and 184 in 1976.[45] But the past 15 years have seen Brazil metamorphosed by industrialization. Coffee comprised half of exports as late as 1964; by 1973 it had fallen under 20 percent. Manufactured exports are about one-third of the total. Brazil produces small computers and a thousand other sophisticated products; it exports such goods as automobiles and light planes. Ford Motor Company has gone to Brazil to make engines for cars sold in the United States. Brazilian construction firms have undertaken many projects in Third World countries using Brazilian machinery.[46]

The policies producing economic growth have been generally but not entirely those approved by both the U.S. government and U.S. business interests. There has been at least a fight against inflation: inflation seems to be the winner, but it has been partly neutralized by a Brazilian invention, indexation, whereby bank deposits, securities, debts, taxes, and so forth are regularly refigured according to the rise of the official price index. The income tax was enforced for the first time in Brazilian history; the number of persons actually paying grew many fold in the first years of the military government. The exchange rate is kept realistic and speculation is discouraged by frequent devaluations of the cruzeiro. Instead of land reform (of which there has been some) the government stressed large, modern farms, with free competition, in the U.S. style. President Figueiredo began his term by moving closer to the U.S. economic model, proposing to phase out export subsidies, cut protective tariffs, and sell shares of state corporations.[47]

The Brazilian economic model, however, is far from the American. Brazilian growth has rested less on market forces than on the ability of the planners, armed with a panoply of credit and regulatory powers, to guide the economy. The technocrats of the ministries have much authority to tell businessmen what they may or may not produce, where they should purchase supplies, and so forth; and permits are required—often in fiendish abundance—for almost any operation. At the same time, a large share of industry is state-owned, and over half of fixed capital investment is ascribable to the state or public corporations. If socialism means state control of means of production, Brazil may be the most socialistic of the important industrial states of the West. U.S. and other foreign interests, however, having suffered the incoherence, instability, and rhetoric of the Goulart period, are relieved by the stability and reliability of the military government, which permits quite reasonable profits for cooperative enterprises.

An incidental benefit of industrial growth and a support for independence in foreign policy is the indigenous armaments industry. The nascent arms industry was nationalized in 1970, and the government determined to limit purchases to companies that would set up plants in Brazil. Only by so doing could the United States sell F-5 fighter planes. The Brazilian aircraft industry has especially prospered; the Air Force procures fighter planes only at home[48] and many small planes are sold abroad. Arms imports have been reduced to special needs, while Brazilian arms exports, including armored cars, tanks, and planes, rose from near zero in 1975 to about $800 million in 1980.[49] Even the Soviet Union has been reported procuring Brazilian armored vehicles.

This economic muscle has permitted Brazil to indulge in a little imperialism of its own. The Brazilian outreach has made itself felt especially in the three weaker countries bordering on Brazil: Uruguay, Paraguay, and Bolivia. Brazil seems to have been involved in the military takeover of Uruguay, at least as an example, and Juan Bordaberry seemed to have been prepared to make his country a political and economic client of Brazil.[50] Bolivia is substantially penetrated by Brazilian capital, and Bolivians complain of Brazilian exploitation of their resources, especially natural gas.[51] Brazil seems to have had a hand in the 1971 military coup in Bolivia, in the failed coup attempt in 1979 of Col. Alberto Natusch Busch,[52] and possibly Gen. Luis García Meza's seizure of power in 1980. There has long been close cooperation between Brazil and Paraguayan dictator Alfredo Stroessner. Although Argentina was formerly economic hegemon over Paraguay, recently there has been much Brazilian development of that country, including acquisition of land.[53]

Brazil has carried on a modest economic aid program for these countries and others on its frontiers, including Peru, Ecuador, and Colombia. Many students, especially from Bolivia, receive scholarships to Brazilian institutions. Brazilian economic relations with other Latin American countries are parallel to those of the United States with Brazil. Brazil imports from Latin America mostly raw materials, while it exports mostly manufactures (largely produced by subsidies of U.S. or European corporations); half of Brazilian manufactured exports go to Latin America.[54] Brazilian investment in less developed neighbors looks, on a smaller scale, like U.S. investment in Brazil. Brazilian geopoliticians, such as Gen. Golbery do Couto e Silva, éminence grise of successive military governments, have long dreamed of Brazilian domination of South America.[55] This is distant, and no country is in any sense a Brazilian puppet; but the sway of Brazil has grown to warm a nationalist's heart.

POLITICAL DIVERGENCE

While Brazil has acquired the material means to go its own way, so far as this is possible for middle-rank nations in this interdependent world, it is evidently somewhat more inclined to do so because it is a rather different kind of polity from the United States with somewhat different values. In Brazil, old and new authoritarianisms have fused with modernizing and democratic strains to produce a new political form. It is not totalitarian, since it makes no effort to organize the entire lives of its citizens and leaves large scope for private or free initiative. It is not democratic, since the input of elected officials to decision making is small. It is not classic dictatorship, such as has reigned over many Latin American states. The dictatorships are unsystematic, nonideological, and personalist; the Brazilian state is the opposite in all respects. It has been called "corporatist," but this term properly refers to an organization built on corporations in the medieval sense; in Brazil only one "corporation," the military establishment, holds the political levers; and there is no formalized representation for any other.

The military rulers would like to think of themselves as an aristocracy in the Greek sense of the word, that is, rule by the best. They regard themselves as better qualified to care for the interests of the nation than civilian politicians, who gave a rather dismal account of themselves during 1945–64, than labor leaders, and than businessmen, who are trained to promote only their own interests and who have no systematic education in government. It is the strength of the military that status in it, more than in any other major sector of Brazilian society, is based on qualifications, primarily education.

Military academy cadets are selected by examination; a large majority are of middle-class origin. Upper-class youths do not find it attractive because they must enter at the bottom and their standing is of no great advantage; those of the poorest classes are excluded because a secondary education is required, and this is not easy for poor boys to get.[56]

The rising officer passes through three or four schools: a four-year course in the academy, one year at junior officers' school before he can become captain, and three years at the General Staff School to qualify for general; to reach top ranks, especially since 1964, he probably has to attend the ESG. Along the way, academic performance is very important, considerably more so than in U.S. forces, for example.[57] The system of merit promotion is the more outstanding because the bureaucracy has no comparable ladder but rests largely on favor. The quality of the upper ranks is maintained by rigorous up-or-out rules. Officers can remain only four years in any rank; if not promoted they are retired, or at age 66 at the latest.[58] Hence there is always a new set of generals coming up.

The new president has been chosen by the outgoing president in the last cases, Geisel and Figueiredo, in consultation with high officers, especially the four-star generals (whom the president himself has selected). Each successive presidential succession through Figueiredo has been smoother than the preceding. A strength of the system is the limitation of the president to a single term of formerly five, now six, years.

The precedent was set by Castelo Branco, and it is supported by the general practice of mobility through the officer's career. Incompetents cannot come to the top; on the other hand, no charismatic leader is likely to be permitted to attain excessive authority over his fellows.

Because of the nature of their careers, officers have few personal links with large landholders, captains of industry, or other civilian leaders. This makes it easier for the military to regard themselves as nonclass and above narrow sectarian interests.[59] This also means that major policy discussions are likely to be kept within the military and out of public view. Proposals emanate from the presidency or ministries, and there is very little information indeed regarding decision making. The quality of decision making seems to be at least somewhat better than before.[60] The military does not seem thus far to have abused its powers for major personal enrichment. Nor has it built itself up as an institution. The army, 273,800 in 1978, included 0.2 percent of the population, very close to the percentage of previous decades. Its budget of about $2 billion was 1.4 percent of the GNP, a figure that has not changed greatly for many years.

The manner of rule of the military government owes more to tradition and the institutions built up by the dictatorship of Getulio Vargas than to foreign influences. Business in Brazil has since colonial days been subject to much regulation, as producers have sought state support while accepting paternalistic guidance. State enterprise became important under Vargas, in steel (Volta Redonda), petroleum (Petrobras), and in several other branches, while state financial powers were preeminent. The state sector is very large in finance and basic industry, accounting for about half of new investment. It is typical that in negotiations for Brazil's nuclear program, the U.S. side was represented by private firms only; the German, by private firms in cooperation with state authorities; the Brazilian, by state enterprises only. To control labor, the military government had only to apply the Vargas system whereby state-directed unions were supported by a compulsory tax, militancy was penalized, and cooperative leaders were rewarded with good jobs. Wages were more or less fixed by the government, which arbitrated disputes, while the unions distributed social security benefits. The bureaucracy, which had functioned as welfare agency for the middle classes, was purged and at the same time given latitude to work without interference from civilian politicians. There are rich rewards within the system: those who are loyal, talented, and educated can move rapidly up to influence and affluence in the service of the technocracy.[61]

The role of the state is justified by the nationalist-authoritarian doctrine of National Security, which despite nebulosity merits being called an ideology.[62] It began as a statement of commitment in the world struggle: "We are in a condition of total war, a war that has become a desperately complex game depending on the political economy, social psychology, general geography, and the latest conquests of nuclear physics. Now in this framework the military authorities will be organs of planning and direction of operations, since the total war calls upon the entire Nation, in the full exercise of its coordinated facilities, for a single superior aim. Hence the basic activities of the Nation are subordinated to the interests of its security."[63] National Security is not only a military but a social condition, something the nation needs for permanent well-being, including maintenance of sovereignty and search for the common welfare. It is apparently almost equivalent to effective government and unity.[64] It assumes that social classes have basically harmonious interests, that the growth of production will provide answers for national needs, and that the Armed Forces must guarantee order for production and prosperity.[65] Capital and labor should not squabble over the division of the product but work together under the guidance of the state,[66] while the government, in the fashion of most authoritarianisms, emphasizes unity, from family to nation. The cold war has receded but National Security remains, linked with Development, upholding the conviction that Brazil can and must become truly great. It is elaborated in many books, a broad legitimating basis for military rule, and a framework for political thought.

The legally constituted and sanctioned guardian, exponent, and developer of the ideology is the ESG, which has acquired an importance far beyond that of its original model, the National War College. More authoritative than any individual president, it is the intellectual center of the regime. As ideological authority it may even be compared (with some exaggeration) to the Central Committee of Communist states.[67]

After 1964, the military, seeking qualified leaders, turned to graduates of the ESG because they had sophisticated general preparation and ideas for national renewal. The ESG, which guides the less exalted officer training schools, provides the basis for unity of general purpose essential to the maintenance and effectiveness of the authority of the armed forces and coordinated thinking on matters outside the military domain. Consequently, to be one of the few dozen generals admitted yearly is valuable for reaching top levels; in particular high officials of the intelligence agency (Servico Nacional de Informacões, SNI) must be ESG graduates.[68] For civilians, who are the majority of students, attendance at the ESG is the best way to get into the charmed circle and so to qualify for responsible office. Civilians graduated acquire high military titles. The ESG thus links the civilian leadership to the military, and promotes a common concept and language of national security.[69]

According to the director of the ESG in 1970, Gen. Augusto Fragoso, the mission of the school was "the formation of the national elite through methodically preparing year after year, officers and civilians of the highest intellectual and moral rank, for the functions of planning and directing the national security . . . involving directly or indirectly all the activities of the nation."[70] By law the ESG has the assignment of fostering "the habit of joint work, looking to the effective collaboration of the different sectors related to problems of National Security."[71]

The elite indoctrinated in this system has maintained theoretical loyalty to the democratic ideal. Along with national integration, territorial integrity, sovereignty, progress, and social peace, a chief stated objective of the elitist ESG is "an ever more democratic form of government and conscious and responsible liberty of the citizens."[72] But it is democracy mostly for the conscious and responsible, according to the judgment of the leadership; and the emphasis is on duties rather than rights. The mentality of U.S. politics is not congenial to the Brazilian power elite, and there have obviously been gaps in understanding.

This reality places certain limits on the cordiality of U.S.-Brazilian relations and the receptivity of Brazil to the needs and ideas of the United States. The centralized, integrated character of the Brazilian state, moreover, probably hinders the exercise of U.S. influence, just as pluralistic countries are handicapped in dealing with highly integrated Communist states. If on some future occasion the Brazilian leadership should decide to turn their country toward strong, even violent nationalism, it could readily and rapidly do so. Such a turn is quite conceivable if it appears that economic collaboration with the United States has become unrewarding; there is a strong current of feeling in the high command that would like to assert Brazilianism much more forcefully. The president would have only to turn the wheel, and the country would follow, perhaps gleefully.

NOTES

1. Ronald M. Schneider, *The Political System of Brazil: Emergence of a "Modernizing Authoritarian Regime"* (New York: Columbia University Press, 1971), pp. 218, 253.

2. Concerning the low profile, see Lawrence E. Harrison, "Waking from the Pan-American Dream," *Foreign Policy*, no. 5 (Winter 1971-72): 163-81.

3. Jan K. Black, *United States Penetration of Brazil* (Philadelphia: University of Pennsylvania Press, 1977), p. 165.

4. John W. Tuthill, "Operation Topsy," *Foreign Policy* 8 (Fall 1972):80.

5. Williard O. Beaulac, *A Diplomat Looks at Aid to Latin America* (Carbondale: University of Southern Illinois Press, 1970), p. 110.

6. Marcos de Sá Correa, *1964 visto e comentado pela Casa Branca* (Pôrto Alegre: L & PM Editores, 1977), pp. 90-91.

7. Tuthill, "Operation Topsy," p. 67.

8. Carlos Estevam Martins, *Capitalismo do estado e modelo político no Brasil* (Rio de Janeiro: Ediciones de Braal, 1977), p. 391.

9. Peter D. Bell, "Brazilian-American Relations," in *Brazil in the Sixties*, ed. Riordan Roett (Nashville, Tenn.: Vanderbilt University Press, 1972), pp. 99–100.

10. *New York Times*, December 8, 1968, p. 44.

11. *New York Times*, March 2, 1969, p. 11.

12. Carlos E. Martins, "Brazil and the United States," in *Latin America and the U.S.*, ed. Julio Cotler and Richard Fagen (Stanford: Stanford University Press, 1974), p. 299.

13. Martins, *Capitalismo do estado*, p. 406; *Visão*, November 4, 1974, p. 28.

14. Martins, *Capitalismo do estado*, pp. 410–11.

15. Ibid., p. 408.

16. Jose Alfredo Amaral Gurgel, *Segurança e democracia: una reflexão político* (Rio de Janeiro: Livraria José Olympio, 1975), p. 174.

17. Michael Morris, *International Politics and the Sea: The Case of Brazil* (Boulder, Colo.: Westview Press, 1979), pp. 35, 47.

18. William Perry, *Contemporary Brazilian Foreign Policy*, (Beverly Hills, Calif.: Sage Publications, 1976), p. 54.

19. Albert Fishlow, "Flying Down to Rio: U.S-Brazilian Relations," *Foreign Affairs* 57 (Winter 1978–79):396.

20. *Visão*, June 11, 1973, p. 23.

21. Walder de Goes, *O governo do General Geisel* (Rio de Janeiro: Editora Nova Fronteira, 1978), p. 30.

22. Wayne A. Selcher, *Brazil's Multilateral Relations: Between First and Third Worlds* (Boulder, Colo.: Westview Press, 1978), p. 251.

23. Peter Flynn, *Brazil: A Political Analysis* (Boulder, Colo.: Westview Press, 1978), p. 497.

24. *New York Times*, July 12, 1974, p. 32.

25. *New York Times*, February 21, 1976, p. 1.

26. *Newsweek*, March 1, 1976.

27. *Visão*, March 8, 1976, p. 22.

28. *Visão*, April 18, 1977, p. 43.

29. *Resenha de política exterior do Brasil*, no. 15 (October-December 1977):3.

30. Roger W. Fontaine, "The End of a Beautiful Relationship," *Foreign Policy* 28 (Fall 1977):166.

31. *Visão*, November 14, 1977, p. 18.

32. *Brazil Today*, January 9, 1979, p. 3.

33. *New York Times*, March 30, 1978, p. 3.

34. *Estado de São Paulo*, July 1, 1979, p. 7.

35. *Brazil Today*, August 21, 1979, pp. 2–3.

36. *Visão*, May 28, 1979, p. 53.

37. Norman Gall, "In the Name of Democracy," *American Universities Field Service Staff Report 1978/9*, pp. 10–11.

38. *Veja*, October 3, 1979, p. 38.

39. *Los Angeles Times*, March 2, 1980, p. VIII-2.

40. *New York Times*, January 17, 1980, p. A-8.

41. *Visão*, May 5, 1980, p. 52.

42. Norman Gall, "The Rise of Brazil," *Commentary* 63 (January 1977):46.

43. *United Nations Statistical Yearbook 1977*, p. 157.

44. *Journal do Brasil*, May 24, 1980, p. 19.

45. *United Nations Statistical Yearbook 1977*, p. 98.

46. *Economist*, October 27, 1979, p. 80.

47. *Business Week*, March 19, 1979, p. 61.

48. *Veja*, July 4, 1979, p. 21.

49. *Business Week*, March 24, 1980, p. 69.

50. Martin Weinstein, *Uruguay, The Politics of Failure* (Westport, Conn.: Greenwood Press, 1975), pp. 134–46.

51. *Veja*, November 4, 1979, p. 41.

52. *Veja*, November 9, 1979, p. 39.

53. Riordan Roett, ed., *Brazil in the Sixties* (Nashville, Tenn.: Vanderbilt University Press, 1972), p. 150.

54. Serge D'Adesky, "Brazil's Rise to Dominance in Latin America," *Fletcher Forum* 3 (Summer 1979):49.

55. Golbery do Couto e Silva, *Geopoliticá do Brasil* (Rio de Janeiro: Olympios, 1967).

56. Alfred Stepan, *The Military in Politics: Changing Patterns in Brazil* (Princeton: Princeton University Press, 1971), p. 41.

57. Georges-André Fiechter, *Le régime modernisateur du Brasil, 1964–1972* (Leiden: Sijthoff, 1972), p. 35.

58. Robert M. Levine, "Brazil: The Aftermath of Decompression," *Current History* 70 (February 1976):55–56.

59. Stepan, *Military*, p. 42.

60. Ronald M. Schneider, *Brazil: Foreign Policy of a Future Great Power* (Boulder, Colo.: Westview Press, 1976), p. 210.

61. Thomas Skidmore, *Politics in Brazil: An Experiment in Democracy 1930–1964* (New York: Oxford University Press, 1967).

62. Expanded in *Doutrina Básica* (Rio de Janeiro: Escola Superior de Guerra, 1979).

63. General Umberto Peregrino, quoted by Fernando Pedreira, *Brasil político 1964–1975* (São Paulo: Difel, 1975), pp. 34–35.

64. Francisco de Souza Brasil, in *Brasil: Realidade e Desenvolvimento* (São Paulo: Editora Sugestões Literarias, 1972), p. 520.

65. C. Neale Ronning, "Military Government since 1964," in *Perspectives on Armed Politics in Brazil*, eds. Henry H. Keith and Robert A. Hayes (Tempe, Ariz.: Arizona State University Press, 1976), p. 240.

66. Oliveira, *As forças armadas*, p. 39.

67. Pedreira, *Brasil político*, p. 34.

68. Ronning, "Military Government," in *Perspectives on Armed Politics in Brazil*, eds. Henry H. Keith and Robert A. Hayes (Tempe, Ariz.: Arizona State University Press, 1976), p. 240.

69. Schneider, *Political System*, pp. 250, 288.

70. Cited by Black, *United States Penetration*, p. 194.

71. de Souza Brasil, *Brasil*, p. 558.

72. Ibid., p. 520.

4

THE CARTER CONTROVERSIES

THE NUCLEAR FIASCO

The new Carter administration in early 1977 undertook to sway the Brazilian government from two important policies: the explicit program to build up nuclear power production with potentials for the manufacture of nuclear weapons; and a policy not publicly admitted but notorious in practice of using inhumane methods against political terrorism or—it was charged—against simple opposition. In the ensuing controversies, the U.S. government undertook to exercise influence it believed that it possessed; the controversies and their results merit attention as the most straightforward attempted application of U.S. influence on Brazil since World War II.

Nuclear energy is attractive for Brazil because that huge country is exceptionally lacking in fossil energy resources. In the south, there are some coal deposits but they are mostly of inferior quality; coal production is not very promising, although it has been increased substantially. Wood is a valuable resource; and in 1946 it furnished 70 percent of the national energy supply. At one time most Brazilian steel was produced by charcoal from eucalyptus plantations. But this option has not satisfied the industrial planners; there are already protests against the removal of land from agriculture to grow trees. In the 1950s it was assumed that Brazil should be rich in oil, as it had once been rich in gold and diamonds; but Petrobras has been disappointed. The Brazilian economy since 1973 has suffered gravely from the high cost of imported fuel and its effects on the balance of payments, and an adequate independent source of energy has a high priority.

Falling water, happily clean and permanent, is the only energy resource with which Brazil is abundantly supplied. Rivers descending from the plateau making up a large part of the country's land mass offer a potential of at least 119,000 megawatts[1] and perhaps as much as 500,000 megawatts.[2] Hydro plants in the vicinity of São Paulo gave the original impetus to the industrial growth of that region, and hydropower has been very helpful for the incipient industrialization of the Northeast. Brazil now has about 25,000 megawatts of installed hydropower capacity, and very large projects underway in the south (especially Itaipu) will raise that figure sharply in coming years. Brazil's other major renewable energy source is the production of alcohol from sugar cane and other crops. This has the advantage, of course, that the liquid product is usable in conventional automobiles; but capital costs are high and it has been possible thus far to raise production only to a small fraction of needs.

Under these circumstances, it is disputable whether it is wise to make a heavy investment in nuclear energy. The government, however, has long favored it. During the first half of the 1970s when basic decisions were made, alcohol was given little consideration; and various arguments were raised against reliance on hydroelectricity. The bulk of hydropower is rather remote from main centers of population—although it has long been a national policy to shift development toward the interior. Curves of exponentially rising power requirements hit the ceiling of hydropower potential some time in the 1990s, at least if the lower estimates were accepted; hence it was considered imperative to proceed to prepare for future needs. It was probably more important, however, that the government and the technocrats have regarded nuclear energy as a symbol of modernization. Going nuclear meant entering the select company of the highly advanced nations; to refrain meant accepting secondary status. Thus, in 1971 the ESG stressed three themes: the East-West ideological opposition, the economic and technological disparity of developed and less developed nations, and the dramatic separation of nuclear and nonnuclear nations.[3] It seemed intolerable for Brazil to remain on the low side of such a division in the world.

There were also more strictly political reasons. One was the old rivalry with Argentina, which undertook a nuclear program well ahead of Brazil. The Argentine Atucha reactor, with a capacity of 360 megawatts, has been on line since 1974, and another was to start up in 1980. Without a strong nuclear program, Brazilian leadership in South America would be incomplete at best. Moreover, there are suspicions—however firmly denied—that Brazil would like eventually to have its own atomic bomb, or at least the capacity to make one if circumstances should require, to affirm its position in the world, amplify its influence in Latin America, and reduce dependence upon the American alliance.

Brazil's interest in nuclear power goes back to the immediate postwar years, when it was much touted as the answer of the future to energy needs, especially of countries short of coal and oil. In 1946 Brazil repudiated at the U.N. the thesis that there was a duty to share resources and rejected the Baruch Plan for international control of atomic energy. Instead, the Brazilians, confident of possessing large uranium deposits, proposed exchanging ore for technology.[4] In 1951 Brazil tried secretly to purchase gas centrifuge equipment for enrichment of uranium from Germany, but the United States stepped in and vetoed the deal.[5] This successful intervention probably encouraged the effort to undo the 1975 German-Brazilian nuclear deal, but in the 1950s Germany was incomparably weaker. Even then, American intervention caused considerable resentment. Brazil (like Argentina) did acquire some nuclear technology in the 1950s under the Atoms for Peace program. Under a 1955 agreement, Brazil received five experimental reactors by 1973.[6]

The Kubitschek government decided on a 150–200 megawatt plant using enriched uranium (the proportion of easily fissionable U-235 being raised from 0.7 percent to about 5 percent), the fuel favored by the United States. Quadros, however, in keeping with his policy of independence from the United States turned to France for a natural uranium reactor—the Argentines having decided to go the natural uranium route. Under Goulart, studies went forward, and engineers were going back and forth between Brazil and France. But the military government cancelled this project, while the French gave up the natural uranium method in favor of the U.S. approach.[7] The preference for enriched uranium over natural uranium was a victory for nonproliferation, because the natural uranium produces more plutonium, which can be fairly easily separated and made usable for explosives. The natural uranium process, moreover, requires the importation or production of heavy water; and the process is reckoned more expensive.

For a few years the post-1964 government let the nuclear question rest. However, it was decided to proceed in cooperation with the United States, because of reliance on U.S. friendship, high technology, and dependability, using the commercially preferred enriched uranium-light water process.[8] In the early 1960s, the United States had plunged into nuclear exports on a large scale (after France and Canada had led the way with reactors for India and Israel). Scores of reactors were sold worldwide, all to use fuel supplied only by the United States, making attractive commercial prospects. The Brazilians agreed in 1967 to buy theirs from Westinghouse, the largest exporter in the field. The plant to be built at Angra, on the coast near Rio, was to have a capacity of 626 megawatts and was to be completed in 1977; a second plant, Angra II, was to come into operation by 1980.[9] They were to be fueled by uranium mined in Brazil and enriched in the United States, according to contracts reached in 1971–72.[10] An Ex-Im Bank credit was extended in 1972. To manage the program, a government monopoly, Nuclebras, was set up in 1970.

Westinghouse seemed to have the nuclear program in its pocket, but the Brazilian government was disposed to broaden its options. In 1967, when attachment to the United States was near its height, it was decided to work toward an independent fuel cycle;[11] the conditions imposed by the United States seemed too stringent and designed to keep Brazil permanently dependent on international interests opposed to the nuclearization of Brazil.[12] The government secretly began work on a 15-year plan for nuclear independence.[13] Early in the 1970s the Soviet Union began offering an alternative source of enriched uranium, and some claimed that a natural uranium-heavy water system like the Argentine would be better for Brazilian independence.[14]

In 1974, discontent was overtaken by crisis. After the boom year of 1973, when exports increased by half, Brazil was hard hit by the fuel crisis. Previously talk of perhaps 50 nuclear plants by the end of the century had seemed rather idle; now nuclear power seemed vital. In May 1974, India entered the club of those possessing nuclear weapons or at least nuclear explosives; this gave Brazil a feeling of lagging and spread the idea that nuclear explosives might be useful. Much more important was the fact that the U.S. Atomic Energy Commission notified Brazil that it could not guarantee delivery of the previously promised enriched uranium; the government even returned an advance payment. This was not discriminatory against Brazil; various other countries received similar notice. But it did not give Brazil the consideration implied by a special relationship, and it contradicted a premise of cooperation with the United States, that this country was a reliable source of fuel. Earlier, the United States had refused to permit Westinghouse to construct enrichment and reprocessing facilities in Brazil on the grounds that Brazil refused to adhere to the Nuclear Non-Proliferation Treaty—a refusal that constituted a minor long-term irritant in U.S.-Brazilian relations. Westinghouse tried to persuade Brazil to participate in an enrichment plant to be built in the United States.[15] The Brazilian government, however, insisted that the entire cycle, from ore to kilowatts, plus facilities for reprocessing spent fuel, must be in Brazilian hands.[16]

The Brazilian authorities for many years had kept in contact with European sellers of nuclear technology, especially France and then more seriously with West Germany. The latter had sold a reactor to Argentina in 1968, and nuclear matters were discussed when Foreign Minister Willy Brandt went to Brazil in 1968. The following year a technical agreement was concluded; Brazilian engineers began traveling to Germany, and nuclear cooperation was formally instituted in 1971. In 1973–74, Brazil began negotiations for the purchase of as many as eight nuclear plants, concerning which the U.S. government was fully informed.[17]

The announcement in June 1975 of a huge contract for West Germany to provide Brazil a large and self-contained nuclear power industry was nevertheless sensational; a Brazilian weekly saw it as, "the greatest diplomatic, economic, and scientific victory of Brazil."[18] Germany agreed to assist with technology and equipment in the construction of eight power reactors, four to be finished by 1986, four by 1990, plus enrichment plants and reprocessing facilities. Brazil was to acquire not only an independent nuclear power industry but all requisites for the production of nuclear explosives. The goal was 10,000 megawatts of nuclear energy by 1990. The basic design for enrichment, the most sensitive part, was one originally developed by Westinghouse, the jet-nozzle process, dubious technology not actually in use anywhere. The Brazilians wanted a centrifuge process, but this was vetoed under U.S. pressure by the Netherlands and Britain who shared in it, and Brazil settled for the less tried and more power-consuming jet-nozzle technology.[19]

Mixed German-Brazilian companies were to be formed for everything from uranium prospecting to the manufacture of reactor parts. Although the reactors and reprocessing were to be entirely Brazilian, Germany acquired rights of exploration for uranium, of which Brazil had at the time known reserves of only 3,000 tons.[20] It was intended that Brazil should become an exporter of nuclear fuels and equipment, and the agreement would be helpful to German as well as Brazilian nuclear ambitions. To some extent, it was a move to independence on the part of Germany as well as Brazil.

This deal foresaw by far the largest transfer of nuclear technology to the Third World. The proposal for enrichment facilities, which could be turned to the production of weapons-grade uranium, and for reprocessing plants, which could produce plutonium equally useful for explosives, as well as recovering the substantial amount of uranium 235 remaining at the end of the fuel cycle, naturally raised fears of radically accelerating the spread of nuclear weapons. To meet this criticism, the agreement included provisions for a system of controls allegedly more stringent than called for by the International Atomic Energy Agency and the Nuclear Non-Proliferation Treaty. The Brazilians undertook not to use information obtained through the agreement to make explosives and not to copy the German technology except under agreed conditions.[21]

This was not absolutely convincing, since the Brazilians refused to admit international controls over any processes that they might invent,[22] and the line between copying and improvement or invention might be thin. The U.S. Congress, moreover, expressed indignation that Germany was profiting from a business that the United States had renounced for the general security. The reaction of the Ford administration, however, was limited to some expressions of pain. Perhaps the State Department was somewhat surprised at the alarm widely expressed in the press and

Congress. In February, when the U.S. ambassador to Bonn was briefed on the negotiations approaching consummation, the administration urged the Germans, not very energetically, to desist. This failing, it asked for the inclusion of safeguards under supervision of the International Atomic Energy Agency (IAEA), to which the Germans agreed.[23] The mood was still of low profile, and no formal protest was lodged.[24] President Ford did not take up the matter when conferring with Helmut Schmidt about the time the deal was announced.[25] The chief concern of the State Department was to meet congressional criticism of dereliction in not pressing the Germans on the issue; the administration had to equivocate slightly, claiming to have evinced opposition without having made loud noises.[26] It is to be noted that the question was raised not with the Brazilian buyers but with the German sellers, presumably because it was felt the United States had leverage with the Germans dependent on NATO and American security forces. The Brazilians saw opposition in the U.S. Congress and press, not the State Department. Not much heed was taken of a French-Brazilian agreement of August 1976 for two late-model reactors and a uranium treatment plant and study of ways to use the large Brazilian thorium reserves.[27]

The issue had over a year and a half to simmer down before the end of the Ford administration, but Jimmy Carter resolved to bring it to a boil. During the campaign he accused the Republicans of failure to address the dangers of nuclear proliferation, and his stronger approach was widely praised.[28] He called for a moratorium on the sale of uranium enrichment and plutonium processing plants, specifically condemning the West German-Brazilian deal and rebuking Ford for having failed to apply pressure against it.[29] Immediately on entering office, President Carter followed through by opposing further development of a U.S. breeder reactor, although this would potentially multiply nuclear resources more than fiftyfold and would reduce waste disposal problems, because the breeder and consequent availability of plutonium would complicate the restriction of nuclear weaponry.[30]

Before the administration was a week old, Vice President Mondale was urging Bonn to pull back from commitments to supply nuclear technology to Brazil; the administration, he told Chancellor Schmidt, was "unalterably opposed" to the contract.[31] The Germans, who claimed to have more than satisfied the Nuclear Non-Proliferation Treaty, declined to be swayed by Mondale; and they would not yield to Warren Christopher, who repeated the message a few weeks later.[32] It is said that the administration, in this stiffest U.S.-German dispute since World War II, went so far as to threaten withdrawal of U.S. troops from West Berlin; but the Germans were unmoved by this bluff.[33]

The Carter administration also turned to press the Brazilians with whom it had less leverage. In February and March Secretary of State Vance several times argued the case with the Brazilian ambassador to no avail, and Carter sent President Geisel a letter on the issue.[34] The Brazilians, on the contrary, were angry because the United States had violated the memorandum of understanding by taking up with Bonn a matter of prime interest to them without prior consultation. At the beginning of March, Assistant Secretary of State Warren Christopher went to Brasília, although the Brazilian government let it be known that it was prepared to discuss only nonproliferation, not the German deal.[35] Christopher is said to have presented the government with a version of the accord as the American administration would like it to be. But his discussions ended after only one day when the Brazilians flatly rejected the suggestion that enrichment be done in the United States or under international or multinational control. It was left to the holdover ambassador, John Crimmins, to try to patch up relations and get on with business as usual.[36]

In May and June 1977, President Carter continued his drive against the spread of nuclear technology to many nations: Brazil, Argentina, Egypt, India, Iran, Israel, South Africa, South Korea, Spain, Taiwan, and Yugoslavia.[37] But in June, he conceded that he had no way to impose his will on Germany and Brazil.[38] Feelings were somewhat assuaged as Carter was scheduled to visit Brazil in November. However, the Carter tour was replaced by a swing through Latin America by Vance; and he returned to the attack when stopping in Brazil. He sought to convince the Brazilians on logical grounds that nuclear energy, or at least the full cycle, was uneconomic and politically dangerous.[39] He predicted that it would probably lead to a nuclear arms race, and reportedly told Geisel that Argentina would renounce reprocessing if Brazil did, although Argentina was going ahead on a complete cycle with German and Swiss assistance and had given no assurances of desisting.[40] As reported by Brazilians, Geisel asked Vance for alternative solutions for Brazil's energy needs, but the Secretary could only suggest awaiting new technology.[41] Shortly before, the administration had tried a little carrot-and-stick diplomacy by recommending the furnishing to Brazil of 54 tons of low-enriched uranium, followed with a warning that future uranium deliveries would be questionable if Brazil proceeded to acquire reprocessing facilities.[42] The Brazilians do not appear to have been impressed.

There were no more practicable steps to take to push or cajole Germany and Brazil to give up their nuclear business, and sundry more urgent matters arose in Europe and the Near East, so the Carter administration tended to drop the cause. It came up again, however, on the occasion of the state visit of Carter to Brazil in March 1978, although much of the controversy was laid to rest in private letters between Carter and Geisel before the visit.[43] Carter then drew a distinction between the development of nuclear power, which the United States continued to encourage, and the production of weapons-grade nuclear materials either through enrichment processes or through reprocessing. In a press interview he diplomatically disclaimed authority over either West Germany or Brazil, but, "as a friend of both countries" he wished to express to them the opinion that it would be both possible and better to have a complete nuclear fuel system without reprocessing. In the United States much money had been spent on reprocessing, but it had not been found economical. He encouraged Brazil to look further to the use of thorium, a safer and more abundant material, and expressed approval of Brazil's desire to have an advanced nuclear power capability. He also suggested that it would be excellent for Brazil to subscribe to the Nuclear Non-Proliferation Treaty.[44]

Little seems to have been said about nuclear problems in the Carter-Geisel talks, which took up trade questions, Cuban-Soviet penetration of Africa, agricultural cooperation, disarmament, and so forth. Although Geisel, who had flown to Bonn less than a month before to sign three additional nuclear agreements, made no concessions, the final communiqué indicated essential agreement on nuclear matters, or at least an agreement to disagree without acrimony or argument.[45]

The Brazilian reaction to the U.S. attack on the nuclear program was the more negative because it came late and seemed a capricious change of the new administration. But to reject U.S. interference was a matter of basic pride, an assertion of economic and political independence. There was no effort to arouse nationalistic passions, and the government wanted to keep the quarrel separate from economic and security bonds with the United States.[46] But passions were fired. Whereas previously, there had been many doubts and reservations, especially among Brazilian nuclear scientists,[47] in the face of the attack, "to support the accord became a matter of national honor, the accord became untouchable."[48] Some sectors wanted a much more forceful affirmation of nationalism and saw an opportunity to bring people and government together:

> The diplomatic struggle for survival of the nuclear agreement with Germany encompasses a great idea, capable of mobilizing the nation and uniting it. The pressure exerted by the North American government against our agreement not only contributes to the mobilization but above all leads the government to perceive the benefits of this general rejoining. [Previously the government was hesitant to bring the people to its side, but] Now, however, things change in tune with the attitudes of Jimmy Carter, with his Southern messianism or his need to uphold the nuclear monopoly because of pressures in his own country. The

question of the threatened nuclear agreement, above all and more than any other, unites the Brazilian nation, and the government perceives that it needs this union.[49]

For Brazil, nuclear development, without conditions imposed from without, was integral to technological maturity and symbolic of modernity; the United States seemed to wish to divide the nations into those entitled to enjoy enrichment and reprocessing facilities, and those unworthy—the industrialized and powerful on one side, the poor and weak on the other. To yield would be to sacrifice both development and security and to admit permanent inferiority.[50]

In 1967, Costa e Silva had expressed a much-quoted sentiment: "Nuclear energy has an exceptional role and is no doubt the most powerful resource in reach of the developing countries to reduce the distance that separates them from the industrialized nations."[51] Nuclearization was seen as a central part of modern science, and to curtail it was to curtail the development of Brazil. It was a matter of pride to stand up to the United States on the issue, a pride the stiffer in compensation for the visible economic dependency. In April 1977, after President Carter had stated that the United States would strongly pursue the effort to secure modification of the nuclear agreement, Foreign Minister Azeredo da Silveira asserted sharply, "Brazil has nothing to fear; we are not frightened. The United States are a powerful country, but Brazil is a sovereign country, and will defend its interests." He went on to call attention to the failure of signatories to the Nuclear Non-Proliferation Treaty to fulfill their obligation to furnish nuclear technology to those lacking it.[52] The Brazilians felt that theirs was the stronger moral position since they were standing up, like India, for the equality of the less developed nations. The Brazilian-German deal represented a major break in the American near-monopoly in the world reactor market, based on dominance in the supply of enriched uranium, and it was regarded as a model for the Third World.[53]

Brazilians were also skeptical of the purity of U.S. motives. Behind the American talk of checking nuclear proliferation for the common security, they saw the interests of the nuclear industry, particularly Westinghouse, to keep them dependent on enriched uranium from the United States. Nuclebras had been set up to exploit Brazilian resources, which were assumed to be enormous; this the United States sought to impede. The material interest was undeniable, and it was easy to equate interest with motivation. Chancellor Schmidt had done as much when he stated earlier that opposition was stirred up by disappointed corporations.

The suspicion that the U.S. interest was basically economic was fueled by a still not fully explained incident. Shortly before the Brazilian-German accord was finalized, a U.S. corporation, Bechtel, offered to build an enrichment plant in Brazil in a desperate attempt to head off the German deal. It was claimed that this was authorized by or at least known in advance by the State Department, but the Department shortly reacted by forcing withdrawal of the offer.[54]

Brazilians also felt that the United States was doing them an injustice by not accepting at face value their repeated assurances of pacific intention and willingness to comply with international safeguards under the IAEA. Brazil had subscribed to and expressed support for the Treaty of Tlatelolco (1967) to prohibit nuclear weapons in Latin America, with a control mechanism. But fears of an eventual nuclear arms race in Latin America were not entirely groundless. The Treaty of Tlatelolco does not come into effect until ratified by all Latin American nations and other nuclear powers, but Argentina, Cuba, and the Soviet Union have abstained and do not seem likely to join. The control provisions have remained on paper.[55] Brazil was at first opposed to Tlatelolco and has steadily rejected the Nuclear Non-Proliferation Treaty, which promised access to nuclear technology and fuels in return for a no-weapon pledge and agreement to international inspection and checking of nuclear activities; this is regarded as an effort to conserve old monopolies and freeze differences.[56] In any case, U.N. International Atomic Energy Agency controls refer only to specific operations and facilities and are no guarantee against the production of bombs, as India showed by making a nuclear explosive device surreptitiously.

Although U.S. experiments with peaceful nuclear explosives ("Operation Plowshare") have been discouraging, the Brazilian government has frequently expressed the need for such a capacity,[57] and peaceful explosives are physically indistinguishable from unpeaceful. The Treaty of Tlatelolco is interpreted as permitting peaceful nuclear explosives.[58] There has been some talk, moreover, of a frankly military application of nuclear capacities. The sober *Estado de São Paulo* has stated that Brazil should have an atomic bomb if other nations do,[59] while from the Argentine point of view it has been self-evident that Brazil wanted the bomb to support its imperialist ambitions.[60] It has been suggested that the military feel it necessary to remain in power in order to assure the procurement of nuclear weapons that a civilian government might not have the resolve to acquire, and Brazilians privately admit the nuclear goal.[61] In 1975, Foreign Minister Azeredo da Silveira stated, "Brazil should not consider spending money to make bombs, but we must have the technology to make them if one day it were necessary to maintain parity in the region,"[62] that is, in case Argentina acquired the bomb. It has often been stated that Brazil could build an A-bomb in a fairly short time, perhaps ten years, and that the deal with Germany is helpful to this end.[63] There have been speculations, probably with little basis, that Germany, prohibited from military use of nuclear force in Europe, might cooperate with Brazil in development of a bomb, and that Germany might contribute toward a Brazilian rocket.

Nonetheless, the Carter administration evidently concluded there was nothing useful to be done, and since the 1978 mission has at least publicly desisted from raising the issue. When Gerard Smith, Carter's nuclear non-proliferation treaty advisor, was in Brazil in July 1978 he did not even bring up the German deal.[64] The United States proceeded in 1978 to provide start-up fuel for the Angra I reactor. The West German and Brazilian governments, on the other hand, have reaffirmed fidelity to the agreement—for a time the Brazilians seem to have been afraid the West Germans would bow and renege.[65]

As U.S. opposition faded, that within Brazil mounted. When the United States withdrew from the fray unofficial influence from the American (and European) antinuclear movement grew, and Brazilians became free to oppose the program without being placed on the side of Carter. By 1980, there were well-organized antinuclear demonstrations, mostly by students and other youth and aligned with ecological and other antiestablishment causes. This, and widespread criticism in the press were made possible by the ending of censorship and the general relaxation of authoritarianism in 1978–80. The superintendent of Nuclebras complained that his work was impeded by the public debate.[66]

As elsewhere, nuclear construction in Brazil was hurt by delays and rising costs. Angra I was to begin operation not in 1978 but early 1981; Angra II was very far behind and unlikely to produce in the 1980s; and Angra III was still on the drawing board in 1980. The cost of the whole program of eight reactors was estimated at $30 billion,[67] when Brazil was in debt almost beyond its capacity. The cost per kilowatt, estimated at $510 in 1971, had risen to $2,000 or more in 1979; and Brazil probably lacked adequate trained personnel for the reactors envisaged. The site was poorly selected, and there were many stories of corruption or gross mismanagement.[68] It was questioned whether the costly program was necessary at all in view of Brazil's abundant rivers; while hydropower was not exactly where wanted, it was fairly well distributed for desired dispersal of industry. Nuclebras was accused of presenting a false picture of hydropower potential.[69] Electrobras, the state electric monopoly, claimed there was almost twice as much, while the slower growth of energy use further undercut the justification of the program.[70]

It seemed, moreover, that the chief cause of American concern might be moot; a reprocessing plant might not be economic unless at least six reactors were built, which appeared increasingly distant.[71]

Brazilian opposition to the nuclear program after Carter's peacemaking visit continued gradually to swell to a protest movement expressive of widespread fears of nuclear pollution or accidents. The contracts were attacked as unduly advantageous to the Germans; under them, in the opinion of some, Brazil bound itself to a new and onerous dependency.[72] Use of the jet-nozzle process, expensive and untried, was seen as a concession to German interests.[73] A legislative committee heard testimony that Brazil was purchasing from Germany much equipment that could be produced in Brazil.[74] Brazilian scientists were generally hostile to the deal, which they saw as favoring German over native talent.[75] In the opinion of physicist José Goldemberg, it was a neocolonial agreement that made Nuclebras a foreign body in Brazil and hindered economic development. For many, the atomic dream had become a nightmare.[76]

The government has taken a defensive posture under the cover of much secrecy—Nuclebras is far more curtained than the U.S. Nuclear Regulatory Commission. Proposed sites of future plants are held secret, as is much that would generally be considered purely commercial. The 1975 agreement, in fact, has not been fully divulged. In August 1979 police confiscated an issue of *Gaceta Mercantil* that published part of the text of the 1975 agreement—the first arbitrary act against the press of the Figueiredo administration. The minister of security was at a loss to explain why a commercial agreement was held confidential but promised an explanation for a closed Senate committee. In a reversal of previous alignments, the government blamed U.S. interests in nationalistic terms. According to the president of Nuclebras, Paulo Nogueira Batista, efforts to publish the agreements were in the interests of those who, "having lost the Brazilian market fear Brazil's taking over the markets they formerly held."[77] It seems that one article provided for the formation of a joint enterprise to export "materials and services related to nuclear plants" to Latin American countries. In the opinion of *Veja*, however, secrecy was a cover for bad business[78] and the chief virtue of Nuclebras was to employ a host of overaged bureaucrats.[79]

The government wished, nonetheless, to go forward, albeit more slowly than originally anticipated. In 1975 a firm commitment was made for only two plants, with an option for six more; recently it was proposed to proceed with one of those under option,[80] and there may be some idea of working on a much more dangerous and costly breeder reactor.[81] It is hardly argued that they are an economic necessity, but Brazil claimed to have some 200,000 tons of uranium oxide, with very incomplete exploration,[82] and it is felt that this resource should contribute to energy independence. Nuclear power is still associated with modernization; Brazil is proud to be able to offer nuclear technology to Iraq in exchange for oil.[83] It is also hoped that work on fission reactors will help to prepare for the day of fusion power, giving technical experience and training scientists and engineers.

It is the less likely that Brazil will renounce nuclear power, even if uneconomic, because Argentina is going ahead with it—and boasting of its nuclear primacy in Latin America.[84] Argentina has a plutonium separation plant and is building heavy water production facilities, with Swiss help and to the impotent displeasure of the United States, in order to expand use of natural uranium.[85] In May 1980 President Figueiredo signed in Buenos Aires an agreement for cooperation in nuclear technology intended to make it more economic for both nations.[86]

Unless discredited by possible accidents, nuclear power seems likely to go forward. France, for example, proposes to rely on nuclear reactors for 62 percent of its electrical energy by 1985, and it counts on uranium ore with the energy equivalent of a billion tons of oil, or 50 times as much if used in breeder reactors, which France is pioneering. Current world nuclear capacity is about 125,000 megawatts, a figure expected to rise to 850,000 to 1,200,000 megawatts by A.D. 2000.[87] Nuclear power is probably not suitable for any but the most advanced industiral countries; hardly anything is more technology-intensive. But many Third World countries want it, for various reasons, as Brazil does; and it may be cheaper than it has been for Brazil. Small prefabricated reactors (about 200 megawatts) have been developed, and they are offered at bargain prices by producers lacking domestic orders because of the current slump in nuclear construction in the United States and Europe.[88] These do not lead directly to nuclear weapons, but the reprocessing of used fuel rods, a chemical process, is much less difficult than isotopic separation for the enrichment of uranium; Brazil could probably manage reprocessing alone. Reprocessing may be uneconomical at present, especially on a small scale, but it becomes more attractive as uranium prices rise.

Although the plutonium produced in reprocessing is not the best mixture for explosives, the potential for proliferation and filling the earth with piles of A-bombs is appalling. The incentives to become an atomic power are strong, mostly because of regional rivalries and insecurity. If Israel has nuclear weapons (as is widely believed), Arab states must obtain them. That China is a nuclear power was reason for India to try to catch up, and India's nuclear progress drives Pakistan. Possibly dozens of countries by the end of this century may have the capacity to wreak nuclear havoc.

Against this danger, America has used a variety of pressures to discourage the export of nuclear technology. The best efforts, however, have suffered from apparent inconsistency. Thus, it seemed remarkable that the United States was so concerned with the German-Brazilian deal when it was prepared to sell reactors to Israel and Egypt, neither of which (unlike Brazil) accepted international controls.[89] Recently the United States objected (vainly) to the French sale of nuclear fuel and equipment to Iraq, although Iraq had ratified the Nuclear Non-Proliferation Treaty permitting international inspection. The United States cut off aid to Pakistan because of its nuclear program, but Carter, overruling the Nuclear Regulatory Commission and going contrary to the spirit if not the letter of the Nuclear Non-Proliferation Act of 1978, authorized continuing shipments of nuclear fuel to India despite the Indian refusal to permit inspections or to promise no more nuclear explosives.[90] It seemed that the United States used influence more or less as believed available; it pressed most in the case of longtime friend if not client Brazil, less toward Pakistan, a semi-ally, and was most compliant to neutralist or Soviet-leaning India, which could easily go to the Soviet Union for uranium.

The Carter administration has tried to use the withholding of nuclear fuel as a means of influence, but this is a markedly shrinking asset. In 1970, Europe bought nearly all its enriched uranium from the United States; in 1980, only 40 percent[91] because of increased supplies from France and the Soviet Union. Moreover, whereas fuel was short in 1975, there is now a surplus.[92] Despite this trend, the U.S. Congress in 1978 passed the Nuclear Non-Proliferation Act (against the judgment of the administration), denying nuclear fuel to any country producing plutonium without American permission. Under the act, recipients of U.S. fuel were required to open installations to international inspection; and inflexible, complex procedures were established for any reprocessing of spent fuel, compromising the independence of cooperative countries.[93] The administration was permitted a certain latitude in waiving requirements as much as a year, but, as the president reported to Congress, the United States was made unreliable as a supplier[94] and various countries were irritated by controls applied retroactively to contracts already made. The one certain effect of a policy of withholding enriched uranium was to make it more important for countries to become self-sufficient.

It thus appeared that efforts to use American influence to restrict the nuclear development of Brazil and other countries were costly in good will and ineffective. It would have been unfortunate if Germany had yielded to the pleas to withdraw from its engagement; Brazil would only have been infuriated and the more determined to secure nuclear technology elsewhere. In any event, the United States appeared as a poor friend and unreliable partner, opposing the progress of a faithful ally; Brazil saw itself treated as untrustworthy and inferior like the rest of the Third World. In any case, there is no technical means, certainly none at the disposal of the United States, for preventing the growth of nuclear plants and attendant risk of the spread of nuclear weapons.[95] Even international safeguards are flimsy and cheatable.

Possibly the most effective leverage the United States could hope to exert would be the example of renouncing nuclear power, as some have urged.[96] If nuclear power is considered too valuable to renounce, it may be that a "free market in nuclear fuel would be the best way to discourage countries from securing their own costly facilities."[97] If the United States had been more willing to sell nuclear technology to Brazil, it would have been easier to keep at least a little control of the uses to which it might be put. The best incentive for Brazil to refrain from seeking enrichment and reprocessing capacities would be to provide a reliable supply of fuel more cheaply than Brazil could hope to produce it, with the condition of returning spent rods. Most of all, if Brazil felt it could count on the United States as the faithful other half of a permanent special relationship, Brazil would feel less need for a nuclear program at all.

HUMAN RIGHTS

The second and broader theme of President Carter's effort to restore idealism to foreign policy was support for human rights; and this, like nonproliferation, caused a stir in U.S.-Brazilian relations, albeit rather less abrasively and more successfully. Human rights in one form or another—democratic institutions, civil liberties, freedom from religious or racial persecution—have been a concern of the United States from the Declaration of Independence onward. Carter's administration however, was the first to speak for the repressed of all lands in assertion of the new widely but partially accepted international right of censure—the license, sanctified by U.N. Charter and other documents and the Helsinki Accord (1975), of denouncing inhumanities even while unable to intervene directly on behalf of the victims.

It had been generally accepted that one government had no business trying to interfere with the way another government treated those under its jurisdiction, at least unless very large numbers were involved. Through the postwar period, however, there has been rising concern about arbitrary treatment; Stalin's murder of millions aroused less protest in the 1930s than did Brezhnev's incarceration of a few thousand in the 1970s. Religious and private idealistic organizations—notably Amnesty International—have striven to sensitize the world to official brutality not only in Communist countries but in dictatorial states everywhere, such as the Phillipines under Marcos, South Korea, Uganda, Iran, and others. There was condemnation for abuses in many countries of Latin America, such as El Salvador, Guatemala, and the military-dominated governments of Chile, Argentina, Uruguay, and Brazil.

Official concern with human rights in Latin America grew in the latter

1960s. In 1967 there was established an Inter-American Commission on Human Rights,[98] charged with promoting their observance; and in 1969 an Inter-American Convention on Human Rights gave a juridical basis for concern. Congress, reflecting citizens' anxieties, showed increasing concern after the end of U.S. military involvement in Vietnam early in 1973. In that year it began conducting inquiries into human rights practices, especially in connection with foreign aid, and attaching human rights amendments to aid appropriations. In 1974 military assistance was prohibited to nations grossly violating human rights, a provision aimed primarily at South Korea and Chile; and the Jackson-Vanik Amendment imposed a rights condition—reasonable freedom of emigration—on commercial advantages for Communist countries. Growing congressional pressure impelled the State Department to undertake the study of human rights practices in many lands and to expand slightly its human rights section, previously occupied by a lone, not very busy, third-rank officer.[99] The principal concern of the State Department with human rights in the Kissinger era seemed to be to brush the question off as far as possible. The Secretary even rebuked his ambassador in Chile for privately raising the rights issue. A department memorandum remarked that, "although the Executive Branch understands why repression is necessary, the emotional Congress . . . may do something irresponsible."[100]

The Nixon and Ford administrations thus did nothing to discourage the Brazilian torture chambers, which aroused the indignation of leftist and liberal circles in the United States and Western Europe. When the military took hold in 1964 there was a strong drive to clean up, as the officers saw it, by ruthless methods if necessary. In the name of combatting subversion and corruption, hundreds were deprived of political rights, thousands were removed from jobs, and thousands more arrested, arbitrarily confined, and interrogated, all too frequently with the accompaniment of refined or simply brutal torture. Castelo Branco, however, was not of dictatorial temperament; and after the revolutionary wave had passed there was considerable relaxation. Shortly after the coup, Vernon Walters went with ambassador Gordon to express to General Costa e Silva the hope of their government for the observance of human rights and freedom of the press under the new regime. Costa e Silva, apparently shocked, replied that they could not proceed exactly as in the United States but had no desire for a brutal dictatorship.[101]

The establishment of a much more dictatorial system under Costa e Silva's Institutional Act V of December 1968 led, however, to the institutionalization of harsh procedures, which constituted an outrage to leftists and democrats. Deprived of opportunities of legal political expression, the more extreme of them went into underground and terrorist activities. By August 1969 there were reportedly ten guerrilla groups in operation, heirs of Ché Guevara and emulators of the Vietnamese fighters against capitalism-imperialism, trying to imitate in the cities of Brazil the irregular warfare successful in Asian jungles.[102] They made illegal broadcasts, robbed banks, assassinated and kidnapped.

The biggest coup of the terrorists was the kidnapping in September 1969 of U.S. Ambassador C. Burke Elbrick. For his release, the radicals demanded the shipment to Mexico of 15 political prisoners. Under U.S. pressure, the government quickly yielded. But as soon as the ambassador was safe, the government declared war on subversives, suspended constitutional guarantees, and arrested thousands. The death penalty was restored for the first time since 1891, and sentences were carried out without review. The security forces were given license to treat their suspects pretty much as they pleased.[103] Torture apparently became the chief means of securing information, and it seems that hundreds died under it, although President Médici repeatedly denied it was official policy. Subordinates seem to have frequently overstepped their mandate. Ironically, abuses were worst in São Paulo and Rio, the richest and most advanced centers. In November 1970 about 5,000 persons were held for political reasons in Rio alone.[104] For several years the government waged something like a war against a fraction of the population. There was also irregular counterterror, as the death squads, mostly off-duty police, murdered both supposed subversives and common criminals at a rate of several hundred yearly.

Thanks to the use of torture or not, the government began getting the better of its violent opponents by a sophisticated and well-organized repressive campaign.[105] Their outstanding leader, Carlos Marighella, was betrayed and shot in a police ambush in November 1969. In 1970, subversive activity crested with several kidnappings of diplomats, and some 15 revolutionary organizations were at work.[106] But the victims of revolutionary terrorism, under 100 since 1964, were far outnumbered by the victims of repression. Amnesty International in 1972 listed over a thousand persons tortured in nearly all Brazilian prisons.[107] Early in 1973, the government claimed victory over the chief guerrilla organization,[108] but repressions continued through the end of the Médici term in March 1974.

Criticism of Brazilian police brutality grew in the United States, especially as the Brazilian Catholic Church increasingly took an antiregime position in defense of popular rights and freedoms, and Catholic activists joined the Marxists in jails. In the Congress, Senator Frank Church and others denounced the program of the Agency for International Development (AID) to supply and train Brazilian security forces, which was responsible in 1971 for the training of 641 out of 271,000

Brazilian police.[109] This program was terminated during 1972–73 by Congress.[110] Other aid, however, continued through the bad years of 1966–75.[111]

Reaction in the executive branch was muted, since Kissinger did not consider human rights an appropriate subject for public diplomacy.[112] The Rockefeller mission to Brazil in June 1969 met deputies of the suspended congress and student leaders, and raised questions of censorship and academic freedom,[113] but neglected political prisoners. When an American missionary-journalist, Fred Morris, was arrested and maltreated in October 1974, the U.S. ambassador John Crimmins sent a strong protest note, and further angered Brazilian authorities by releasing it to the press. The *Washington Post*, Senator Edward Kennedy, and others reacted with indignation; but Kissinger ignored the matter.[114] When Kissinger was in Brazil in February 1976 to sign the memorandum of special relationship, the question of human rights was apparently not raised.

The problem became less acute after 1975, as President Geisel undertook to ease authoritarian rule. On the human rights docket Brazil fell behind Argentina, Uruguay, Chile, and others. Geisel discouraged arbitrary and secret arrests and torture and permitted more open protest. Some continued to disappear, but it was possible to ask questions and demand explanations.[115] Direct censorship was ended, except for a few outstanding papers, where censors lingered; and the feud with the church was mended.[116] Terrorism was under control, Geisel said, so redemocratization could proceed.[117]

In the first part of 1975, however, arrests continued as though by inertia of the apparatus. Hundreds were detained monthly, and detention still probably meant unpleasant experiences.[118] A turning point came with the torture and probable murder of a São Paulo journalist, Vladimir Herzog, a few hours after being arrested on October 25, 1975, by military opponents of Geisel. The resulting wave of protest and indignation led Geisel to dismiss the army commander responsible; and the course since then has generally been toward legality. The human rights issue, like the nuclear issue, climaxed long before President Carter raised it to prominence.

In his campaign for the presidency, Jimmy Carter took up the question of promotion of human rights, and he spoke of it in his inaugural address. In part an extension or continuation of the civil rights drive against racial discrimination—several human rights advocates in the Carter camp were veterans of the marches of the 1960s—the idea appealed to a nation looking for a better expression of national purpose after Vietnam and Watergate.

The application of the human rights policy to Brazil, however, was rather incidental. The prime target was the Soviet Union and Eastern Europe. There is no evidence that Carter intended in advance to make a great issue of human rights, but they were brought to center stage by repressive measures taken by the Soviet and Czechoslovak governments about the time Carter entered office. In effect repudiating the indifference of his predecessor, he took up the challenge and expressed sympathy with the dissidents, even writing a letter to Andrei Sakharov. But if condemnation of Soviet maltreatment of intellectuals was not to be merely anti-Soviet or anti-Communist politics, it had to be generalized as an ideal and applied to friends and allies such as Brazil, as well as nonfriends. In fact it seemed to many that the policy in fact penalized pro-American governments much more than anti-American, since the sanctions behind it were denial of assistance and loans, which anti-American governments would not be likely to get in any case.

Many legislative enactments sought to deny aid to at least the worst violators of human rights—concern being chiefly for rights of personal security, immunity from arbitrary arrest and mistreatment, rather than political rights of participation (support for which is more intrusive) or economic rights (which require positive action and which are in many cases difficult or impossible to achieve). No less important, the Export-Import Bank and U.S. representatives on international lending agencies were instructed to take into account the rights record of applicants, unless the loans directly aided the poor. By the end of 1978, the United States had opposed international loans to 16 countries on human rights grounds.[119]

Brazil, however, did not figure prominently in discussions of rights violations in the first months of the new administration, perhaps because by then the intensity of repression had substantially diminished; and it would not appear that the Carter administration especially desired to press Brazil on that topic. It came to the fore because a law for which Carter had no responsibility; the International Security Assistance Act of 1976, required the State Department to submit to Congress a report on all 82 countries receiving military or security assistance. The report, in which Brazil had a minor place, was given to the Senate Committee on Foreign Relations in March 1977.

The section on Brazil was not severe. It noted "real but gradual" liberalization under Geisel in the face of difficulties and opposition from "conservative elements," especially concerned by antigovernment majorities in relatively free local elections. It linked political arrests and "reports of abuses" in 1975 with activities of the Communist party and noted that "reports of abuses of political prisoners immediately declined sharply" after the removal of the commanding general of the São Paulo district. Regarding integrity of the person:

> Some infringements by the government upon the right to life, liberty, and security of the person continue to be reported. . . . Political detainees and others acting on their behalf have charged the government with torture, cruel, inhuman and degrading punishment in earlier years. These accusations, including detailed excerpts of depositions by the detainees, have been publicized in the media in Brazil and other countries. The government has in some instances launched inquiries into reports of abuses. Corrective actions have included removal from office of persons responsible for the mistreatment of alleged subversives. Since January 1976, moreover, human rights advocates within and outside Brazil have stated in public reports and interviews that persons arrested in security cases are for the most part not being subjected to torture or harsh conditions of interrogation or confinement; very few charges of abuse have arisen in this period involving political detention.

Note was taken of irregular police abuses, including "death squad activities, and the frequent unavailability of legal redress of victims," while "Fair hearings by impartial tribunals are not consistently available to political detainees." It was remarked, however, that many or most of those brought to trial were acquitted.

The government was otherwise given good marks regarding sex, race, and religious discrimination; travel was reported free except for a tax for balance of payments purposes. Media censorship was rated at the lowest level since the mid-1960s.[120]

As a courtesy and perhaps to give an opportunity for refutation, the embassy gave a copy of the report to the Brazilian government prior to submission. The Foreign Office did not appreciate the courtesy and indignantly returned the report as "intolerable interference." Within a few hours the Brazilians denounced the military aid agreement in effect since 1952. They had previously rejected a $50 million military aid package.[121] It is said that some military hotheads talked of breaking diplomatic relations.[122] Yet the Brazilian public position was moderate. When the government denounced the military agreements, it prohibited radio and television from commenting on frictions with the United States.[123] It is possible that the government was less infuriated by a relatively mild statement of well-known facts than it was glad for an excuse to break formal ties which the Armed Forces had been considering terminating for a year or more in any case.[124] The reaction was conditioned, moreover, by irritation at American pressure in the nuclear question—the report was presented to the Brazilian government at the very time Warren Christopher came to argue the nuclear case. Some Brazilian military men contended that Carter was using the campaign for human rights as a means for forcing modification of the nuclear power program.[125]

The Geisel government emphatically claimed that it was already checking excesses of security agencies and needed no prodding from Americans,[126] who failed to appreciate the necessity of harsh measures against terrorism. When the question of human rights was taken up by a meeting of the Organization of American States (OAS) in June 1977— Carter had just signed the Inter-American Convention on Human Rights, which had been waiting nearly a decade—Brazil took a stand for noninterference on national sovereignty grounds but was less indignant than Chile, Argentina, and Uruguay, the record of which was worse. Foreign Minister Azeredo da Silveira called the issue exaggerated, pointed to the importance of other rights such as to nourishment, education, health care, and so forth, while expressing Brazil's broad desire to cooperate for the fulfillment of human rights in general and urging that there be no pointing of fingers.[127]

Ambassador to the United Nations Andrew Young and others expressed criticism of Brazilian human rights practices, but the Carter administration began to back away from the issue as it concurrently did from the nuclear question. The administration assured the Brazilians that they were in no way being singled out, and the Brazilians took no obvious economic retaliatory moves. Rosalynn Carter, welcomed in Brazil in June 1977, was able to speak with Geisel about both human rights and nuclear proliferation without acrimony.[128] There was little objection to her meeting American missionaries who claimed to have been treated like animals in Brazilian jails. She said she had discussed rights at length with President Geisel.[129] Subsequently Brazil rejected the visit of Allard K. Lowenstein, U.S. representative on the International Human Rights Commission.[130] In September the Brazilians completed the erasure of old military agreements by terminating the U.S. naval mission[131] and the U.S.-Brazil Joint Military Commission, left over from World War II. Cooperation was continued, however, through the chiefs of staff and joint exercises.[132] In November, Secretary Vance took with him to Brasília Patricia Deriam, human rights advisor for the State Department, but she does not seem to have played any role.[133]

Shortly before Carter's March 1978 visit to Brazil, Ambassador John Crimmins, who had sometimes ruffled the Brazilians, was replaced by Robert Sayre, who took a milder tone on human rights and other issues. Those who regarded pressing Brazil on human rights as provocative of a valuable ally feared that Carter would feel impelled to make some dramatic political statement,[134] but he took a conciliatory position. He spoke with several oppositionists, two cardinals, a lawyer, a newspaper publisher, and a few others, but avoided any hint of intervention. In statements to the Brazilian press he spoke of the two countries being committed to enhancing human rights but acknowledged that a major difference existed, the U.S. desire to marshal world opinion and to publicize proven violations against the Brazilian opposition to bringing international organizations into the picture. He also noted that Brazil supported the Inter-American Human Rights Commission and suggested that it or the United Nations should be allowed to investigate allegations. The principal accomplishment of a rights policy, he felt, was to call the attention of world leaders to the problem.[135] The Carter visit was generally seen as putting an end to the asperity that marked the first year of the new administration.

The effort of the administration to inject itself or international organizations into the Brazilian human rights problem to some extent aroused nationalistic forces in Brazil, as in other countries under similar or stronger attack, such as Argentina.[136] Hard-liners in the government and doubtless many outside it regarded foreign censure of any kind as intolerable meddling. Foreign Minister Azeredo counterattacked by saying that the real fault lay with the developed countries' failure to do enough to eliminate the problems that led to abuses.[137]

The State Department, however, believed that the policy earned good will for Carter and the United States among the majority of Brazilians. Carter was cheered in Brasília when he spoke about human rights.[138] An outstanding Brazilian publicist, Celso Lafer, called human rights "one of the worthy items of the Carter administration's foreign policy."[139] Some complained that the chief fault of the policy was that it did not go far enough and push for more political rights.[140]

A Brazilian journal saw the Carter policy helping Brazil toward liberalization of the idea of National Security.[141] It is hardly accidental that in May 1977, a few weeks after Carter's appearance, there were student demonstrations, like none for many years, in São Paulo, Rio, and other cities, calling for amnesty for political prisoners, an end to repressions, and free elections. In March 1978, shortly before the Carter visit, the Brazilian lawyers' association unanimously demanded restoration of rule of law, human rights, freedom of expression, and security for judges. It is reasonable to guess that the moral support of the U.S. government made it at least more difficult to go back to large-scale repressions. Figueiredo in an interview agreed with the human rights policy as "a weapon in the fight against ideological totalitarianism" but not so far as it was "an attempt to interfere in the internal affairs of another country," and hoped this was no longer at issue.[142]

It has never been officially admitted, of course, that Carter policies had the slightest influence on Brazilian performance. They were hardly decisive, because improvement began with the beginning of the Geisel administration and was marked, as noted earlier, from the end of 1975. But the respect for human rights gradually improved through 1977, despite some reversal of the process of liberalization in April, and the course continued through 1978 and 1979. In 1978, according to Amnesty International, there were 180 political prisoners in Brazil, not a very large number for a large country. By 1979 the number was down to 73.[143] According to a British writer, Michael Scammel, in mid-1979 three Brazilian journalists were still imprisoned.[144]

The last admitted political prisoners—held in connection with terrorist acts—were set free in 1980. Police brutality was still occasionally reported in the Brazilian press in 1980, but it was directed against common criminals and was due at least in part to public pressure for measures against rising crime.[145] Permissible periods of detention incommunicado were reduced, and provision was made for examination of detainees to preclude torture. The police, however, claimed that freedom of torture was necessary for their work, and they protested the punishment of officers responsible for the death of a victim.[146] They exercised de facto powers of preventive detention, and for them to threaten to make arrests only by warrant or flagrante delicto was like a threat to go on strike.[147] A high police administrator, while admitting the difficulty of preventing the abuse of prisoners, considered torture a subhuman degeneration of which few were guilty and insisted that the question of torture of political prisoners was bygone.[148] But death squads were still active, and political oppositionists could hardly feel very secure unless the rule of law prevailed.

A major step toward national reconciliation was the amnesty of September 1979 that permitted some 5,000 exiles to return to Brazil. Only a few, some 200, were excluded because of violent acts; many former terrorists were amnestied. The few still living leaders from Kubitschek-Goulart days, such as Leonel Brizola, Miguel Arraes, and the perennial Communist chieftain, Luis Carlos Prestes, trooped back from New York, Algeria, and Moscow, to resume political activities, in trust that the government would respect its pledges. It seemed either that the government felt confidence in its own stability or a need to improve its legitimacy by concessions to humanity and legality.

It seems probable that the official human rights policy—although less important than the pressures of public opinion and private organizations in the United States and Europe—contributed to an improvement in civil and political freedoms in Brazil. It may have had a broad impact, indeed, on dictatorship in Latin America.[149] Human rights policies and the implied support for democracy very likely had something to do with the holding of elections and the renunciation of power by the military in the Dominican Republic, Peru, and Ecuador in 1978–79; and it may have contributed to moderation of dictatorship in Chile and Uruguay.[150]

It seems clear that the rights policy, while irritating some in such countries as Brazil and Argentina, generally improved the U.S. image in

Latin America.[151] It helped to erase the identification of the United States with dictatorial regimes and earned the applause of many otherwise anti-American intellectuals. Its purposes included the restoration of trust in the United States and its foreign policy, taking the ideological initiative from the radical Left and providing a basis for communication with opposi-tionists and alternative claimants to power, as well as helping the persecuted;[152] and to some extent it achieved these objectives, while giving Americans a slightly better feeling about their country.

The means employed have been primarily informational, but the U.S. Congress tried to give the policy teeth by linking foreign aid and commercial or financial advantages to human rights performance. In 1978 the prohibition on aid or military sales to Brazil, Argentina, Paraguay, El Salvador, and Guatemala was reaffirmed—in part superfluously since these countries had mostly already rejected military aid after the 1977 report. Likewise investment insurance was prohibited (with some excep-tions) in countries found to be violating human rights. But such measures as holding up Ex-Im Bank loans have not proved very effective and have been largely given up. Most emphasis has gone to publicity, such as the country reports—in 1979 and 1980 reports were made, as legally required, on not only aid recipients but all U.N. members. It is questioned whether a quiet, a private approach might not avoid antagonizing and ultimately prove more effective.[153] However, foreign interference in this regard does not seem to have been widely resented. There is little coercive threat and the cause is highly credible, coinciding with world opinion and the feelings of many Brazilians; and there was no evident selfish U.S. interest, as in the nuclear issue. U.S. loss of influence in Brazil from 1977 to 1980 was certainly far less from preaching human rights than from the perceived inconsistencies and unreliability of U.S. foreign policy. The fact that the human rights issue was pressed so closely in conjunction with the nuclear issue made it harder for the Brazilian government to be receptive in regard to either.

Some friction may have been a necessary price. It is surely appropri-ate for the United States to offer moral support to Czechs or Russians pleading for decent treatment, but this can hardly be done effectively unless the policy is morally consistent. Brazil never ranked high in the human rights concerns of the American administration, but it could not be ignored.

It is a difficult question how far the United States should endeavor to impose moral-political standards upon governments over which it has more influence—how far it should try to turn Nicaraguan, Chilean, or Iranian autocrats into democrats (which would mean causing them to lose power) or should support them as better for the United States than a likely alternative. It has frequently seemed that the United States has tended to stand by its friends or dependents even when they lacked popular support—and lack of popular support made them more dependent on the United States. It is not possible to dictate the political institutions of other countries with the kind of influence the United States had in Japan and West Germany through military occupation; any attempt to shape other countries' governments would be interpreted as imperialism. But the United States can apparently, as it seems to have done in Brazil, exert a generalized and diffuse influence in favor of its values if it proceeds with discretion and tact.

NOTES

1. *Veja*, October 25, 1978, p. 140.

2. Norman Gall, "Noah's Ark: Energy from Biomass in Brazil," *American Universities Field Staff Reports, 1978*, no. 30, p. 5.

3. *Veja*, September 20, 1978, p. 33.

4. Carlos de Meira Mattos, *Brasil: Geopolítica e destino* (Rio de Janeiro: José Olympios, 1975), p. 93.

5. John R. Redick, "Nuclear Proliferation in Latin America," *International Organization* 29 (Spring 1975):276.

6. Juan E. Gugliamelli, *Argentina, Brasil, y la bomba atómica* (Buenos Aires: Tierra Nueva, 1976), p. 8.

7. Norman Gall, "The Twilight of Nuclear Exports: Brazil and Iran," *American Universities Field Staff Reports, 1979*, no. 2, p. 186.

8. Redick, "Regional Nuclear Arms Control in Latin America," p. 420.

9. John R. Redick, *Military Potential of Latin American Nuclear Programs* (Beverly Hills, Calif.: Sage Publications, 1972), p. 21.

10. *Visão*, September 9, 1974, p. 27.

11. Edward F. Wonder, *Nuclear Fuel and American Foreign Policy* (Boulder, Colo.: Westview Press, 1977), p. 287.

12. Ronald M. Schneider, *The Political System of Brazil: Emergence of a "Modernizing Authoritarian Regime"* (New York: Columbia University Press, 1971), pp. 49-50.

13. *Visão*, September 9, 1974, p. 25.

14. José Goldemberg, *Energia nuclear no Brasil* (São Paulo: Hucitec, 1978), p. 11.

15. Testimony of Walter O. Enright, U.S. Congress, Senate, Committee on Foreign Relations, Subcommittee on Arms Control, *Nonproliferation Issues*, 1977, p. 127.

16. *Resenha de Política Exterior do Brasil* 12 (January-March 1977):11.

17. Testimony of Enright, *Nonproliferation Issues*, p. 130.

18. *Visão*, July 1, 1975, p. 25.

19. Gall, "Noah's Ark," pp. 171-72.

20. *Visão*, July 7, 1975, p. 16.

21. Wonder, *Nuclear Fuel*, p. 286.

22. *New York Times*, June 10, 1975, p. 13.

23. Wonder, *Nuclear Fuel*, p. 289.

24. *Die Zeit*, June 27, 1975.

25. *New York Times*, June 10, 1975, p. 13.

26. As evident in testimony, Senate, Committee on Foreign Relations, *Nonproliferation Issues*.

27. Mattos, *Brasil: Geopolítica*, p. 98.
28. *New York Times*, May 31, 1976, p. 7.
29. *New York Times*, May 14, 1976, p. 1.
30. *New York Times*, April 8, 1976, p. IV-1.
31. *New York Times*, January 26, 1977, p. 5; Ibid., January 27, 1976, p. 4.
32. *New York Times*, March 13, 1977, p. 13.
33. *Visão*, November 14, 1977, p. 19.
34. *New York Times*, March 31, 1977, p. 2.
35. *Visão,* November 14, 1977, p. 19.
36. *Isto É*, March 16, 1977, p. 8.
37. *New York Times*, May 17, 1977, p. 3.
38. *New York Times*, June 7, 1977, p. 5.
39. *New York Times*, November 23, 1977, p. 9.
40. Jorge Antonio Aja Enfil, "Nuclear Energy in Argentina," *AEI Foreign Policy and Defense Review* 1, no. 6 (1979).
41. *Brazil Today*, January 9, 1979, p. 3.
42. *New York Times*, November 17, 1977, p. 12; November 23, 1977, p. 9.
43. *Isto É*, March 29, 1978, p. 24.
44. *New York Times*, March 31, 1978, p. A-12.
45. *Isto É*, April 5, 1978, pp. 14–15.
46. Walder de Goes, *O governo do General Geisel* (Rio de Janeiro: Editora Nova Fronteira, 1978), p. 158.
47. *Visão*, July 7, 1975, p. 20.
48. *Visão,* February 21, 1977, p. 14.
49. *Isto É*, March 16, 1977, pp. 5, 23.
50. de Goes, *O governo*, p. 164.
51. Mattos, *Brasil: Geopolítica*, p. 94.
52. *Brazil Today*, April 26, 1977, p. 3.
53. José Enrique Greno Velasco, "El acuerdo Brasil-RFA y la noproliferación nuclear," *Revista de la Política Internacional* 154 (November-December 1977):113–43.
54. *New York Times*, December 11, 1975, p. 19; Robert Gilette, "Nuclear Exports: A U.S. Firm's Troublesome Flirtation with Brazil," *Science* 189 (July 25, 1975):267–69; Wonder, *Nuclear Fuel*, p. 294; Zdenek Červenko and Barbara Rogers, *The Nuclear Axis* (New York: Quadrangle, New York Times, 1978), pp. 292–93; Norman Gall, "Atoms for Brazil, Danger for All," *Foreign Policy* 23 (Summer 1976):191–92.
55. Redick, *Military Potential*, p. 428.
56. *Resenha de Política Exterior do Brasil* 12, (January-March 1977):14.
57. Gall, "Atoms for Brazil," pp. 159–60; *New York Times*, March 31, 1967, p. 14; Ibid., July 5, 1967, p. 16.
58. Redick, *Military Potential*, p. 423.
59. *New York Times*, June 12, 1975, p. 11.
60. Gugliamelli, *Argentina*, p. 37; Gall, "Atoms for Brazil," pp. 159–60.
61. Serge D'Adesky, "Brazil's Rise to Dominance in Latin America," *Fletcher Forum* 3 (Summer 1979):48.
62. *Visão*, July 7, 1975, p. 16.
63. As in *O Comercio* (Brasília), March 28, 1980, p. 11.
64. *Visão*, September 18, 1978, p. 32.
65. *Visão*, April 2, 1979, p. 22.
66. *Jornal do Brasil*, May 23, 1980, p. 17.
67. *Estado de São Paulo*, April 6, 1980, p. 3, *Visão*, June 30, 1980, p. 21.
68. Gall, "The Twilight of Nuclear Exports," p. 1.
69. *Estado de São Paulo*, April 6, 1980, p. 3.

70. *Jornal do Brasil*, May 23, 1980, p. 17.

71. *Der Spiegel*, September 18, 1978, p. 132.

72. Goldemberg, *Energia nuclear*, p. 5.

73. *Visão*, April 2, 1979, p. 22.

74. *Veja*, August 29, 1979, pp. 80–90; Ibid., October 17, 1979, p. 139.

75. *Segurança e Desenvolvimento* 28, no. 176 (1979):77; *Veja*, November 7, 1979. p. 32.

76. *Visão*, June 30, 1980, p. 16.

77. *Veja*, September 12, 1979, p. 32.

78. *Veja*, October 12, 1979, p. 32.

79. *Veja*, August 29, 1979, p. 91.

80. *Jornal do Brasil*, May 15, 1980, p. 22.

81. *Der Spiegel*, September 18, 1978, p. 132.

82. *Segurança e Desenvolvimento* 28, no. 177 (1979):60.

83. *Business Week*, December 3, 1979, p. 62.

84. As in *Technology Review* 82 (May 1980):21.

85. Ata Enfil, "Nuclear Energy in Argentina," p. 6.

86. *Visão*, May 26, 1980, p. 21.

87. *Scientific American* 242 (May 1980):78.

88. Joseph R. Egan and Shem Arungu-Olende, "Nuclear Power for the Third World," *Technology Review* 82 (March 1980):47.

89. Stockholm International Peace Research Institute *Yearbook 1977* (Cambridge, Mass.: The MIT Press, 1977), p. 10.

90. *New York Times*, June 26, 1980, p. A-4.

91. *New York Times*, March 16, 1980, p. E-3.

92. Thomas L. Neff and Henry D. Jacoby, "Nonproliferation in a Changing Nuclear Fuel Market," *Foreign Affairs* 57 (Summer 1979):1134; *Technology Review* 83 (June–July 1980):80.

93. Neff and Jacoby, "Nonproliferation," p. 1128.

94. *Congressional Record* 125 (March 22, 1979):S3162.

95. As concluded by an international conference, *New York Times*, November 4, 1979, p. 1.

96. Amory Lovins, L. Hunter Lovins, and Lenard Ross, "Nuclear Power and Nuclear Bombs," *Foreign Affairs* 58 (Summer 1980):1159.

97. Bertrand Goldschmidt, "A Historical Survey of Nonproliferation Policies," *International Security* 2 (Summer 1977):86.

98. G. S. Starke, "Human Rights and International Law," in *Human Rights*, eds. Eugene Kamenka and Alice Erh-Soon Tay (New York: St. Martin's Press, 1978), p. 129.

99. Roberta Cohen, "Human Rights Decision-Making in the Executive Branch," in *Human Rights and American Foreign Policy*, eds. Donald P. Kommers and Gilburt D. Loescher (Notre Dame, Ind.: University of Notre Dame Press, 1979), p. 219.

100. Ibid., pp. 220, 221.

101. Vernon Walters, *Silent Mission* (Garden City, N.Y.: Doubleday, 1978), p. 390.

102. *New York Times*, August 16, 1969, p. 2.

103. Tad Szulc, "Letter from Brasilia," *New Yorker*, March 10, 1975, p. 80.

104. *New York Times*, November 7, 1970, p. 6.

105. Thomas E. Skidmore, "Brazil's Chaging Role in the International System," in *Brazil in the Seventies* ed. Riordan Roett (Washington, D.C.: American Enterprise Institute, 1976), pp. 20–21.

106. *New York Times*, December 14, 1970, p. 15.

107. *New York Times*, September 7, 1972, p. 10.

108. *New York Times*, January 12, 1973, p. 2.

109. *New York Times*, July 25, 1971, p. 5.

110. U.S., Congress, House, Committee on International Relations, Subcommittee on International Organization, *The Status of Human Rights in Selected Countries and the U.S. Response*, 1977, p. 2; William L. Wipfler, "Human Rights Violations and U.S. Foreign Assistance: The Latin American Connection," in *Human Rights and U.S. Foreign Policy: Principles and Applications*, eds. Peter G. Brown and Douglas McLean (Lexington, Mass.: Lexington Books, 1979), pp. 186–87.

111. Ibid., p. 46.

112. Albert Fishlow, "Flying Down to Rio: U.S.-Brazilian Relations," *Foreign Affairs* 57 (Winter 1978–79):399.

113. *New York Times*, June 18, 1969, p. 21.

114. *Visão*, November 4, 1974, p. 26.

115. Szulc, "Letter from Brasilia," pp. 80–81.

116. *New York Times*, February 23, 1974, p. 37.

117. *New York Times*, March 2, 1975, p. 3.

118. Adam Matthews, "Surveillance—and Worse—in Brazil, 1975," *Christian Century* 92 (December 31, 1975):1205.

119. Ronald M. Schneider, "A New Administration's New Policy," in *Human Rights and U.S. Foreign Policy: Principles and Applications*, eds. Peter G. Brown and Douglas MacLean (Lexington, Mass.: Lexington Books, 1979), p. 10.

120. U.S., Congress, Senate, Committee on Foreign Relations, Subcommittee on Foreign Assistance, *Human Rights Reports Prepared by the Department of State*, 1977, pp. 111–12.

121. *New York Times*, September 20, 1977, p. 8.

122. *Visão*, November 14, 1977, p. 20.

123. *Isto É*, March 18, 1977, p. 7.

124. *Isto É*, March 16, 1977, p. 6.

125. House, Committee on International Relations, *Status of Human Rights*, p. 46.

126. Álvaro Valle, *As novas estructuras políticas brasileiras* (Rio de Janeiro: Nordica, 1977), p. 223.

127. *Brazil Today*, June 23, 1977, p. 1.

128. *Isto É*, June 15, 1977, p. 12.

129. *New York Times*, June 9, 1977, p. 1.

130. *New York Times*, August 12, 1977, p. 5.

131. Michael Morris, *International Politics and the Sea: The Case of Brazil* (Boulder, Colo.: Westview Press, 1979), p. 201.

132. U.S. Congress, House, Committee on Government Operations, *U.S. Embassy Operations, Rio*, 1978, p. 34.

133. *Isto É*, November 30, 1977, p. 30.

134. *Visão*, November 14, 1978, p. 20.

135. *New York Times*, March 31, 1978, p. 12.

136. de Goes, *O governo*, p. 157.

137. *New York Times*, September 24, 1978, p. 4.

138. *Wall Street Journal*, March 31, 1977, p. 1.

139. *Estado de São Paulo*, July 1, 1979, p. 7.

140. See for example Helio Bicudo in *Estado de São Paulo*, July 1, 1979, p. 8.

141. *Veja*, September 20, 1978, p. 47.

142. *Brazil Today*, September 18, 1978, p. 3.

143. Joan R. Dassin, "Press Censorship—How and Why," *Index on Censorship* 8 (July–August 1979):13.

144. *Veja*, August 1, 1979, p. 6.

145. *New York Times*, October 5, 1979, p. 10.

146. *Veja*, October 17, 1979, pp. 29–30.

147. *Veja*, October 29, 1979, pp. 22–26.

148. *Veja*, August 29, 1979, pp. 3–4.

149. George W. Grayson, "The United States and Latin America: The Challenge of Human Rights," *Current History* 76 (February 1979):53.

150. As suggested in the case of Uruguay by *Isto É*, April 2, 1980, p. 15.

151. As testified by James Theberge, U.S., Congress, Senate, Committee on Foreign Relations, Subcommittee on Western Hemisphere Affairs, *Hearings on Trends and Issues October 4–6, 1978*, 1979, p. 15.

152. Abraham Lowenthal, "Latin America: A Not-So-Special Relationship," *Foreign Policy* 32 (Fall 1978):114–15.

153. A. Glenn Mower, Jr., *The United States, the United Nations, and Human Rights: The Eleanor Roosevelt and Jimmy Carter Eras* (Westport, Conn.: Greenwood Press, 1979), pp. 138–45.

5

ECONOMIC INFLUENCE

AID

Discussion of U.S. hegemony or dominance in Brazilian (and Latin American) affairs has emphasized economic factors as both means and purpose—the imperialism of the rich power using economic leverage in an insatiable urge for more riches. There are various ways in which the economic preponderance of the United States might influence Brazil: through dependence on imports to or exports from the United States; through the activities of American corporations in Brazil, and through favor or disfavor of the U.S. government.

The last category includes credit furnished by international lending and monetary agencies subject to U.S. influence or control, and outright economic aid furnished through the U.S. Agency for International Development (USAID), gifts, loans, or project assistance.

Economic aid is supposedly intended to help governments improve the productivity and well-being of their people; Congress is persuaded to vote for foreign aid (a never popular expenditure) because it helps keep governments and peoples more friendly to the United States and less susceptible to blandishments of the major world antagonist, while foreign aid helps American exporters and may even, in sum, assist the balance of payments. According to a critic, aid is intended not only for more or less defensible although selfish purposes, such as a bribe to secure the adoption of certain measures and help to multinational corporations (through providing infrastructure and increasing demand) but also for reprehensible ends, such as making nations worse indebted and hence more dependent, to stabilize repressive social structures, and to impoverish the masses.[1] To what extent U.S. aid to Brazil has served these purposes is controversial. It is clear only that whatever purpose or utility it may have had has been worn out.

The U.S. foreign aid program was, practically speaking, an outgrowth of the cold war; previously it had been only disaster relief, albeit on a large scale, as in the aftermath of the world wars. Brazil was not regarded as critically endangered during the first years of the cold war, and priority went to the Marshall Plan and the rebuilding of Europe—to some disappointment of the Brazilians. Kubitschek's proposal in 1958 of "Operation Pan America," by which the United States was called upon to provide liberal loans and price supports for Latin America, was not taken seriously in Washington. Brazil received some loans, however, as noted previously, most to help over balance-of-payments difficulties. There was controversy from time to time as the IMF tried to impose conditions of monetary stabilization and fighting inflation. Unable or unwilling to meet such conditions, at one time Kubitschek broke off negotiations with the IMF, to the general applause.[2]

Attention turned to Latin America and Brazil only after Castro became involved in an escalating quarrel with the United States and promised to revolutionize Latin America. The Alliance for Progress was the Kennedy administration's response: by a large injection of public and private capital, supported by technical skills and backed by democratic reform, the Latin American states in cooperation with the United States could improve their conditions and societies and enter a new era without violent upheaval. The Alliance, however, was always more rhetoric than substance. The promised billions of dollars of public aid and private investment failed to appear, while the effort to couple aid with reform ran into opposition from both nationalists (often leftists) and conservatives. Qualified personnel was lacking both on the U.S. and the Latin American side, and those technically qualified were usually politically insensitive. There was a contradiction between using aid in effect to buy friendship or to support existing power structures and the use of aid to improve living standards and promote the reforms that were desirable, by U.S. standards of democracy, in most of Latin America.

The beginning of the Alliance for Progress coincided with the beginning of the Quadros-Goulart period of instability and U.S. concern about Brazil's drift toward radicalism. Differences quickly arose. For example, early in 1961 Assistant Secretary Adolf Berle allegedly offered Quadros a package of $300 million in exchange for support of the U.S. position in Cuba; Quadros either spurned the offer as offensive[3] or felt that he had to decline it because of nationalistic sentiments. The difficulty of agreement was illustrated by a minor altercation between Quadros and the AID mission. Quadros wanted the mission to select among a set of projects it endorsed for the use of PL 480 funds (derived from sale of U.S.

foodstuffs in Brazil). The Americans, not wishing to have the responsibility of designating particular projects, declined and proposed joint selection. The Brazilians in response decided not to use any of the funds, although they had earlier committed three times the PL 480 funds available.[4] Because of such friction and inefficiency, as well as increasing reluctance to finance a leftist state, less than a fifth of approximately $600 million of loans approved during the Quadros and Goulart administration was actually disbursed. The fiscal stabilization upon which the United States insisted was not a Goulart priority.

RESCUING THE NORTHEAST

Brazil was the most important target of the Alliance for Progress, and one of the first Alliance projects was aid for the impoverished Northeast, the same region that had worried the United States in 1940–43. Radical forces were at work there, generated by and seeking to mobilize the rural desperation; and the area seemed in the eyes of Washington planners on the way to Castro-style revolution. The American press discovered the Peasant Leagues seeking to overthrow the oligarchic order, and built up their leader, Francisco Julião, as a major radical figure. In 1961, Julião declared himself a Marxist and a Communist and called for a Soviet-type government in the Northeast. He was supported publicly and privately financed by Castro to an unknown but modest extent.[5] The peasant leagues swelled to a membership estimated at 100,000.[6] A peasant congress sponsored by the Communist party in November 1961 was attended by not only Julião but also Goulart. The leftist forces had no common program except overthrow of the semifeudal rule of the large landholders. Peasant leagues, leftist Catholic groups, the Communist party, sundry splinters of Maoists, Trotskyites, and others, and political leaders following Goulart or on their own were all working more or less at odds. The U.S. embassy, however, saw potential revolution or guerrilla war, and Castro's hand, and felt it was urgent to show the people of the Northeast that their better future lay in cooperation with this country. Aid should shape politics; the Brazilian economic problem was an American security problem.

President Kennedy saw the Northeast as a proving ground of the hopeful theory that economic development could do away with the conditions generating discontent and Communism, and the administration moved with energy and dispatch. A study of the problem led to the Bohen report (February 1962) for a short-term impact program to meet immediate needs and a longer-term program for basic development, from literacy to water conservation measures. To implement it, the

United States would work with Sudene (Superintendencia de Desenvolvimento do Nordeste), the Brazilian development agency for the Northeast created by Kubitschek in 1959 but funded against much resistance only in 1961. In April 1962 an agreement was signed for collaboration between USAID and Sudene over the next two years in a $131 million program.

Considering the alarm over radicalism in the Northeast, the amount was not large, but USAID moved in force to Recife. A mission was established, which grew to 113 U.S. personnel by 1963,[7] the only USAID mission in the world outside a national capital. It was eagerly watched; Kennedy for months wanted daily progress reports.[8] But difficulties began quickly despite the fact that the approach of the Bohen report and that of Celso Furtado, director of Sudene, were close together. The Brazilians wanted the program to be administered by Brazilians as a Brazilian undertaking with little U.S. participation beyond endorsing and paying for projects; any closer control was regarded as interference. USAID wanted to be at least codirector of specific projects. The Brazilians did not understand U.S. procedures and paperwork. Moreover, USAID wanted considerable freedom to deal with other Brazilian authorities; Sudene wanted all dealings to be with itself. At the same time, USAID was very short of suitably equipped personnel. Technical experts with a knowledge of Portuguese and/or familiarity with the region were hardly to be found, while morale suffered from poor housing conditions, oppressive climate, and lack of schools and health facilities.[9]

However, the chief cause of the rapid breakdown in communication between USAID and Sudene was the difference of priorities. The former thought of the program as primarily anti-Communist. But where USAID saw subversion, Furtado saw poverty and ignorance; and he did not mind having in Sudene radical leftists or Communist party members who would cooperate in the projects of the program. In fact, the leftists were the most interested in and supportive of Sudene. For Goulart, Sudene was a means of appealing to the left without much offending the right. U.S. personnel saw in Sudene the political tendencies that they were in the Northeast to combat and found it no help in the immediate objective of turning back radicalism; if this could not be done first, there was not much point in the long-range program. A typical concrete conflict arose over an educational program. American administrators saw the literacy campaign being used to indoctrinate in leftist ideas and wished to be able to withdraw aid where they disapproved of the content of teaching. The Brazilians resented this as an effort to assert foreign control of education.[10] The sensitivity to Communism was exaggerated, one can say with hindsight; and it impeded cooperation with non-Communist nationalists and reformers.[11] The result, however, was that USAID came to find Sudene uncooperative and to distrust it and its goals of social change—

although these were close to the proclaimed reform goals of the Alliance for Progress.

Consequently, within months, USAID was looking to working directly with state governments, bypassing Sudene, hoping to find in them not only more politically acceptable leadership but also more efficient administration. The state leaders, mostly anti-Goulart in any case, were prepared to cooperate,[12] since it freed their own funds for other uses. USAID hoped that the nine Northeast governors would compete for U.S. funds and thus advance the program. At the same time, it could strengthen anti-Goulart forces and enable them to withstand pressure from the federal government. As Goulart turned left in 1963, USAID increasingly emphasized loans for projects to be undertaken with state and local administrations or other agencies. Theoretically all such arrangements were subject to approval by the federal government in Brasília, but it was hardly in a position to veto states getting a handout from the United States. At one time, Sudene tried to block a USAID agreement with the state of Rio Grande do Norte for help to education; but it was overruled by Goulart. All the "islands of sanity" expenditures, however, added up to considerably less than $100 million.

Although any help for anti-Goulart governors amounted to a slap at Goulart, the most blatant political use of aid was in the effort to prevent the election of Arraes to the government of Pernambuco in 1962. He had close ties with the pro-Soviet Communist party, and he made statements such as, "Large land-holdings are allied with North American imperialism and must be liquidated,"[13] while Julião was talking revolution. The election was seen as crucial for the future of the Northeast. To help his moderate opponent, USAID undertook a crash program to build schools as showpieces—a program previously opposed by Sudene on practical grounds. But only $1 million was spent,[14] a tiny fraction of the planned schools were built and fewer were put to use, and the anti-Arraes candidate was a washout as a campaigner. Elected governor by a modest margin, Arraes took revenge by abrogating the accord negotiated by USAID with his predecessor, although USAID was still prepared to work with him[15] as it had when he was mayor of Recife. However, Arraes in office moved somewhat away from radical positions and came into conflict with Goulart.

In sum, American interests were not significantly advanced. Washington turned to short-term political goals and thus became in effect supporter of the traditional landholding aristocracy that regarded land reform or mobilization of the masses as poison, the more dreaded as talk of revolution rose, while the broader idealistic goals of the Alliance for Progress were abandoned. The Northeast lacked political structures suitable for modernization, and USAID was incompetent to take their place and carry out a program on its own because of shortage of suitable personnel, unfavorable conditions, bureaucratic incompetence, and confusion of objectives. For example, a public health program came to nothing because of lack of doctors and nurses willing to work in the countryside, fear and hostility of the intended beneficiaries, red tape and procedural hassles.[16] An attractive proposal to make synthetic rubber from surplus sugar never got off the ground.[17]

Whether the USAID program influenced the brewing of the 1964 revolution and its outcome is speculative. It may have at least slightly dampened the zeal of the radicals. Julião, for example, by early 1964 had largely forsaken the leagues for the fleshpots of Rio; and there was no move in the Northeast to challenge the military coup that went against all the rhetoric of the preceding years. It may be significant that in a poll conducted for the United States Information Agency (USIA) in March 1964, the largest number of respondents (38) named economic aid to Latin America as a reason for a favorable view of the United States, the next largest (19) picked a similar response, aid to the poor of the world, while fewer (8 or less) pointed to promotion of peace, democracy, freedom, and so forth.[18]

HELP FOR THE MILITARY GOVERNMENT

With the coup-revolution of March 1964, both the atmosphere for U.S. aid efforts and their purpose changed entirely. The program was now to support the government, not forces opposed to it; and the urgency of forestalling violent revolution was replaced by the urgency of underpinning the political status quo. As noted above, credit was immediately made available to the new government, and Castelo Branco received some $900 million in loans[19] to underwrite its economic stabilization program, of which the United States thoroughly approved. There was an abundance, perhaps a plethora of projects, accompanied by a swarm of advisers. USAID continued trying in the Northeast to build up the infrastructure of transportation, health care, and education, while promoting agricultural modernization and new industries, hydropower projects and irrigation. Although there was no longer a contradiction between purposes of the aid program and those of the government, there were still difficulties with inadequate staff on both sides and confusion regarding direction by USAID, Sudene, the American embassy, and ministries in Rio. Only a tenth of the 11,000 schools projected were finished by 1971.[20] It proved impossible to reorganize the educational system on the U.S. model.[21] The approach continued to be favorable to the established class structure, with hopes that benefits of modernization would seep down to the masses. The United Nations, the World Bank, and the Rockefeller Fund got into the action, and USAID spent $249 million up to June 30, 1968,[22] without important results. One showcase project flopped when housing was built where there were no jobs.[23]

Aid was halted late in 1968 as a token of displeasure at the suspension of Congress and the imposition of stricter rule under Institutional Act V. In a few months it was quietly resumed on a smaller scale on condition that the Costa e Silva government not play it up as a sign of U.S. approval. However, economic aid, of either loans or grants, dwindled to insignificance by 1974. In 1980 there remained a single AID official in the embassy in Brasília who lacked funds to do much more than counsel private organizations and distribute useful information about raising goats and bees, a presence more indicative of bureaucratic inertia than foreign policy.

Aid, in any case, became less necessary with the economic takeoff beginning in 1968–69. There were (and are) still millions of malnourished Brazilians, but the government acquired resources much beyond anything the United States is prepared to offer. Most importantly, the country's credit rating improved while the amount of dollars available in Europe swelled because of the U.S. balance of payments deficit. Whereas Kubitschek or Goulart was desperate for a loan of a few hundred million dollars, in the 1970s Brazil was borrowing billions from the World Bank, the Inter-American Development Bank, the IMF, the International Bank for Reconstruction and Development, and most of all from private lenders. Typically in 1979 Brazil got a $1.2 billion loan from a Eurodollar syndicate for the production of alcohol.[24] In 1977 Brazil got $27 billion, and the debt had ballooned to $50 billion early in 1980, the servicing of which strained the already burdened balance of payments.

Aid has thus ceased to play a role in U.S.-Brazilian relations after 1968. Before 1964, the Brazilian government was inclined to look to Washington and may have been somewhat deterred from independent actions by the need for bailouts. But Goulart plunged onto his leftist course in defiance of the displeasure of the United States. The aid program then served to encourage anti-Goulart forces, but it did not greatly help them materially. After the coup, aid helped to shore up the new regime and make its path easier, but it did not confer a great deal of leverage, and there were inevitable frictions in the relationship of donor and recipient. Both sides were satisfied to wind it down.

U.S. policy prefers that developing countries obtain credits, so far as feasible, from international and private sources. Yet any reliance on foreign capital represents dependence of a kind.[25] It ties the country to the world economic system, and it tends to open the economy by requirements of procuring equipment from the least expensive sources.[26]

Need for foreign capital doubtless also inhibits populist-redistributionary, anti-foreign corporation policies, and may make a congenial climate for foreign investments. On the other hand, there is created an interdependence, and Brazil's hand is strengthened as its debt mushrooms. Any hint of repudiation would send tremors through the world financial community, and a Brazilian finance minister must be treated with great respect lest he recur to measures that would be disastrous for the international credit system.

TRADE

Critics of relations between less and more developed economies have seen trade relations as a prime means of maintaining and using the dominant relation. The economically developed power, it is argued, manipulates the interchange, manages prices, sells high-priced manufactures and buys cheap raw materials. To keep the less developed country in a situation of inferiority, the industrialized country hinders technological progress in the semicolonial state, at least in areas competitive with its own goods. It also works in league with local agents, "compradors" in Marxist terminology, a sector of the local bourgeoisie that profits by acting as agents for foreign commercial interests. The argument is not strictly Marxist, because in classical Marxism capitalism is international—a point emphasized by Marx—and it should make no difference to the capitalist whether a plant is located in the United States or in Brazil—indeed, it should be preferable to locate in Brazil because labor is cheaper and less organized there, and should permit more extraction of surplus value. The thesis is Leninist, dealing in terms not simply of exploiting classes but exploiting nations.

Trade is, in any event, a potential means of U.S. domination in Brazil, since the United States has been the largest single buyer from and seller to that country for some 60 years. Before World War I, the U.S. share of Brazilian imports was about 15 percent and behind that of Britain. Because of wartime disruptions, the U.S. share rose to 22 percent in 1923, ahead of any other power, and remained around that figure, or increased slightly, up to World War II. Only briefly in 1938, Nazi Germany pulled slightly ahead. During the war, with other suppliers and markets cut-off, the U.S. share approached 70 percent.

Since then, however, the trend has been gradually down. The import substitution policy of the 1950s was in effect directed mostly against American manufacturers, with tariffs on manufactured goods averaging over 250 percent,[27] but capital goods imports continued to come predominantly from this country. As late as 1969 the United States accounted for nearly half—48 percent—of Brazilian trade, but by 1973 this figure had shrunk in the "economic miracle" to 34 percent. Meanwhile the West European and Japanese share had gone in the opposite direction, from 36 to 48 percent. The U.S. share of Brazilian trade has since then continued to shrink. In 1977, the EEC took 30 percent of Brazilian exports of $12.1 billion; the United States, 16.5 percent; Latin America, 12 percent; and Japan, 7 percent. The EEC furnished 34 percent of $12 billion imports; the Middle East, 30 percent; the United States, 20 percent; Japan, 7 percent; and Latin America, 6 percent. The U.S. share of Brazilian imports has decreased for various reasons: the loosening of political ties, the conscious effort of the government to diversify foreign trade, the decline of the U.S. share in the world economy, the end of the aid program, Brazil's increasing ability to make for itself manufactures formerly procured in the United States, the high cost of petroleum imports, and the expansion of exports to the Third World, partly to pay for petroleum. Over the period 1967 to 1979 Brazilian exports to less developed countries expanded more rapidly than to any other category, at over 20 percent yearly.[28] In 1979, a quarter of Brazil's exports went to other Third World countries, and they furnished 40 percent of imports—a decade earlier the figures were 9 and 27 percent.[29]

Because of such factors, U.S.-Brazilian trade, long heavily imbalanced in favor of the United States, has since 1978 been approximately balanced. Since 1974, Brazilian imports from the United States have grown only slightly, while exports to the United States have nearly doubled. The Brazilian share of U.S. trade has remained constant or tended to shrink slightly, while the Brazilian share in German and Japanese trade has grown considerably. The United States and Brazil have become less close and special economic partners of each other.

That the United States was formerly preponderant in Brazil's foreign trade and is still the largest single market and supplier has clearly been of importance for Brazil and the shape of Brazilian life. To what extent it has been translatable or translated into direct political influence remains doubtful. The fact that Brazilian coffee and other raw material exports are not competitive with the United States, whereas Argentine grain is, doubtless has had something to do with better relations with Brazil than Argentina. But the United States has not made, perhaps could not make, any effort to turn a strong market share into control; the United States has not hindered Brazil from opening doors to competitive suppliers. Nor has it been attempted, so far as appears, to keep Brazil a mere supplier of raw materials. Thanks in large part to foreign, preeminently U.S. corporations, the share of manufactures in Brazil's exports has steadily increased, while coffee, formerly dominant, has retreated to a minor fraction, although its weight varies with prices and the weather.

It has not been practicable for the United States to use its commercial position concretely to shape Brazilian conduct because virtually everything that Brazil procures in the United States is obtainable elsewhere, and any attempt to cut off supplies would not only hurt U.S. sellers but might permanently injure U.S. exports as Brazilians found other suppliers. It may be possible to inconvenience the Soviet Union by halting grain sales because the U.S. position is very strong and the Soviet need is great, but even here it is doubtful that the Soviet loss is much greater than the American and the import of the embargo is as much moral as economic. Comparable measures against Brazil might have come into question only if the trends of 1964 had led to a Castro-like regime. A threat to refuse to buy Brazilian products, primarily coffee, might be more realistic; but for various reasons it would be very difficult to implement except under extreme circumstances when relations had gravely deteriorated, as the breakdown of relations between the United States and Cuba led to the exclusion of Cuban sugar.

TRADE CONTROVERSIES

The difficulty of using economic superiority as a bargaining lever is well shown by the negotiations that have taken place over trade between the two countries, mostly dealing with trade barriers, since 1964. Controversies arose almost entirely from efforts to protect American consumers from lower prices on grounds that certain Brazilian exports (like those of many other countries) were too cheap, that is, were subsidized, hence represented unfair competition and under an 1890 law had to be burdened with compensatory duties or limited by quotas. The arguments were about no question of foreign policy and represented no major effort of the United States to influence Brazil but answered internal political needs and pressures broadly contrary to basic foreign policy objectives of expanding trade and winning the good will of an important ally.

Brazil, badly needing to push exports in the face of chronic deficits on the balance of payments and a huge debt and certainly not desirous of selling more cheaply than necessary, has seen restrictions on its exports as irrational and unfair. Like most other nations, Brazil has employed export stimulants, chiefly partial or complete exemption from sales and income taxes.[30] It has seemed to Brazil that instead of restricting its exports the United States should favor imports from developing countries and particularly from such a faithful ally as Brazil; at most protection should be limited to cases of genuine injury to local industry.[31] Brazil, as close economic partner of the United States, would like a system of preferences instead of relying on Most Favored Nation treatment. From the Brazilians' point of view, they were being penalized for doing what they should. Under the import substitution policies of the 1950s and early 1960s, exports were neglected to the detriment of monetary stability, and it was in the U.S. interest then as it is now for Brazil to become more export oriented. It was the pro-American government of 1964 that took many measures to promote exports.[32]

The first important trade issue to arise was also the largest and most sensitive, because the amounts involved were greatest. It seemed to Brazilians that by restricting imports of instant coffee the United States was trying to deprive them of benefits of industrialization. Brazil saw the export of instant coffee instead of beans as not only an advance in processing but also as an effort to restore Brazil's share of world coffee sales, which had fallen by 1967 to 37 percent from 80 percent a generation earlier.[33] What to the United States was proper protection for domestic industry for the Brazilian was economic aggression; violent emotions were avoided only because of the Brazilian government's disinclination to nationalistic appeals. Many, indeed, saw it as a First-Third World confrontation and a matter of national prestige. In the rhetoric of a deputy of the progovernment party:

> As a leader of the despoiled, Brazil will secure a real and undisguised, crude examination of the crushing relations of the First and Second Worlds with the Third. It will be a case for these times, the unmasking of a hypocritical policy of aid with money taken from the aided nations and on the condition that the aided nation remains stuck in the swamp. On the one side, at the top of the mountain, the developed wolf; below, the undeveloped lamb.[34]

From 1966 the U.S. National Coffee Association was grumbling about the import of Brazilian instant coffee at prices substantially below those of the equivalent amount of coffee beans, hence undercutting the costs of U.S. instant coffee producers. Imports from Brazil reached about 14 percent of U.S. production in 1967; moreover, U.S. producers lost export markets.[35] Green coffee cost $40 per bag in the United States, but only about $4 in Brazil for producers of instant, partly because they, unlike shippers of bean coffee, paid no export tax, partly because they could use grades unsuitable for export. The United States wanted to eliminate as much as possible of the difference and demanded that Brazil tax exports of instant equitably with exports of beans. It was preferred not to apply a U.S. duty in order to avoid outright protectionism.

Negotiations were conducted in the framework of the International Coffee Organization and an arbitration commission. Issues were complicated by the fact that the U.S. importers of beans and makers of instant and Brazilian exporters of beans and of instant all had somewhat different interests.[36] The United States had claimed to favor Latin American processing of raw materials; and AID funds, in fact, had helped establish the Brazilian manufacturing of instant coffee.[37] Amid complaints of "colonial style imperialism," the U.S. position consequently appeared decidedly inconsistent, as this country exerted pressure and even threatened to wreck the International Coffee Agreement, which it had helped to sponsor. The Costa e Silva government at first took an unyielding line but then gave way and fixed an export tax of $0.13 per pound on instant.[38] While the Brazilians saw this as an imposition, U.S. producers regarded it as inadequate and demanded that it be raised considerably. As the dispute dragged, Chairman Wilbur Mills of the House Ways and Means Committee threatened to oppose renewal of the International Coffee Agreement.[39] A settlement was finally reached in 1971 whereby Brazil agreed to sell 560,000 bags of green coffee without export duties to U.S. makers.[40] The whole argument has become moot in recent years because nearly all U.S. instant and much of Brazilian is made of African beans, cheaply available to both.

Less weighty differences regarding many commodities, textiles, shoes, handbags, pig iron, soybeans, and so forth have caused occasional friction from the time of Costa e Silva, whose government did not mind expressing resentment about U.S. trade policies. Foreign Minister Magalhães Pinto, having accused the United States of trying to prevent the formation of Petrobras and then sabotaging it, complained that manipulation of the market for Brazilian goods took away what was given as foreign aid. He wanted preferential treatment for Latin American goods, a bigger sugar quota, and lifting of the quota for certain Brazilian textiles that had only a trivial market share.[41] In the view of another minister, Horacio Lafer, "America was marching on one leg, political solidarity, while the other, economic cooperation was ever more atrophied."[42] There was even speculation that Brazil might switch to "positive political neutralism," because of its irritation.

For the most part, however, American administrations have tried to resist pressures from American industries and have used authority granted by Congress to waive at least temporarily compensatory duties called for under the old law. They have avoided finding subsidization or injury to U.S. producers, or in the worst case have kept countervailing duties rather low. Shoes presented the most difficult problem, as the U.S. industry was in doldrums for many years while imports grew steadily. A tariff of 4.8 percent was imposed on Brazilian shoes in 1974; U.S. manufacturers complained not only that the Brazilian shoes were undercutting them but that Brazil refused to export cheap hides that would have made it easier for U.S. manufacturers to compete. The duty on Brazilian shoes was increased to 9 percent, although imports surged much more from Italy, the Philippines, Hong Kong, and Singapore than Brazil. There were also moves to penalize cotton yarn, towels, pig iron, and ferroalloys in 1977-78, but most of these were disapproved.[43]

Negotiations in 1976-77 settled many differences, and in March 1979, a U.S.-Brazilian agreement cleared most of the rest. Brazilians agreed to phase out export subsidies, while the United States required the showing of definite injury prior to imposition of countervailing duties. After many years of haggling over leather jackets, boys' apparel, sundry textiles, and the like, with studies and petitions one after another, in 1980 the issue seemed to have receded to insignificance, as only scissors and shoes remained dutiable at a rate of 1 percent, while pig iron was under study.[44]

In these controversies, the United States was generally very hesitant to take steps injurious to Brazil, and the weight of the superpower hardly seemed decisive. Brazil usually had a negative balance of trade with the United States, and this gave leverage to the former. It was not easy to object to Brazilian exports to the United States when U.S. exports to Brazil were larger and vulnerable. Moreover, the trade issues were considerably more important and emotional for Brazil than for the United States. The American government wanted to avoid noisy confrontations partly because they were not worth the trouble, partly because they would make a bad impression so far as publicized around the world. The Brazilians had no such inhibitions; to the contrary the government could improve its image by standing up against the Americans, although it showed restraint and turned the negotiations into a nationalist cause only mildly and occasionally. The U.S. side of the argument also suffered moral weakness. Any exclusion or restriction of exports from developing countries ran counter to expressed principles and ideas and to the claim of the poorer countries for assistance in raising their productivity and standard of living. When many voices claim that the rich owe large reparations to the poor, the demand to be allowed to sell their wares in the markets of the rich is moderate and reasonable. The United States cannot push Brazil to lower its own very high barriers to American exports because this would conflict with a goal accepted by all, the industrialization of Brazil, while Brazil is in a position practically to demand free entry for its products, raw and manufactured, to the U.S. market—a position accepted in theory by the United States. Finally, the Brazilian government can push its case in fairly monolithic fashion, while most of the energies of the U.S. government go to internal disputes, the administration against congressional backing for special interests, the Tariff Commission against the State Department, and so forth. The bargaining power of the United States has been consequently weak, and the Brazilians have been led to make only a few compensatory concessions, such as lowering duties on U.S. apples and pears.[45]

It must be conceded, however, that the recurrent friction over minor trade questions has been negative for U.S. influence; it grates on Brazilian sensitivities that their president has to plead for a lower duty on towels. Any restrictions on their products, especially manufactures, strikes Brazilians as an unjustifiable attempt to keep Brazil inferior. It has long been dogma that the terms of trade are unfavorable to the weaker economy, a means of extracting wealth from the poor, and that the situation only worsens in capitalistic-monopoly conditions. Nearly all Brazilian unions separated from the Inter-American Regional Labor Organization and the International Confederation of Free Trade Unions, dominated by the AFL-CIO, in 1971 in protest against U.S. protectionism.[46] Much of the intensity of protest has vanished, however, after the rise of the Organization of Petroleum Exporting Countries (OPEC) and the growing difficulties of the industrial nations. Brazil, too, has profited; its terms of trade improved from 100 in 1965–67 to 125 in 1977.[47]

While trade thus involves frictions (generally unnecessary, to be sure), it clearly has broad effects on society and polities. The Brazilian economy is not strongly export-led—foreign trade accounting for less than 10 percent of GNP—but it is substantially meshed into the world economy. The fact that the United States was the principal buyer, supplier, and source of credit in 1964 made a radical course more difficult—although certainly not impossible, as demonstrated by the divorce of Cuba from the American orientation. It has seemed increasingly advantageous through the postwar years for nations to participate fully in the world economy; maximizing foreign trade has been, for many nations such as Japan, Singapore, and West Germany, equivalent to maximizing growth. The Soviet Union, China, and many other countries have seen economic slowdown at least in part because they have denied themselves much of the advantages of trade. So far as orientation to the world market remains evidently advantageous for Brazil, that country is tied to a liberal economic system with whatever political consequences may be entailed. Unless it is prepared to pay a high price, it must remain basically a friend of the Western "capitalist" world and of the United States.

MULTINATIONAL CORPORATIONS

Brazil has long been a favored field for foreign investment because of its agricultural and mineral potential and large market; and Americans have seemed drawn to it, perhaps because they feel at home there. For most of the history of Brazil, however, Americans paid little attention to enterprises abroad, and the British were the dominant foreigners. In Brazil, as in many countries of Latin America and elsewhere, in the latter decades of the nineteenth century British capitalists were constructing railroads, utilities, and processing plants, improving the ports, lighting the cities, and transporting goods from the interior for shipment to Europe.

In the 1930s, foreign investment was prominent in Brazil in mining, airlines, telephones, and a variety of manufacturing enterprises; about half of it was British, one-fourth American, one-fifth Canadian—an overwhelmingly Anglo-Saxon presence.[48] The foreign sector in the Brazilian economy did not really surge, however, until after World War II. The British stake had then been largely depleted, but the American nearly tripled from 1945 to 1960.[49] The flow of investment slowed to a trickle in 1962-63 because of economic and political uncertainties. After the antileftist revolution, foreign capital began again coming in, but only slowly; the influx in 1965-67 was still not back to the 1958-61 level.[50] Only after 1968, with the full restoration of confidence, did the flow become and remain quite large. In 1967, the foreign stake was $3.7 billion; in 1972, $7 billion; at the end of 1979, $16 billion.[51]

Since World War II, and especially since 1964, foreign investment in Brazil has gone mostly into manufacturing, seeking to profit not so much from low labor cost or local raw materials as from access to a large market surrounded by high tariff and monetary barriers.[52] Brazil has generally been rather hospitable to this invasion—with nationalistic exceptions—because it has filled genuine needs. Foreign capital has facilitated growth—not only because of shortage of native capital but also because of the reluctance of Brazilian capitalists to venture into unfamiliar undertakings in the face of family business traditions and the preference for more solid investment, principally real estate. Not only foreigners but Brazilians of foreign background have been very prominent in industry and commerce, especially in southern states, with Italians, Germans, and Lebanese heading the list. In 1964, only 16 percent of São Paulo industrialists were sons of Brazilians.[53] The most important function of the foreign corporation, however, is to introduce modern management and technology in a country equipped with labor and resources to make good use of advanced equipment and techniques.

There have been claims or accusations that the Brazilian government, to some extent before 1964 but especially afterwards, has positively favored foreign producers. In any case, foreign firms have generally been permitted to operate without prejudice. They have been excluded by law from certain fields, chiefly coastal shipping, domestic air traffic, printed and broadcast media, and production of petroleum, coal, and uranium. State enterprises dominate steel, generation of electricity, and utilities generally. Commerce, construction, and small manufacturing enterprises are very largely in the hands of Brazilian capitalists. The most conspicuous and largest corporations that make up industrial Brazil are (except for some state corporations) foreign.

Just what proportion of Brazilian industry is foreign-owned is unclear, partly for lack of solid statistical data, partly because ownership and control are often mixed—there are many joint ventures, licensing arrangements, and so forth—and partly because the more small businesses are counted, the larger the Brazilian share. It is clear, however, that foreign enterprises are dominant in the most dynamic sectors of the economy and in areas requiring high technology, product differentiation, special managerial skills, and world marketing capabilities.[54] The chief exception is tobacco, totally controlled by foreign firms by virtue of their psychological advantage. Foreign firms have led the industrial boom, and they produce almost all Brazilian manufactured exports.[55] They strongly dominate or perhaps monopolize such sectors as pharmaceuticals, household appliances, automobiles, tobacco, and electrical goods—more or less the branches that have achieved best growth in the past few years. In the pharmaceutical industry, for example, there are some 400 manufacturers, but 20 multinationals have 73 percent of the trade and the Brazilian firms do very little research and development.[56] The sway of foreign firms may extend much beyond their immediate organizations; for example, in the early 1970s, some 1,500 Brazilian suppliers depended on the eight foreign automobile makers.[57]

There have been estimates that half of Brazilian industrial production comes from foreign firms.[58] Of the 100 largest nonstate firms in 1972, according to a Rio paper, 37 were American, 12 German, 8 Argentine, 4 Swedish, and 4 French; of the 20 largest in 1974, 7 were American; 2 German; 2 British; 1 each of Argentina, Switzerland, France, and Italy; 4 were Brazilian.[59] In 1975, 59 of the 100 largest were foreign.[60] In 1980 it was calculated, however, that corporations more than half foreign-owned had 19.45 percent of the capital of the 200 largest enterprises.[61]

What proportion of foreign holdings in Brazil pertain to the United States cannot be stated with exactitude because of many complications and ambiguities of ownership. For example, various corporations with home offices in London or Toronto may be more or less U.S.-owned; one of the largest foreign interests in Brazil, the Canadian Brascan, seems to be one-third U.S.-held. However, it appears that about half of total foreign investment in 1960 was from the United States. In 1965, it was slightly under 40 percent; by 1967 it was back to 48 percent; by 1975, it was down to 32 percent.[62] According to the Banco Central do Brasil, at the end of 1979 net U.S. capital was $4.375 million, or 27.4 percent of all foreign capital. At this time, the European Economic Community was responsible for 33.1 percent, of which nearly half, or 15.4 percent, was West German. Japan accounted for 9.5 percent and Switzerland for 12.0 percent.[63] The latter three countries have all expanded their holdings in recent years, more or less in the same measure as the U.S. share has decreased. However, it is assumed that a considerable part of Swiss holdings represents non-Swiss ownership; and figures would be somewhat different if debt capital were included along with equity. The Brazilian government has slightly encouraged non-American investment for the sake of diversification and immunity to economic pressure from the United States.[64] The recession of the U.S. share is gradual, and it may be reversed slightly by $1.5 billion of new investment in 1980.[65] It is sufficiently pronounced, however, that the Brazilian press ordinarily refers simply to "multinationals," all lumped together, without pointing especially to American corporations, as was customary 20 years ago.

The sector of industrial capital that has expanded most during the past 15 years has been that of state enterprises. They offset the growth of the multinationals; to a large extent, they have been set up and fostered to defend the Brazilianness of the economy, "the national parry to the foreign threat."[66] State enterprises have nearly half the invested capital of the hundred largest firms,[67] and the only really important expansive native operations are government-controlled.

Extensive state participation in the economy is in the Brazilian tradition from colonial days, when mercantilist regulation of commerce and industry was customary. Its modern beginnings stem from Vargas' New State, which not only increased official direction of the economy but began large-scale state ownership of industry. After American corporations had declined to build a steel plant, Vargas undertook it with U.S. governmental assistance. The Volta Redonda steel works began production in 1946 and became symbol and leader of Brazilian industrialization. Wartime demands led to more official participation in the economy and to economic planning. In the 1950s, state guidance and investment seemed necessary to promote industrialization. Petrobras, the state petroleum monopoly, was established in 1954, partly because of a conviction that the American companies were not actively enough developing Brazilian resources, partly to keep the assumed riches of the land in Brazilian hands. It has been followed by a train of "bras" giants, such as Electrobras and Nuclebras. Second to none is the mining corporation, Campanhia Vale do Rio Doce, an industrial empire and multinational engaged in many branches; it accounts for as much as 10 percent of all investment in the Brazilian economy.[68]

The big expansion of the state sector came under the procapitalist military government. The state share of fixed investment, around 15 percent shortly after World War II, rose in a few years after 1964 to nearly half, near which figure it has remained.[69] To achieve growth where private investment was unavailable or inadequate, or to develop resources that were not to be turned over to foreign interests, the state moved in. Between state ownership of a large part of the economy and extensive regulation of most of the rest, through monetary, foreign exchange, and credit controls, subsidies, fixing of prices, and planning authority, Brazil has become in effect a substantially socialistic state. Taxes as percentage of GNP also rose markedly after 1964.[70] It seems that the state enterprises have been in general fairly efficient and well-managed.[71]

In theory the state opposes socialism and prefers private enterprise; with some encouragement from the United States—in 1976, for example, Secretary Kissinger urged less state intervention.[72] Such ideological reasons, many complaints from the Brazilian private sector,[73] and a feeling that state management and investment have become less essential in the maturing economy have brought some tendency to retreat from public ownership. In 1974, the government got out of the coffee marketing business. In 1976, Petrobras began contracting with foreign companies for the prospecting and development of offshore oil resources,[74] partly to deflect criticism of Petrobras for failure to find more oil. There have also been joint ventures of state corporations with multinationals, giving the former power of direction, the latter protection.[75] The state turned more definitely away from economic interventionism under Figueiredo, apparently as part of the policy of "abertura." Before his inauguration, Figueiredo stated, "We should privatize all state companies that we can, keeping under government ownership only those that are necessary for national security or that cannot attract private capital."[76] State enterprises in 1979 had run up a foreign debt of $20 billion,[77] and Finance Minister Delfim Netto was reported desirous of removing many costly subsidies.[78] Official policy proposes the gradual elimination of state competition with private enterprise[79]—by no means an easy objective.

For the most part, the public sector supplies basic needs of the private—steel, electricity, oil, transportation, and so forth—providing, some say, the means for higher profits for private, especially foreign capital. It is the foreign firms that dominate the advanced and most remunerative lines of production, and they are the conspicuous participants in Brazil's industrial modernization. The Brazilian finds their advertisements throughout his slick magazines, and neon lights proclaim hundreds of foreign brands—the multinationals flaunt their alienness by using English, sometimes French or German names. It is an intrusion, and it is widely if not generally disliked; Brazilian capitalists join leftist nationalists in damning the penetration. Many of the arguments and the facts supporting condemnation, it may be noted, are drawn from U.S. critics of international capitalism.

There are many charges against the multinationals in Brazil, as in other Third World countries, some of which appear borne out by economic data, others of which may have a more emotional basis.[80] The biggest fault attributed to them is, naturally, that they serve their own interests, as judged from the viewpoint of a foreign headquarters. Thus they buy preferentially from their own sources and gear their export sales to the advantage of the foreign directors. They may transfer funds through pricing mechanisms and various payments in lieu of frank remittance of profits. They may weigh on the balance of payments; for example, 74 percent of the materials used by multinational drug firms are imported.[81] On balance, they seem to reduce competition.[82] They avoid bringing in new capital so far as possible—capital import is the least of their virtues—but use their position to mobilize local capital. In a third[83] or a half of cases[84] entry is by takeover of an existent Brazilian firm. On the other hand, it appears that, on the average, the foreign subsidiaries are somewhat more capital-intensive than national firms, pay about a third higher wages to more qualified labor, are more flexible in labor relations and readier to accept collective bargaining, and are somewhat more inclined to invest in poorer regions in accordance with government incentive programs.[85] U.S. multinationals in Brazil reported 14 percent return in 1972; broadly, rates of profit of foreign and Brazilian firms may be about roughly the same.[86] The foreign firms provide only a small fraction of employment in Brazilian manufacturing, perhaps under 10 percent, but they produce nearly half the output.[87]

Political rhetoric goes well beyond economists' reckonings, and when U.S. corporations are widely suspect in the United States, it is not surprising that many Brazilians take their evil for granted. Since Vargas' last term, anti-foreign capital talk has been part of the Brazilian scene, only more or less repressed during the early years of the military regime. There are many charges of unfair or unscrupulous practices. They represent the crafty and powerful foreign interests wanting to maximize lucre at the expense of the Brazilian people and their God-given resources. The biggest complaint is probably that they take more money out of Brazil than they put in, although there is no logical relationship between new investment and earnings or repatriation of old. Corporations are accused of exporting goods needed in Brazil, such as shoes when millions of Brazilians are shoeless, or producing crops for export when Brazilians are undernourished. It is not generally claimed that foreign firms treat their workers worse than do Brazilian, but the foreigners are accused of using capital-intensive technology that creates few jobs. They also use only imported technology, whereas national firms make use of some Brazilian technology.[88] They force suppliers to underpay their workers[89] and make Brazil a dumping ground for obsolete capital goods at inflated prices.[90] A mild accusation is that foreign tobacco companies sell high-tar, high-nicotine cigarettes to addict Brazilians.[91] Health care is a sore subject. The Brazilian Medical Association protested the "commercialization" and exploitation of health care by foreign (U.S.) organizations such as American Medical International and threatened a strike if they were not curtailed.[92] Brazilian doctors denounced that multinational drug companies produced medicines only to alleviate, not cure, chronic diseases, such as Chagas disease and schistosomiasis, in order to keep the patient a permanent consumer,[93] or that the companies produce expensive drugs and neglect the inexpensive.[94] "Mercantilist international groups," it is said, want to profit by the sickness of Brazilians.[95]

Much protest stems from fear that the natural riches of which Brazil is proud may be lost to greedy and unscrupulous foreigners—feelings behind the national monopolies of petroleum and uranium. It was considered scandalous, for example, that U.S. firms held 93 percent of the iron ore of Minas Gerais in 1963;[96] and Hanna Mining Company has been especially unpopular. There is reluctance to see *any* foreign investment in land, and big holdings in the interior—Amazonia and Matto Grosso—by foreign land companies are particularly resented. Visceral feelings about minerals merge into the enduring anxiety over the Amazon region. "The Amazon is ours" and "The people will defend the Amazon" have been common graffiti.

This preoccupation has come strongly to the fore in regard to the agro-industrial empire of Daniel K. Ludwig, American billionnaire (born 1898). He invested over $780 million in a swatch of jungle larger than the state of Connecticut on the Jari river, a tributary of the Amazon. On this estate, he built four towns, schools, a hospital, pulp mill, communications, and accessories. The population of the area increased from near zero to over 30,000, with a work force of 8,500, only 40 being non-Brazilians. Wages were three times the national average for rural labor. The main products were rice and pulp from fast-growing introduced trees, both sold in Brazil.[97] It would seem, prima facie, that this was not far from the bright dreams of Amazonian development, and the Médici and Geisel governments so regarded it. It was surely more promising than the much commoner practice of stripping the jungle and turning the land into low-grade pasture. But critics in Congress and out charged that Ludwig was running a slave camp, sheltering an American base, building up his own armed forces, and devastating the land for profit.[98] The developers made the error of administering the property as virtually a foreign enclave exempt from Brazilian police, schools, municipal authorities, and so forth.[99] This was at least partially corrected by an agreement of early 1980; thenceforth automobiles in Jari would use Brazilian plates. It was slightly ironic, however, that the individualistic Ludwig was berated as a multinational corporation.

The broadest complaint against the foreigners is simply against their intromission into Brazil. Even if what they are doing is good, they are doing what Brazilians should be doing for themselves; one can hardly doubt that a Brazilian entrepreneur making the Amazon productive in the way of Ludwig would be a general hero. The foreign corporations transfer decision making abroad, reducing the role of Brazilians in their own country and making Brazil subject to distant international forces.[100] There is no reason a priori to assume that foreign corporations are more predatory than Brazilian ones, and foreigners may be sensitive to the delicacy of their position. But they are less identified with the land, presumably readier to make their profit and depart if the climate turns hostile, and supposedly under the influence of their own governments.[101] Dependence on foreign capitalistic interests seems like a continuation of colonial dependency, and feelings against the multinationals are reminiscent of antipathy for Portuguese merchants in colonial days[102]—antipathy for people who have jobs and wealth that should be for Brazilians.

It is commonly taken for granted that economic presence equals political power, and that all United States or all foreign corporations are linked to form a single force. In the complex and tangled interrelationships of international trade and finance, it seems hardly necessary to prove that the United States, as the stronger power, gets the better of affairs. This logic cannot easily be applied to Swiss, Dutch, or Argentine firms, which operate successfully in Brazil, unless one assumes that all are simply capitalists—together with their Brazilian counterparts. From the leftist ideological point of view, there is not much difference; capitalism is capitalism. But, in the general attack on capitalism, shafts were directed preferentially at "U.S. imperialism," which virtually stands for the entire capitalist order. European and Japanese corporations were seen as "indirect" U.S. capital,[103] and the multinationals are blamed generally for the ills and abuses of the Brazilian economy; for example, the high accident rate in Brazilian industry is laid to their influence.[104]

The trusts represent a general evil; thus they plotted the assassination of President Kennedy because of his popular policies.[105] The multinationals caused the superinflation of 1964 in order to destabilize the populist Goulart government.[106] Just as Vargas in his suicide note and Quadros in his resignation message, the Brazilian Left mixes the foreign interests with the selfish and reactionary forces of Brazilian society, down to the exploitation of the peasants by feudalistic landholders. The multinationals are seen as a powerful conspiracy behind Brazilian politics. The theme of a recent play, "Brazil from Censorship to Opening," by Sebastião Nery, was that Vargas, Quadros, and Goulart were all forced out when they tried to control the superprofits of the foreign corporations.[107] When Figueiredo was asked during a conference, "Why, when Brazil has such problems with its balance of payments and foreign debt, don't you cut down a little on the profits of the foreign corporations?" he replied, "Do you want the CIA to overthrow me?"[108] Figueiredo was exercising his well known sense of humor; but to Brazilians it seemed a sober reply, especially because Figueiredo, as former chief of the Brazilian counterpart of the CIA, was assumed to be familiar with the mysterious powers of that agency. According to one-time agent Philip Agee, the chief purpose of the CIA in less developed countries is to help the multinationals.[109]

Criticism of the multinationals has varied in intensity from time to time, becoming more muted in prosperity, harsher as difficulties accumulate. There was rather less in the years of very rapid growth but has been more since 1979, with the soaring of inflation and the national indebtedness. Usually critics do not attack multinationals in general but certain ones or certain practices, and hardly anyone urges prohibiting foreign investment but making it serve national needs. Brazilians in talking with foreigners commonly discount antimultinational talk as empty rhetoric. However, even those who may recognize that charges are untrue or exaggerated probably feel some satisfaction at seeing Goliath taunted; few are disposed to expose themselves as defenders or collaborators of the unpopular interests. Deputies to Congress speak of the need for organizing a national front against foreign capital and propose new controls and limits on remittance of profits,[110] although their opinions can at best have a moral effect on the government. Within the military regime itself such sentiments are strong. In April 1980, Gen. Antônio Carlos de Andrade Serpa was relieved of his position as chief of the army personnel department because of his escalating attacks on the "savage capitalism" of the multinational corporations, but he received messages of support from hundreds of fellow officers.[111]

The feeling is visceral. Thus Brazilian authorities, proud and jealous of their alcohol fuel program, want to keep it, like petroleum under Petrobras, uncontaminated by foreign capital.[112] The feeling is strong enough that technical cooperation with the United States has been inhibited. Foreign investment is to be allowed only in the production of alcohol for export to the investing country.[113] The multinationals are likely to be blamed for rather contrary things. For many years, they were held responsible for fastening military rule on the country in order to assure favorable conditions for themselves; recently some say that they promote "abertura" in order to check Brazilian economic competition. Formerly the corporations were blamed for holding down wages with the assistance of a cooperative government; recently they have been accused of fostering independent unions in Brazil because they are in a position to pay higher wages than Brazilian firms. A Ford director charged that a strike in the automotive industry was Communist-backed; a labor leader laid responsibility to the CIA.[114] In 1980, a deputy alleged that the multinationals were behind the metalworkers' strike, the direct victims of which were all foreign enterprises.

Anti-multinational feeling thus complicates many questions of labor policy, taxation, exchange controls, and so forth, turning economic into political questions; any major economic move is subject to interpretation in the context of foreign versus national interests. Effects on U.S.-Brazilian relations are less intense, however, than in the early 1960s, because of the internationalization of foreign holdings. German and Japanese firms frequently seem as conspicuous as American, or more so; and Germany and Japan, like the United States, have to be concerned with their image as exploiters. Moreover, the U.S. government has tended to dissociate itself from U.S. corporations operating abroad. Undersecretary of State Richard Cooper, for example, said the United States would remain neutral in quarrels of multinationals with the host government instead of automatically siding with the corporation.[115] In fact, there has been concern in Congress lest the strength of American corporations weaken private enterprise in Brazil. Not everyone has been impressed by this modesty; the multinationals are still associated with the United States, and they obviously have negative effects on U.S. influence among most social groups.

There is no doubt, however, that the multinationals have no little influence with the governing powers, an influence that in some ways and to some degree means U.S. influence in Brazil. The leftists regularly speak of the "anti-Brazilian government in the service of the multinationals."[116] This is somewhat rhetorical, but the state has made a frank effort to gain the confidence of the foreign corporations. The policy has been to make conditions as favorable as possible for them subject to their serving the economic purposes of the state.[117] A regulation of 1955 even made it easier for foreigners than Brazilians to import equipment.[118] A law of February 1965 provided that "Foreign capital invested in Brazil shall enjoy the same legal treatment as that given domestic capital,"[119] and it has often been claimed that the government has actually shown favoritism for the foreigners. For example, it was claimed that a native poultry industry was destroyed to make a monopoly for U.S. producers.[120] The policy of the military government to restrict wage increases, control unions, and prohibit strikes, was allegedly intended primarily to benefit foreign corporations; and the policy of monetary stabilization was seen as a safeguard for foreign profits,[121] the more plausibly because U.S. and international monetary authorities strongly advocated stabilization. It has been regarded as discrimination in favor of foreign interests that the state generated electricity and (until recently) permitted foreigners to handle the more remunerative and less capital-demanding retailing of it.

Concretely how multinational corporations can manipulate the Brazilian state is much less discussed. One means is their influence on the press through advertising. Scanning weekly and monthly publications, to a lesser extent the dailies and broadcast media, one cannot fail to be impressed by the importance to the media of advertising by foreign corporations; the effect is increased by the domination of the advertising industry by American agencies.[122] Perhaps more important, however, is the general community of interests of the multinationals with the Brazilian upper classes—not precisely a conspiracy but a shared interest, in the leftist view, of exploiting and repressing the popular majority, a union strengthened by snobbery and imitation of the foreigners on the one hand, by bribery in the form of good jobs on the other. Such closeness may influence state policy; for example, Daniel Ludwig was a good friend of President Geisel. Several high government officials sit on the board of Souza Cruz, subsidiary of Philip Morris and chief cigarette producer.[123] This may have something to do with the fact that the government authorized a price raise even when it was not requested; on the other hand, the fact that the price of cigarettes is more than half taxes may have influenced the price fixers. Henrique Simonsen, finance minister under Geisel, was a member of Citibank Corporation of New York. Perhaps most significant is the fact that Gen. Golbery do Couto e Silva was formerly president of Dow Chemical's Brazilian subsidiary. Do Couto e Silva has been the brain behind most presidencies since 1964, possibly the most influential single individual of the entire period; and he was reported to have helped Dow's business while in the cabinet.[124] Such links do not seem to have been numerous, however, and it is possible that far more high figures have been associated with Brazilian firms.

Whatever the influence and advantages of the multinationals, they have suffered increasing pressure, especially since about 1974. The growth of the Brazilian economy and greater availability of local capital and diversification of sources of capital, the tough posture of the Andean Pact, the greater confidence and aggressiveness of the less developed nations, and the assistance of the U.N. in dealing with the multinationals have all tilted the balance of power toward government and away from the corporations. For some years they have been complaining of various restrictions and raised taxes. Following a patent law of 1971 designed to facilitate transfer of modern technology, measures have curbed the powers of foreign banks, created trading corporations to get the best prices on imports and exports, required competitive bidding, and sought to force multinationals to do more research in Brazil.[125] Import controls were stiffened in 1976.[126]

There has been some reversal of the alienation of the Brazilian economy since 1975, when President Geisel vetoed the takeover of a domestic appliance manufacturer by the Phillips Corporation.[127] In July 1976, a Brazilian sugar and coffee group purchased Hills Brothers Coffee for $38.5 million, the first reported major turnaround of the common acquisition of Brazilian firms by Americans—keeping the English brand name. From 1976 to 1979 the foreign share in electronics sales sank from 64.8 to 45.3 percent; in plastics, from 38.2 to 30.5 percent; in drugs from 74.5 to 70.4 percent; in textiles from 13.5 to 12.7 percent.[128] In 1978, it was decided to Brazilianize the rapidly growing minicomputer industry. When the chief producers, IBM, Burroughs, NCR, and others, declined conditions proposed, a monopoly was given to four national companies, which purchased technology from Canada, France, Japan, and Germany. IBM lost 60 percent of its Brazilian production.[129] In 1978, Brascan sold its Brazilian electrical distributor to Electrobras for $380 million.[130] In April 1980 the last foreign-owned brewery was bought out by Cervejaria Brahma. Brazilian policy is to encourage joint enterprises, whereby Brazil acquires technology and skills without losing control, while the foreign firms gain access to the Brazilian market with less capital outlay; and foreign operations have been tending away from manufacturing to technical assistance and marketing.

The position of foreign enterprises remains strong, however, because of their financial resources—their operations in Brazil usually represent only 1 to 2 percent of their worldwide assets and sales.[131] The government probably finds them more promising for modernization because of their resources and technology, and it is hence constrained to make them feel secure and welcome. Their chief influence, consequently, seems to be like that of foreign trade. Through them Brazil is part of the world economic system led by the United States. They are often targets of resentment, but on balance they seem clearly to make Brazil more receptive to ideas and policies of the United States, especially in the elite circles that have powers of decision. How much influence the U.S. government may exert through them or on their behalf is necessarily obscure, but they are the most conspicuous and perhaps most important form of interaction, a vital part of the complex and multiform web of relationships binding the two countries.

DEPENDENCY

The alien enterprises dominating the economic landscape may be judged in terms of the economic and political detriments or benefits they bring. To many, however, they represent not merely intrusions upon the national life, but the most visible manifestation of the fundamental political and economic reality, the condition of dependency shared with all Latin America. Dependency, variously interpreted and with different emphases on historical and recent, native and foreign, political and economic factors has overshadowed Latin American and Brazilian thinking about the present and future to a degree outsiders often fail to realize.

If it is somewhat less dominant than in the 1970s, it remains strong. Dependency is held responsible for most of the disappointments of the region, economic troubles and backwardness, social injustice, and corrupt and repressive government.[132]

Latin American intellectuals see poor people in rich lands, unmodern despite long contact with the modern world. The outwardly simplest answer, and in some ways the most satisfying, is that they have not been free to improve themselves. For three centuries or more they formed a frankly colonial empire; since the 1820s, for the most part, they have been nominally sovereign but, in the common interpretation, subject to disguised domination and exploitation first by Great Britain and, especially since World War II, by the United States.

The attack on "dependency" has varied in intensity with troubles and prosperity. It goes back in Brazil at least to unhappiness with the coffee-based economy of the 1920s. It became acute as growth slowed down and debts piled up in the early 1960s and was much strengthened by the conviction that the military government of 1964 was more or less an imposition of the dominant power. Opposition to authoritarian rule merged with anti-U.S. and anticapitalist feelings; for Marxists and near-Marxists, U.S. capitalism-imperialism became the full and simple answer to all problems. The kidnappers of Ambassador Elbrick, for example, attributed all the troubles of Brazil to U.S. imperialism.[133] Brazilian writers of the late 1960s, conceding that only 6 percent of capital was foreign, saw it dominant because it held the crucial modern sectors, and concluded that, "Dependence is the key to reality. Once you recognize it, the world comes into focus."[134] "Imperialism" comes up whenever foreigners are involved.

The sense of dependency has lessened with the growth of Brazilian industry and the Brazil-centered foreign policy of recent years, but it persists when there is frustration. For example, General Serpa in April 1980 pointed to the danger of "neocolonialism" and attributed the present crisis to internationalization of the economy, causing inflation, indebtedness, and concentration of wealth.[135] A substantial part of the Catholic hierarchy in Brazil attributes the woes of the land to capitalism, which is quintessentially foreign. Archbishop Helder Câmara has been accusing the government of working against the poor in league with foreign imperialism for more than a decade.[136] A poster issued under the auspices of Archbishop José Maria Pires of Paraíba showed a steer mounted by President Figueirero and a very obese figure labeled "Multinational" carrying big bags with dollar signs on them.[137]

The chief denunciation, of course, is exploitation, the unfair ability of the foreign corporations to squeeze huge profits from Brazil and suck money out of the country. The terms of trade are regarded as unfair, and the United States is or was credited with the power to control the rules of the world economic game. There has been small hope of change. Development by foreign firms does not lead to overcoming dependence, because they perpetuate their control of technology and capital, while state enterprises furnish them a needed infrastructure.[138] Only a socialist revolution could really help, for ". . . while the present power system survives, the state has no alternative but to survive and protect itself as a function of the world capitalist system."[139] A satellite country like Brazil may hope to get heavy industry (as André Gunder Frank conceded in contradiction to his earlier theses), but it cannot hope to catch up in modern technology, the new basis of superiority.[140]

Dependency theory charges that the foreign corporations are responsible for the political troubles of Brazil, that the generals are creatures of the capitalists, allied with Brazilians but primarily foreign, and supported by the U.S. government. Latin Americans generally have a flattering estimate of the power of the United States, exercised in a variety of ways, through diplomacy, military contacts, the CIA, the press, foundations, and corporations (either servants or masters of the imperialist state); they also see a high degree of coherence and purposefulness of actions by the various agencies of foreign power. The "finger of imperialism" then may be found in almost anything, such as the attempted assassination that brought down Vargas in 1954.[141] General Serpa, who was demoted in April 1980 because of his insistence on speaking out against the multinationals, blamed the United States for high petroleum prices. He also accused the Ford and Rockefeller Foundations of trying to keep Brazil weak by reducing the birth rate or sterilizing millions.[142] The president of the Brazilian Association of Medical Units said of the agencies seeking to check population growth, "They are forces represented by savage capitalism that wants to consolidate a colonial bond on the country as an economy peripheral to the great economies."[143]

The references to sinister "international" and "foreign" forces made at dramatic times by Vargas, Quadros, and Goulart made a deep impression; and they seemed to be confirmed by the orientation of the post-1964 government to the United States. The feeling has not been dissipated during years when Brazil has made many minor steps contrary to U.S. wishes. There is even a current of opinion attributing to the mysterious Trilateral Commission vile powers over Brazil (and much of the world).

To what extent the corporations, supported by or supporting U.S. official policy, uphold repressive power structures for their own benefit is a question regarding which evidence is so multiform and contradictory that proponents and opponents hardly hope to convince one another. Even the relatively simple factual issue whether the military government has intentionally favored the corporations, especially foreign, and helped them to exploit and impoverish the working masses is unclear.

It has become evident in Brazil that the foreign presence has not prevented but has probably promoted a large increase in total production. It is urged, however, that the people in general have not benefited. The big modern corporation going into a developing country like a mechanized army, causes maladjustments and unequalizes groups and regions. "Dependent industrialization," it is urged, concentrates income and increases relative deprivation[144] (as independent industrialization frequently does). But the military government, its critics charge, has not moderated but accentuated these trends by neglecting social consequences in focusing on gross national product.

It has been rather generally accepted by both Brazilian and U.S. writers that the post-1964 government, prohibiting unions and strikes (until 1978) and raising the minimum wage less than the inflation rate, was seeking to assure the profits of the multinationals. Hence, while the rich became much richer—Brazilian executives earn more after taxes than many of their American counterparts—the poor became poorer, not only relatively but absolutely. Theoretically, the benefits of industrialization should trickle down; but many statistical data have been cited by various authors to show a relative or even absolute decline of standard of living of wage earners and the less favored sectors of the population as wages failed to keep pace with inflation; and this has been a widespread subjective impression of Brazilians.[145]

Income trends are complicated, however, by regional migration, as millions have left the penurious Northeast for the flourishing South and have shifted from low-paying agriculture to better-paying industry. When the per capita GNP more than doubled from $625 in 1960 to $1,566 in 1976 (in 1978 dollars),[146] it is unlikely that any large group would be worse off in real terms. This would require an extreme change of income structures. But data showing increased inequality refer mostly to the 1960s, and the trend since 1970 has apparently been reversed.[147] Arruda and coauthors, no friends of the multinationals, found that from 1958 to 1969-70, covering the worst period, the percentage of the wage earners' budget devoted to food declined (from 45 to 39 percent) while that going to recreation sharply increased (from 0.5 to 4.1 percent),[148] a good indication of rising standard of living. A poll of July 1970, as the boom was getting underway, showed 57 percent seeing their conditions improved, only "3 percent considerably worsened."[149] One study of income data showed that, while all classes benefited, the poor gained the most.[150] Another set of figures shows that, from 1960 to 1976, all sectors gained, but the poorest decile gained least (35 percent) while the richest two deciles gained 221 percent and 267 percent. However, the next-poorest rose 170 percent, and all those above gained over 100 percent.[151]

If the military regime showed much less concern for the standard of living of the masses than for creating a favorable climate for business, this may or may not testify to the influence of the multinationals. Some insensitivity on the part of the generals is not surprising, and the unions were regarded as politically dangerous from Goulart days. Perhaps the urge to national power more than consideration for anyone's profits dictated a low priority for the living standards of the masses while rewarding those most responsible for pushing industrialization, the managers and technocrats. Communist states have also imposed forced savings on workers and peasants for the sake of capital formation while making engineers and managers relatively rich.

It is not clear what leverage foreign capitalists might exert over Brazilian generals, who are prima facie likely to be proud and nationalistic; bribery is a difficult explanation. As observed by a Brazilian journal at the time of heavy pressure on the nuclear issue, "The heavy bonds of economic dependence are not necessarily translated into effective instruments of intervention in situations like last week's."[152]

It is not even clear how Brazilian capitalists could lead the officers to do their bidding. If the military leadership came out of a landholding or entrepreneurial elite, it might be assumed that officers would serve the needs of their class; but the Brazilian military do not have such origins. The armed forces organize and indoctrinate boys of mostly lower middle-class background, and their ideology of National Security certainly implies no subservience to capitalistic interests, much less to a foreign power. As holders of instruments of force, they would seem quite as capable of exerting pressure on the capitalists as vice versa.

It is doubtful how far the U.S. government may exert itself on behalf of its corporate subjects in Brazil or other Latin American countries or whether the corporations use the government or the government uses the corporations. Overt interference would be counterproductive; there can only be some covert or subdued pressure. Total U.S. investment in Brazil is of the order of 4 percent of the U.S. defense budget or around 0.3 percent of the national product, and the administration is not much inclined to exercise itself unnecessarily on behalf of interests not of major weight. The Congress passed the Hickenlooper Amendment calling for a cutoff of foreign aid to countries confiscating American properties without proper compensation, but the executive has never seen fit to apply it in Brazil or anywhere else; it has been only an irritant, possibly a useful threat. It is desirable to protect commercial interests and a trading system based on respect for property and contracts, but it is equally desirable to avoid ruffling relations with an important country.

In the view of the U.S. executive branch, the security concern in Brazil outweighs most economic interests. Gordon and Kennedy, mindful of bigger interests in Brazilian affairs, were anything but enthusiastic about pushing the cases of expropriated utilities.[153] In many small matters, U.S. business interests are very influential on policy, because they are the chief groups with a solid and permanent stake in the foreign country. They may, indeed, restrict somewhat the freedom of action of the government by pressing it to avoid as well as to take certain actions. We may well guess that U.S. firms in Brazil endeavored to lower the key of the Carter human rights policy. It may be speculated whether the American business community in Brazil has been sufficiently coherent and purposeful to exert pressure in favor of Brazilian interests, which became its interests, in controversies over trade barriers, instant coffee, and the like. On the other hand, the American stake in Brazil is potentially a hostage, restricting the freedom of the government in the unlikely case that it should desire to take action inimical to Brazil.

Some Brazilians have seen advantages for Brazil in the work of the foreign firms. The opening after 1964 to American (and other) business was certainly intended to serve Brazilian interests. In many ways the Brazilians have used foreign capital for their benefit; for example, requiring foreign manufacturers to increase year by year the locally produced content of their product, they have spawned countless smaller Brazilian enterprises. The foreign corporations have become chief earners of foreign exchange, and no one denies that they have created jobs and paid taxes. A dependency theorist such as Fernando Henrique Cardoso concluded that dependency was indeed compatible with growth,[154] and Hélio Jaguaribe saw failure to take advantage of foreign capital and technology as a grave mistake.[155] Valle conceded that reliance on internal capital would require long forced sacrifices and that the centralized military government was less vulnerable to pressures from multinational corporations.[156] The logical policy for rapid economic growth is to rely chiefly on state and foreign enterprises, as Brazil has done.[157] In the view of Peter Evans, "dependent development" is at least a big advance over "classic dependence."[158]

The strongest Brazilian argument against dependency ideas has been made by Roberto Campos, onetime ambassador to Washington and economic planner for the Castelo government, who has been derided by the nationalists as pro-American. He saw not the "occult force" of Western or U.S. "imperialism" but populism, inflation, official paternalism, and instability as the obstacles to development. He cited such facts as that the least imperial country of Europe, Sweden, was the richest, while the most imperial, Portugal, was the poorest. Foreign investment he found valuable both for import substitution and production of exports, introduction of technology, and promotion of efficiency. Multinationals were not to be considered as instruments of a powerful government; corporations of small countries, such as Switzerland or Holland, were as successful as those of the United States.[159]

Not only is dependency theory difficult to reconcile with such facts as the impoverishment of the holders of empire, such as Portugal and Spain, and the rise of powers with no possessions, such as postwar Germany and Japan, but it does not explain why the most prosperous areas of the Third World are those overrun by foreign corporations, such as Taiwan and Singapore. Political control by the United States has not brought foreign economic domination, subservience, and backwardness to Japan and Germany, occupied and governed by U.S. forces after World War II but now enjoying prosperity roughly equal to that of the United States. The problems of the United States and other Western countries with petroleum-exporting nations are hard to square with the vision of all-powerful capitalism. It is also significant that U.S. investments have grown since the 1920s less in Latin America than in any other major area.

The subservience of the Brazilian government to foreign capital is hardly complete. The military regime has never repressed criticism of foreign investments[160] (except by members of the government) and has encouraged inquiry into their role and utility.[161] Brazil has moved considerably away from the old dependence on U.S. trade and capital, partly as a matter of choice; in particular, the government gave preference to European and Japanese firms in 1977–78 in reaction to Carter administration policies. Whatever the common interests of capitalists, the government has gained in bargaining power. If the United States was reluctant to transfer certain technology, as in the case not only of nuclear energy, Brazil could look elsewhere.[162] The government, controlling credit and basic resources and possessing ample regulatory powers, has made something of an art of playing firms of different countries against one another.[163] The interests of multinationals often conflict with those of one another, of local capital, and of the home government.

Various writers urge minimal foreign ownership in the economy. It is far too late, of course, to take this road, but Jaguaribe would like to see Brazil go in that general direction, reducing dependency by disciplining the corporations and building up Brazilian competitors. He would have Brazil not so much rebel against the American penetration as emulate it, pushing Brazilian multinationals in a strengthened Latin American economic community.[164] Even Campos, friendliest to the foreign interests, proposes preferential financing for national enterprises, encouragement for foreign corporations to sell shares locally, and application of antitrust laws against the absorption of local enterprises.[165] No one contends that a very large foreign-owned sector of the developing economy is inherently desirable.

In a sense, the very prominence of dependency theory is a sign of independence; if the foreign interests thoroughly controlled Brazil, they should (as Marxist theory indicates, stressing the primacy of the economic) dictate Brazilian ideology. Dependency theory became more prevalent in the 1970s as Brazil became more autonomous; such ideas were hardly acceptable in the first postwar years when U.S. hegemony was more of a reality.

If control is dubious, however, influence is incontestable. The very pervasiveness of dependency theory in some form or degree is significant, and indeed negative, so far as the foreign corporations are perceived as fatefully dominant or as part of a great malevolent external potency controlling Brazilian destinies. This implies hopeless and helpless inferiority, in the face of which resignation comes easy. Dependency, in the leftist version at least, is self-reinforcing; the only salvation is to come from the overthrow of the world capitalist system, which is beyond the powers of Brazil. A country like Brazil has too much self-confidence to accept fully such implications of futility, but any feeling that destiny is alien-held and uncontrollable undermines self-will—charity and exploitation have the same result.

It is possible, although unproved, that the foreign economic presence may be a factor for repressive or authoritarian government. Foreign investors have even more reason than Brazilian capitalists to be fearful of mass mobilization in a country of such deep class differences as Brazil. It is undeniable that foreign ownership of a large part of the economy complicates the politics of Brazil, as of other Latin American countries. But if it fastens obsolete political structures on them, as contended by Celso Furtado,[166] it is much less because of a conspiracy of domination than indirect effects of the social and political order.

The American economic stake in Latin America and Brazil gives this country an interest in the status quo and puts it on the side of the possessors, favoring a government that is legal and orderly but not too responsive to mass opinion. Popular and democratic movements incline to be anticapitalist and especially anti–foreign capitalist, by extension anti-United States, because the foreign corporations are the natural targets. To a remarkable extent, despite this fact the United States has favored popular, democratic government, at least in form, in Brazil and other Latin American countries. Hence the presence of the multinationals complicates Brazilian politics and makes U.S. influence at the same time stronger and more equivocal, contradictory at the unofficial level, ambivalent at the official.

NOTES

1. Teresa Hayter, *Aid as Imperialism* (New York: Pelican, 1971), pp. 9–10.
2. Moniz Bandeira, *O governo de João Goulart* (Rio de Janeiro: Editora Civilização Brasileira, 1978), p. 398.

3. Jan K. Black, *United States Penetration of Brazil* (Philadelphia: University of Pennsylvania Press, 1977), p. 39.

4. Riordan Roett, *The Politics of Foreign Aid in the Brazilian Northeast* (Nashville, Tenn., Vanderbilt University Press, 1972), pp. 72–73.

5. John W. F. Dulles, *Unrest in Brazil* (Austin, Tex., University of Texas Press, 1970), p. 183; Joseph A. Page, *The Revolution that Never Was: Northeast Brazil 1955–1964* (New York: Grossman, 1972), pp. 98–99.

6. Roett, *Politics*, p. 76.

7. Page, *Revolution*, p. 136.

8. Roett, *Politics*, p. 107.

9. Page, *Revolution*, p. 126.

10. Ibid., p. 136.

11. Ibid., p. 133.

12. Roett, *Politics*, p. 75.

13. Cited by Dulles, *Unrest*, pp. 218–19.

14. Black, *United States Penetration*, p. 67.

15. Ibid., p. 67.

16. Roett, *Politics*, p. 129.

17. Page, *Revolution*, p. 150.

18. Data of Roper Public Opinion Research Center, Williamstown, Mass.

19. Abraham Fishlow, "Flying Down to Rio: U.S.-Brazilian Relations," *Foreign Affairs* 57 (Winter 1978–79):392.

20. Roett, *Politics*, p. 165.

31. Page, *Revolution*, p. 229.

22. Ibid., p. 230.

23. *Wall Street Journal*, March 29, 1967, p. 1.

24. *Wall Street Journal*, November 27, 1979, p. 37.

25. As expressed, for example, by Peter Flynn, *Brazil: A Political Analysis* (Boulder, Colo.: Westview Press, 1978), p. 478.

26. José Roberto Mendonça and Douglas H. Graham, "The Brazilian Economic Model Revisited," *Latin American Research Review* 13, no. 2 (1978):13.

27. Werner Baer and Carlos von Doellinger, "Determinants of Brazil's Foreign Economic Policy," in *Latin America and the World Economy: A Changing International Order*, ed. Joseph Greenwald (Beverly Hills, Calif.: Sage Publications, 1978), p. 148.

28. *Estado de São Paulo*, July 1, 1979, p. 15.

29. *Brazil Today*, October 17, 1979, p. 1.

30. *Visão*, November 14, 1977, p. 64.

31. *Visão*, December 16, 1977, p. 54.

32. Baer and von Doellinger, "Determinants," pp. 148–50.

33. *Veja*, December 11, 1968, p. 27.

34. *Veja*, December 11, 1968, p. 28.

35. William G. Tyler, "A política dos EUA e o café soluvel," *Revista Civilização Brasileira* 18 (March-April 1968):92–93.

36. *Brazil 1969: Articles from Latin America* (New York: Center for Inter-American Relations, 1970), pp. 54–56.

37. Tyler, "A política dos EUA," p. 88.

38. Carlos Estevam Martins, *Capitalismo do estado e modelo político no Brasil* (Rio de Janeiro: Ediciones de Braal, 1977), p. 395.

39. *Wall Street Journal*, August 29, 1970, p. 10.

40. U.S., Congress, House, Committee on Ways and Means, *Sixth Annual Report to the President of the United States on the International Coffee Agreement*, April 5, 1971.

41. *Brazil 1969*, pp. 76–80.

42. Celso Lafer and Félix Peña, *Argentina y Brasil en el sistema de relaciones internacionales* (Buenos Aires: Nueva Visión, 1973), p. 91.

43. U.S., Congress, House, Committee on Ways and Means, Subcommittee on Trade, Hearing, February 9, 1979, pp. 65–68.

44. Information of American embassy, Brasília.

45. *Wall Street Journal*, December 13, 1978, p. 13.

46. William Perry, *Contemporary Brazilian Foreign Policy* (Beverly Hills, Calif.: Sage Publications, 1976), pp. 83–84.

47. *Conjuntura Económica* 32 (June 1978):148.

48. Frank D. McCann, Jr., *The Brazilian-American Alliance 1937–1945* (Princeton: Princeton University Press, 1973), p. 378.

49. U.S., Congress, Senate, Committee on Foreign Relations, Subcommittee on Multinational Corporations, "Multinational Corporations in Brazil and Mexico: Structural Sources of Economic and non-Economic Power," August 1975, p. 96.

50. Ibid, p. 98.

51. *Visão*, April 21, 1980, p. 80.

52. Carlos von Doellinger and Leonardo C. Calvacanti, *Empresas multinacionais na industria brasileira* (Rio de Janeiro: IPEA/INPES, 1975), p. 15. For full data, see Sylvia Ann Hewlett, *The Cruel Dilemmas of Development: Twentieth Century Brazil* (New York: Basic Books, 1980), tables 8–11.

53. Georges-André Fiechter, *Le régime modernisateur du Brésil, 196421972* (Leiden: Sijthoff, 1972), pp. 18–20.

54. Stefan H. Robcock, *Brazil: A Study in Development Progress* (Lexington, Mass.: D.C. Heath, 1975), p. 59.

55. Serge D'Adesky, "Brazil's Rise to Dominance in Latin America," *Fletcher Forum* 3 (Summer 1979): 62.

56. *Visão*, April 21, 1980, p. 56.

57. Doellinger and Calvacanti, *Empresas multinacionais*, p. 59.

58. Black, *United States Penetration*, p. 238; *New York Times*, January 26, 1976, p. 35; February 19, 1978, p. F-3.

59. Marcos Arruda, Herbert de Souza, and Carlos Afonso, *Multinational Corporations and Brazil* (Toronto: Latin American Research Unit, 1975), pp. 210, 216.

60. *New York Times*, January 26, 1976, p. 35.

61. *Visão*, August 31, 1980, p. 33.

62. Riordan Roett, *Brazil: Politics in a Patrimonial Society* (New York: Praeger, 1978), p. 156. Hewlett, *Cruel Dilemmas*, table 10.

63. *Visão*, April 21, 1980, p. 80.

64. Walder de Goes, *O governo do General Geisel* (Rio de Janeiro: Editora Nova Fronteira, 1978), p. 164.

65. *Visão*, April 21, 1980, pp. 78–79.

66. Senate, Committee on Foreign Relations, "Multinational Corporations," p. 150; *Visão*, December 6, 1976, p. 5.

67. Mendonça and Graham, "The Brazilian Economic Model Revisited," p. 8.

68. Hewlett, *Cruel Dilemmas*, p. 117.

69. Lafer and Peña, *Argentina y Brasil*, pp. 80–81; Norman Gall, "The Rise of Brazil," *Commentary* 63 (January 1977):52.

70. Andrea Maneschi, "The Brazilian Public Sector," in *Brazil in the Sixties*, ed. Riordan Roett (Nashville, Tenn.: Vanderbilt University Press, 1972), p. 189.

71. Mendonça and Graham, "The Brazilian Economic Model Revisited," p. 33.

72. Flynn, *Brazil*, p. 499.

73. Mendonça and Graham, "The Brazilian Economic Model Revisited," p. 13.

74. Robert M. Levine, "Brazil, the Aftermath of Decompression," *Current History* 70 (February 1976):55.

75. Baer and von Doellinger, "Determinants," p. 158.

76. Quoted by Norman Gall, "In the Name of Democracy," *American Universities Field Service Staff Report 1978*, no. 3, p. 5.

77. *Veja*, November 7, 1979, p. 35.

78. *Business Week*, November 19, 1979, p. 58.

79. *Visão*, April 21, 1980, p. 79.

80. For a sober study, see von Doellinger and Calvacanti, *Empresas multinacionais*, passim.

81. *Visão*, April 21, 1980, p. 56.

82. von Doellinger and Calvancanti, *Empresas multinacionais*, pp. 101–2.

83. Senate, Committee on Foreign Relations, "Multinational Corporations," p. 143.

84. von Doellinger and Calvacanti, *Empresas multinacionais*, p. 109.

85. Ibid., pp. 63, 69, 76.

86. Senate, Committee on Foreign Relations, "Multinational Corporations," p. 139; von Doellinger and Calvacanti, *Empresas multinacionais*, p. 84.

87. Hewlett, *Cruel Dilemmas*, p. 154.

88. *Visão*, February 28, 1972, p. 144.

89. Arruda, de Souza, and Afonso, *Multinational Corporations*, p. 4.

90. Moniz Bandeira, *Presença dos Estados Unidos no Brasil* (Rio de Janeiro: Civilização Brasileira, 1973), p. 391.

91. *New York Times*, January 21, 1980, p. 2.

92. *A Crítica* (Manaus), April 23, 1980, p. 7.

93. *Jornal do Brasil*, April 28, 1980, p. 13.

94. *Jornal do Brasil*, May 23, 1980, p. 9.

95. *A Crítica* (Manaus), April 17, 1980, p. 2.

96. Arruda, de Souza, and Afonso, *Multinational Corporations*, p. 81.

97. *Time*, September 10, 1979, pp. 76–79.

98. *New York Times*, November 30, 1979, p. 2; Arruda, de Souza, and Afonso, *Multinational Corporations*, pp. 131–208.

99. *Visão*, March 20, 1973, p. 23.

100. Celso Furtado, *Economic Development of Latin America* (Cambridge, England: Cambridge University Press, 1970), p. 69.

101. Hélio Jaguaribe, *Brasil: Crise e alternativas* (Rio de Janeiro: Zahar Editores, 1974), p. 72.

102. E. Bradford Burns, *Nationalism in Brazil: An Historical Survey* (New York: Praeger, 1968), pp. 33–34.

103. Robinson Rojas, *Estados Unidos en Brasil* (Santiago: Prensa Latinoamericana, 1965), p. 59.

104. Arruda, de Souza, and Afonso, *Multinational Corporations*, p. 13 and passim.

105. Rojas, *Estados Unidos en Brasil*, pp. 59, 156.

106. Bandeira, *Presença*, p. 161.

107. *Correio Brasilense* (Brasília), April 12, 1980, p. 7.

108. Ibid.

109. *Visão*, January 12, 1976, p. 54.

110. *A Crítica* (Manaus), April 28, 1980, p. 7.

111. *Visão*, April 28, 1980, p. 17.

112. *Estado de São Paulo*, April 9, 1980, p. 29.

113. *Visão*, April 14, 1980, p. 97.

114. *Veja*, August 16, 1978, p. 114.

115. Abraham Lowenthal, "Latin America: A Not-So-Special Relationship," *Foreign Policy* 32 (Fall 1978):118.

116. *Visão*, April 14, 1980, p. 19.

117. von Doellinger and Calvacanti, *Empresas multinacionais*, p. 134.

118. Senate, Committee on Foreign Relations, "Multinational Corporations," p. 97.

119. Arruda, de Souza, and Afonso, *Multinational Corporations*, p. 59.

120. Bandeira, *Presença*, pp. 391, 393.

121. Ibid., p. 396.

122. Genival Rabelo, *O capital estrangeiro na imprensa brasileira* (Rio de Janeiro: Editora Civilização Brasileira, 1966) devotes much attention to this thesis.

123. *New York Times*, January 21, 1980, p. 2.

124. *Veja*, October 18, 1978, p. 29.

125. Richard J. Barnet and Ronald E. Muller, *Global Reach: The Power of the Multinational Corporation* (New York: Simon and Schuster, 1974), p. 192.

126. *Wall Street Journal*, October 8, 1976, p. 1.

127. Levine, "Brazil, the Aftermath of Decompression," pp. 53–54.

128. *Visão*, April 21, 1980, p. 79.

129. *New York Times*, February 19, 1978, p. F-3.

130. *Wall Street Journal*, December 19, 1978, p. 6.

131. von Doellinger and Calvacanti, *Empresas multinacionais*, pp. 44–45.

132. For a moderate statement of dependency see Peter Evans, *Dependent Development: The Alliance of Multinational, State, and Local Capital in Brazil* (Princeton: Princeton University Press, 1979).

133. *New York Times*, September 9, 1969, p. 1.

134. Marcio Moreira Alves, *A Grain of Mustard Seed: The Awakening of the Brazilian Revolution* (Garden City, N.Y.: Doubleday, Anchor Press, 1973), p. 163.

135. *A Crítica* (Manaus), April 24, 1980, p. 7.

136. *New York Times*, December 17, 1968, p. 1.

137. *New York Times*, June 18, 1980, p. 2.

138. Jaguaribe, *Brasil*, pp. 70–71.

139. Arruda, de Souza, and Afonso, *Multinational Corporations*, p. 10.

140. André Gunder Frank, *Capitalism and Underdevelopment in Latin America: Historical Studies of Chile and Brazil* (New York: Monthly Review Press, 1967), pp. 211–12.

141. By the Marxist Nelson Werneck Sodré, cited by Álvaro Valle, *As novas estructuras políticas brasileiras* (Rio de Janeiro: Nórdica, 1977), p. 215.

142. *A Crítica* (Manaus), April 16, 1980, p. 2.

143. *A Crítica* (Manaus), April 17, 1980, p. 2.

144. Celso Furtado, *A hegemonia dos Estados Unidos e o subdesenvolvimento da América Latina* (Rio de Janeiro: Editoro Civilização Brasileira, 1973), pp. 147–49.

145. Detailed figures are given by Hewlett, *Cruel Dilemmas*, tables 12–17.

146. *Veja*, July 18, 1979, p. 89.

147. Grey P. Pfeffermann and Richard Webb, *The Distribution of Income in Brazil* (Washington, D.C.: World Bank, 1979), pp. 77–78.

148. Arruda, de Souza, and Afonso, *Multinational Corporations*, p. 45.

149. Fiechter, *Le régime modernisateur*, p. 214.

150. Gary S. Fields, "Who Benefits from Economic Development? A Reexamination of Brazilian Growth in the 1960's," *American Economic Review* 67 (September 1977):577.

151. Hewlett, *Cruel Dilemmas*, table 13.

152. *Isto É*, March 16, 1977, p. 23.

153. Valle, *As novas estructuras*, p. 214.

154. Fernando Henrique Cardoso, "Associated-Dependent Development," in *Authoritarian Brazil*, ed. Alfred Stepan (New Haven: Yale University Press, 1973), p. 149.

155. Jaguaribe, *Brasil*, p. 49.

156. Valle, *As novas estructuras*, pp. 212–13, 215.

157. Hewlett, *Cruel Dilemmas*, p. 73.

158. Evans, *Dependent Development*, chap. 6.

159. Roberto Campos, *O mundo que vejo e não desejo* (Rio de Janeiro: José Olympio, 1976), pp. 208–13, 221.

160. Roger W. Fontaine, *Brazil and the United States: Toward a Maturing Relationship* (Washington, D.C.: American Enterprise Institute, 1974), p. 50.

161. Flynn, *Brazil*, p. 488.

162. *Visão*, May 28, 1978, p. 54.

163. Fiechter, *Le régime modernisateur*, p. 239.

164. Jaguaribe, *Brasil*, pp. 73–74, 136.

165. Campos, *O mundo*, p. 222.

166. Furtado, *A hegemonia*, p. 85.

OFFICIAL PROGRAMS

While dependent-interdependent economic relations tie Brazil to the United States (and to other major trading nations), materially restricting its freedom of action, the cultural relations of the two countries have broad and deep effects on Brazilians, predisposing them in favor of—or in some ways against—ideas and policies favored by the United States.

The U.S. government was made aware of the possible importance of information or propaganda by the Nazis in the 1930s; it seemed indispensable, if the United States did not want to see Brazil fall under the spell of the Axis powers, to present American views and virtues. Shortwave radio broadcasts were begun to counter Nazi versions of the news, and the U.S. government sponsored personal missions in the conviction that acquaintance promotes friendship. In 1940–41 Brazil was awash with a tide of goodwill visitors, film stars, scientists, musicians, artists, and intellectuals, who caused a little annoyance but at least gave Brazilians the feeling that they were not being neglected.[1] There was also inaugurated a program to translate American books into Portuguese.

The cultural program has never ceased since, although it has expanded and contracted according to the mood of Congress. The Voice of America broadcasts daily to Brazil in both English and Portuguese. A random survey of 466 persons conducted by the USIA in March 1964 in Rio turned up four listeners, none oftener than twice weekly—not an impressive audience, especially considering that several times as many turned to various other shortwave stations.[2] The USIA, recently renamed International Communication Agency (ICA), carries on in Brazil its largest single country program, costing roughly $6 million yearly. Under its aegis, from 1954 through 1979 some 14,000 long-term scholarships were granted to Brazilians; the Fulbright Commission also administered from 1957 to 1979 1,131 fellowships for Brazilians and 511 for Americans to study in Brazil, most of them in the humanities and social sciences.[3] There has also been some assistance for U.S. students and teachers going to Brazil, Brazilians making short visits to the United States, and a few artists and speakers. The ICA assists the publication of a few books in Brazil by agreeing to purchase a certain number of copies, mostly of works about democratic government.[4] "Project Outreach" has tried to make U.S. publications more easily available. The cultural officer of the embassy also distributes material for the press, radio, and television, and helps communications between U.S. and Brazilian media. A few short films have been produced for Brazilian theaters and television. There are occasional ad hoc programs; for example, under arrangements with the Ministry of Education a group of Brazilian publishers and educators was sent to the United States for study of textbook publishing, and a few U.S. publishers were brought to Brazil.[5]

Perhaps the most significant work of the ICA has been to foster binational centers, which chiefly teach English but which also maintain libraries and reading rooms and carry on a varied program of cultural events. There are some 73 such centers in Brazil, operated with minimal cost to the U.S. taxpayer. Supervised by local boards, usually binational, they were formerly provided with an American director paid by the USIA (or ICA); for the most part, they have been able, thanks to the eagerness of Brazilians to learn English, to become self-supporting through student fees. For example, in 1977 the Casa Thomas Jefferson in Brasília had an income of some $600,000 from about 3,000 students, mostly government employees.[6] For many years there have been a few score Peace Corps volunteers in Brazil, 150, for example, in 1977.[7]

Those who administer these programs have more faith than certitude in the results of their work. It seems likely that opinion leaders sent to the United States return with more realistic, if not more sympathetic, views; and the binational centers are filled with a friendly atmosphere toward things American. Despite the American penchant for commercial advertising, some other nations seem to believe more strongly in such efforts to spread a good opinion of the country. In proportion to the amount of their trade with Brazil, the French have a much larger program for spreading their language and culture via the Alliance Française. The work of the British Council and the German Goethehaus is also impressive, while the Japanese, too, have entered the field. The American program is made possible much more by the eagerness of Brazilians than the appreciation of the Congress.

CULTURAL PENETRATION

Whatever the frictions and suspicions of the multinationals, Brazilians are generally well-disposed toward the United States and things American. A large and perhaps growing share of Brazilian culture is derived from this country; and while Brazilians are still Brazilian, they have absorbed enough of American culture for easy understanding.

Basic Brazilian culture is, of course, of Portuguese origin, with a small Indian (Tupi) and a considerably larger African admixture. After independence, Brazil looked primarily to Britain, the richest nation, and to France, the most elegant. Around the beginning of this century, the literary and artistic influence of France still predominated, but the U.S. presence was becoming prominent, culturally as well as economically, from the 1920s. The strong influx came with World War II. As the *Estado de São Paulo* summarized, "Since then, the North American presence grew in intensity and sophistication and, despite the first signs of political and diplomatic independence of the Brazilian government in relation to the U.S., we remain in the cultural and social orbit, as regards consumption, of the American model. . . . There is nothing more natural than that our children play Bat Man, our artists admire Andy Warhol, or newspapers use imported techniques. . . ."[8] In television, cinema, journalism, book publication, music, and education, U.S. influence is conspicuous if usually not dominant.

A concrete means of cultural influence is advertising—not without reason, Brazilians see the multinationals imposing culture and fashions on their country. Advertising carries an especially American flavor because of the American hegemony in the agencies. Modern advertising came to Brazil in the 1930s to serve branches of U.S. corporations, such as General Motors, and thereby implanted U.S. methods and gained a market position never lost. In the 1970s, of the 20 or so largest agencies, a majority have been American;[9] all of the 12 largest in 1967 were foreign, 8 of them American.[10] They have inevitably conveyed American tastes and attitudes, while subtly or not so subtly shaping, to some degree, the outlook and policies of those dependent on their trade.

The most important medium in Brazil is television, chief source of entertainment and news, since magazine and newspaper readership is not large. Unlike the press, television is subject to censorship, and producers recur the more to imported, mostly American programming. This is cheap, Brazil being a secondary market, abundant, and regularly available. By virtue both of imports and advertising, television becomes, in Brazilian eyes, the fundamental vehicle for the consumer mentality fostered by the multinationals.[11] It would be an error, however, to assume that the U.S. programs in any real sense overwhelm Brazilian television. Late shows are probably American serials, but prime time is generally given to native production. Foreign ownership of broadcasting stations is forbidden. In the 1960s Time-Life endeavored to secure control of TV-Globo, with some dozens of stations, without direct ownership. One device was to acquire the property of the broadcasters and "rent" it to them for a portion of profits. Another was to provide technical assistance, in return for which the Brazilians agreed to take U.S. programs.[12] Since then, U.S. enterprises have not been so aggressive, and Brazilian television is by no means an obvious vehicle of propaganda for foreign or U.S. interests, although it clearly contributes to a favorable atmosphere.

U.S. influence is stronger in the magazines, which have far less mass impact but are influential with the more educated. *Newsweek* and *Time* have Latin American editions (in English) and there are English-language newspapers in Rio and São Paulo. Leading Brazilian weeklies get their world news directly from *Newsweek* or *Time*. A Portuguese edition of *Reader's Digest* has a mass circulation. Dailies rely on U.S. news agencies, such as UPI, although European sources are also used; columnists are borrowed preferentially from the *New York Times*. Brazilians regard U.S. news sources as honest, and they are impressed by the independence and professionalism of American journalism.[13] Major papers have correspondents in New York or Washington, fewer in Europe. Like braodcasting enterprises, the press is legally restricted to Brazilian nationals. However, shortly before leaving office, Castelo Branco exempted "scientific, cultural, and artistic publications" from the law requiring Brazilian ownership,[14] and this has been interpreted rather liberally. One of the leading newsweeklies, *Visão* was for many years under the auspices of a New York firm, but it was at least outwardly separated in 1967 after the scandal arising from the effort of Time-Life to gain control of a television network. *Visão* in 1965 launched a series of trade magazines for industrialists, construction managers, and agriculturists, subsidized by large corporations, mostly foreign. It is typical of the problem of foreign penetration that most comics are of U.S. provenance because they are cheap, easily available, and of usually tolerable quality.[15] They are not overtly ideological, but it has been contended that they have an insidious imperialist influence.

Like television shows and cartoon strips, foreign films can be brought in cheaply because costs of production have been already covered in the home market; at the same time, they are popular. Of 600 to 800 motion pictures released yearly in Brazil, only 80 to 100 are Brazilian,[16] while foreign films have about four times as many viewers,[17] and the take on foreign films is larger.[18] Somewhat more than half the foreign films are from the U.S., "monopoly," as Nelson Werneck Sodré calls it. The strongest competition for the U.S. cinema in the last decades has been French, but since 1964 the American has prevailed. In popular music, likewise, jazz and rock reign in the "Hit Parade" with the assistance of the "DJ," much as U.S. pop music is the leading edge of Western decadence in Eastern Europe. In the early 1960s there was something of an upsurge in Brazilian art, music, literature, and cinema, and Brazilian artists received considerable international recognition; but a slump followed, attributable either to censorship or intellectual demoralization under the authoritarian government,[19] leaving the field more to the imports. It may be that in the recently more relaxed atmostphere the tide will be partly reversed.

In regard to books, a third to a quarter of the titles on the lists of fiction best-sellers[20] are ordinarily by U.S. authors, a smaller but significant fraction of the nonfiction list. Roughly half of translated books year by year are from English, under one-fourth from French, followed by a few percent each from German, Spanish, and Italian. It has been claimed that Brazilian book publishing is dominated by U.S. capital, especially in the production of textbooks and comic books that deform young minds.[21] U.S. influence on Brazilian literature, however, has not been nearly so strong as European, especially French, which has had high prestige with intellectuals. It may be noted that Brazilian Portuguese has been extensively infiltrated by Americanisms, more so than Spanish; and there has been little tendency to reject them, in the French fashion, on nationalistic grounds.

Not only media but people spread culture. In 1977 there were 109,317 tourists from the United States, 89,788 from Argentina, 10,012 from West Germany, 19,975 from France, and 18,175 from Great Britain.[22] Many Brazilian universities have exchange programs with U.S. universities, and of Brazilians going abroad to study by far the largest contingent goes to the United States—2,160 in 1975, compared to 1,122 to France, 369 to West Germany, 256 to the United Kingdom, and so forth.[23] There is much academic travel. Results are not always positive—Herman Kahn once offended Brazilian hosts by casting doubts on 'Brazil's potentials—but much is learned. Brazilians concede that the most significant study of their history is done abroad, principally, the United States.[24] In 1974 there were 700 professors of Portuguese or Brazilian studies in the United States. It is conceded that facilities for study of Brazil are better at good libraries in the United States, such as that of the University of Texas, than at any Brazilian library.[25] Many Brazilian scholars write with an eye to publication in the United States.

The number of persons of U.S. origin in Brazil is relatively small, compared to Germans, Italians, and so forth; but the Americans are mostly in leadership positions. The styles and manners of São Paulo businessmen are notably like those of their U.S. counterparts in dispatch and aggressiveness; this may owe something to Paulista traditions, but it is reasonable to guess that something has been taken from the U.S. business people in their midst. Protestantism, largely propagated by U.S. missionaries, stresses work, family morality, and abstinence, none of which have been traditional Portuguese-colonial specialities, and in effect represents a degree of Americanization. The Protestant population expanded from one million in 1940 to about eight million in 1976.

In these many ways, Brazil receives cultural outflows from the United States and is modified thereby in its views, values, and attitudes, both toward modern life and the outside world, especially toward the area from which most cultural diffusion comes. The effects are complex and ambiguous. In part, they are favorable to U.S. purposes, in part unfavorable, in that they are defensive and negative. They are very little studied, but it cannot be doubted that much of the willingness or unwillingness of Brazil to cooperate with U.S. purposes depends upon their cultural interactions. At best, it facilitates communication; at worst, it generates antipathies directed more strongly against those familiar than distant strangers. Admiration for American achievement and many qualities of American life and ideas goes with resentment of material superiority, intrusion, and sometimes patronizing attitudes.

REACTIONS

Many Brazilians castigate the consumption-oriented society, with its passion for domestic appliances, blue jeans, supermarkets, television, and the thousand things accompanying the conventional "good life" of American suburbia.[26] Yet the chief aspiration of the enlarging middle class is for material conveniences, U.S. style, status symbols of the nouveaux riches.[27] Consumerism and materialism are among the charges thrown at the tide of cultural imports; although Brazil was materialistic enough long before U.S. influence could be blamed, it was so in different and perhaps less conspicuous ways. Americanization is seen as destruction or subversion of native culture.[28] The writer Lygia Fagundes Teller complained of "continual infiltration of foreignisms," resulting in a "language that is neither Portuguese nor English."[29] The United States allegedly exports a mentality of sex, drugs, and violence, "commercialized fakery" and the "cultural patterns of a civilization in crisis,"[30] with an insidious ideological message. The weakness for foreign styles is deemed a disgraceful reflection of economic dependency.

The basic negative reaction to what is called "cultural imperialism" is protest against foreign intrusion. The intellectual Marxists and near-

Marxists are joined by many who abhor Marxism in decrying alienation from the Brazilian heritage, as children play Indians and cowboys instead of bandeirantes. That Donald Duck, Superman, Tarzan, and company are exponents of imperialism is widely believed throughout Latin America (as expounded in several books by the Chilean Armand Mattelart).[31] This brand of imperialism, mostly incorporated in movies, is held responsible for "this process of social, mental, and moral deterioration of Rio society," with its neuroses of emptiness, dissatisfaction, consumerism, and false liberty.[32]

The military government was probably not unhappy for criticism to turn against the United States instead of itself,[33] and many anti-U.S. tales were going around in the late 1960s and early 1970s, for example, that Brazil was being exploited by the export of cadavers to U.S. medical schools.[34] Reproduction was a more frequent theme than death; American missionaries were using birth control to depopulate Amazonia to make room for prison colonies for troublesome blacks, or U.S. AID in the Northeast was putting contraceptive drugs in milk, and agents disguised as missionaries were sterilizing women.[35] The student movement took up the slogans current around American universities in the early 1970s, expressing outrage not so much against specific misdeeds of the United States in Brazil as against the general order of things, for which the United States was held responsible.[36] The government of Castelo Branco wished to depoliticize higher education and make it more productive, but the fact that educational reforms were sponsored by the United States was sufficient to unite students, professors, and government officials against them;[37] hard-liners in the military joined leftist students. The plan to introduce a tuition charge was rejected as a plot to "Americanize" Brazilian universities.[38] Material for anti-Americanism was furnished by the literature of protest in the United States, and American critics furnished ammunition for attacks on the American government. For example, *Newsweek*[39] told much more about complicity in the 1964 coup than Brazilian nationalists had charged.

Partly to give a little protection to Brazilian culture, perhaps more to assist Brazilian producers, some barriers have been erected against the cultural flood. All films shown commercially must be copies made in Brazilian laboratories—a requirement that sometimes raises problems of quality. There is also a tax on foreign films, the proceeds of which go to subsidize Brazilian filmmakers. More important, there have been laws from the 1950s providing that one Brazilian film be shown for every eight foreign, or since 1966 that theaters show Brazilian films at least 56, more recently 84, days per year. Producers have urged that the number of days be much increased to enable them to get their product onto the screen; theater owners have objected to being compelled to give so much time to unpopular shows.[40] A 1976 law required showing a Brazilian short with the foreign feature.[41] The effect on quality of Brazilian productions is not entirely positive; there seems to have been some incentive to produce cheap X-rated films to fill the time requirements. There has also been pressure against foreign stage plays, and comic strip artists demanded 30 percent of the space.[42] It it proposed to require publishers to produce a Brazilian book for each foreign one.[43]

For the leftists or Marxists, the government, subject to foreign capitalist pressure if not control, cannot meet the threat; thus Sodré claimed that the state, in cooperation with foreign interests, sabotaged the Brazilian film industry.[44] In the leftist view, economic and cultural imperialism are all one, economic exploitation reinforced by cultural blockade.[45] In cooperation with U.S. monopolies, the international banks, USAID, the IMF, the Pan-American Union, the Peace Corps, and many foundations have endeavored to buy out and corrupt Brazilian higher education, or limit it to serving the purposes of capitalism.[46] Any such effort must have been counterproductive because for many years students have been in the vanguard of leftist nationalism. The universities above all consume Marxist writings, scorning those of more liberal bent, as leftist instructors turn out Marxist students, and leftist students demand Marxist courses.[47]

Nonetheless, resentment of the cultural invasion seems to have ebbed as U.S. political influence has declined. Even in the bad times, when the United States was regarded as the bulwark of the dictatorship, something of the long-term cordiality of U.S.-Brazilian relations remained. There seems to have been less anti-Americanism in Brazil than in most of Spanish America, perhaps mostly because of basic confidence in the Brazilian destiny. Brazilian intellectuals have not ceased to admire U.S. culture; and the middle classes, although nationalistic, like U.S. products and study English. They do not want Brazil to be in any way subservient but neither do they want it to take an anti-U.S. course.[48] They see unofficial and noncommerical America as honest, disinterested, and generally admirable.

A few polls taken prior to March 31, 1964, at a time when anti-U.S. agitation was at its height, showed basically pro-U.S. sentiments. Of 383 persons questioned in March 1963, 45 percent had a "good" or "very good" opinion of the United States, only 4 percent "bad" or "very bad." Of the Soviet Union, 15 percent had "good" or "very good" opinions, 21 percent "bad" or "very bad." Further, 26 percent felt that Brazil should side with the United States; 3 percent, with the Soviets, 40 percent with neither. Of 350 industrial workers polled by the USIA, only 9 percent knew the United States had proposed the Alliance for Progress, but 35 percent professed a good opinion of this country, only 3 percent a bad opinion. A USIA poll of 466 miscellaneous people of Rio in March 1964 gave very similar results. Asked which country was the best friend of Brazil, 133 named the United States, 105 various West European countries, 5 the Soviet Union, 6 various Latin American countries, and 1 Cuba; 216 had no choice, 33 percent had a "good" or "very good" opinion of the United States, only 4 percent a "bad" or "very bad" one; the remainder had an indifferent opinion or did not know. Asked to choose sides in the contest then seen as constituting the substance of world politics, 25 percent picked the United States; 1 percent the Soviet Union; 30 percent chose neutrality.[49]

In the late 1960s, Brazil saw the United States engaged in a confusing war in Vietnam and torn by disruption and law defiance at the same time that it was identified with the repressions of the military regime. Since the early 1970s, the American image has gradually improved, as Brazil asserted more independence, the United States left Vietnam, and the administration opted for a low profile. The frictions of 1977 between the Geisel and Carter administrations do not seem to have angered many Brazilians, and since then anti-U.S. feeling has clearly diminished, or pro-U.S. sentiments have grown. A Gallup poll in São Paulo, taken just after the cancellation of military agreements, showed the following judgments of U.S. policy toward Brazil (with "no opinion" eliminated): excellent, 5 percent; good, 32 percent; fair, 41 percent; bad, 22 percent. Comparable 1975 results were: excellent, 4 percent; good, 34 percent; fair, 42 percent; bad, 2 percent. The 595 Paulistas were also asked how they viewed U.S. and Brazilian interests regarding specific issues, with the following results:[50]

	Nuclear Deal	Human Rights	Shoe Exports
Close	12	18	20
Fairly close	8	4	17
Slightly different	10	12	11
Very different	36	26	18
No opinion	34	30	34

The cultural presence of the United States in Brazil seems to be in principle like the economic presence. It has caused some resentment (although far less than the multinationals), but it integrated Brazil into the Western world system of which the United States is still the leading part and brings the two countries closer together. As a Brazilian commented:

The enormous presence of the United States produced two compulsions in our intellectuals, artists, and public men: the compulsion to imitate and the compulsion to warn against imitation. In these past two hundred

years, many found in the U.S. the prototype to imitate or the prototype
of what was to be rejected.[51]

It is a perennial dilemma how far to accept the foreign product or to
prefer Brazilian art, movies, books, plays, toothpaste, or drugs for the
sake of Brazilian identity and self-respect. Brazilians want to be independent and also to measure up by world standard; the latter may require
more borrowing. But even in rejecting, the Brazilian intellectual uses
concepts drawn from the American storehouse of ideas of protest.

THE DEMOCRATIC SET

If Brazilians are led to use cornflakes, this is of no tremendous
political significance, although it may conceivably immunize them to
some extent against radicalism. But it may be that the most significant
political influence of the United States on Brazil is the creation of a
climate of opinion in which undemocratic government is illegitimate. The
United States is at least as responsible for the values of free political
institutions in Brazil as for the values of consumerism.

Brazil has for many decades borrowed very broadly from the
patterns of the United States, not only a longtime friend and ally but the
richest, most powerful, and most innovative of states, freely taking over
such things as industrial organization, functional architecture, commercial
spirit, informality of manners, and fondness for computers.[52] The United
States has been the model of the free enterprise economy, and labor
organizations have been built up in the manner of, to some extent under
the direction of, the American labor federations. Movements of opinion in
the United States echo in Brazil. For example, in regard to rights for those
of African descent, an area in which Brazil is often credited with being
especially advanced, influence has been strong. In the 1960s, the U.S. civil
liberties movement made Brazil more aware of the reality of informal
racial prejudice and bars to the advancement of Blacks, who are grossly
underrepresented among university students, civil servants, and army
officers. There were vogues for Afro hairdos and dashikis, as Brazilian
Blacks began to organize and express ethnic feelings almost for the first
time.[53]

Most importantly, despite resentments against actions and policies of
the U.S. government, American political institutions have long been
broadly admired. For Americans, by and large, the only decent political
system is one more or less like their own, with free press, elections for
high office contested by freely operating political parties, independent
courts, and other accessories of pluralistic, democratic, representative

government. This basic view is shared by the generality of Brazilians, at least those who incline to express views on the subject; it is regarded as only natural that Brazil should have a government based on institutionalized popular consent. In the words of the governor of Guanabara, Rafael de Almeida Magalhães, "The American institutional model in which only the power coming from the people is legitimate, became the national ideal. The Brazilian elite decided to govern itself in the democratic way, under which elections and representation of the people are essential instruments."[54]

From the eighteenth century Brazilians were perusing not only Voltaire, Rousseau, and Locke but also Thomas Paine, Benjamin Franklin, Thomas Jefferson,[55] and other pioneers of American political thinking. In the nineteenth century they came to assume that a republic like that of the United States was the proper form of government, and after casting away the monarchy they naturally gave themselves a federal-presidential constitution like that of the United States. Brazilian administrative theory since the 1930s has been almost entirely U.S.-derived, and the United States was seen as the model for an efficient nonpolitical civil service[56] (which failed because it did not correspond to the values of those called upon to implement it). The decision to join the United States in World War II was a decision in favor of the democratic system, despite Vargas' authoritarian rule. When Vargas was retired in 1945, the Brazilians produced a new constitution close to the American model.

In 1964, the generals declined to follow U.S. wishes that power be turned over to a constitutional civilian regime. Castelo Branco called the revolution a democratic movement, but when the Congress hesitated to enact full powers for the military government, it simply asserted the powers it required by virtue of its revolutionary victory. In 1965, when politicians of the old school won important governorships, Castelo Branco—reluctantly—by decree reorganized the parties and reinforced the presidency. Yet the military regime did not undertake complete dictatorship or organize a one-party mobilizational state. Always under more or less pressure to permit a return to normal representative politics, the regime has never claimed permanent dictatorial powers or abolished parties and elections. Now and then the government has made concessions in fact or appearances to the forces of liberalization, and it has repeatedly drawn back and reasserted a firm hand; but the goal of ultimate democratization has never been lost to sight.

Each president has spoken hopefully of decompression, normalization, or "abertura," opening of the political process, it being taken for granted that the democratic way is normal. Castelo Branco said in 1964, "The Revolution is legitimate if within a period that is not unreasonable it guarantees the legitimacy of its continuation by vote."[57] The constitution of 1967 was again cast in the American mold; it particularly paid tribute by organizing the Supreme Court like the American with powers of judicial review. Costa e Silva opened his presidency with an encouraging dialogue with labor leaders, students, and the Congress. However, disorders late in 1968 created a sense of insecurity; and when Congress tried to defend its prerogative by refusing to lift the immunity of an outspoken deputy, it was suspended by force, stringent censorship was imposed, and the president took virtually unlimited authority. Even so, Costa e Silva professed, "I believe in freedom of the press."[58]

It was felt necessary to recall the Congress in order to legitimize the accession of Médici in October 1969, and Médici pledged a reform program to restore democracy.[59] Acting a little more like a popular leader than his predecessors, he tried to conciliate the church and improve the image of his government. There were stern represssions, however, and the severity of the regime continued through his tenure. A censor sat in the editorial room of major papers, which might fill empty spaces with classical poetry. Médici retreated from his promise of democratization by indicating that military rule would have to last until it was possible to assure the well-being of all citizens,[60] and that economic-social democracy must precede political democracy[61]—presumably postponing the latter until well into the next century.

Thus around 1970 the military had advanced from caretaker regime to indefinite guardian, and a considerable sector of the leadership was highly scornful of Congress and electoral processes. Their position was confirmed, moreover, by the rapid economic growth that began more or less coincidentally with the tightening of the regime in 1968 and went on vigorously through the years of iron grip.

Yet the intellectuals, with support from the United States and Europe, were never reconciled to military authoritarianism; and from 1974 the prevalent tide was, albeit slowly and unsteadily, toward democratic government. President Geisel, who took office in March 1974, belonged to the more moderate or Castelista persuasion. Although he did not go so far as Médici in promising democracy at the outset, he sought to reduce the influence of the hard-liners to permit release of tensions, and to coopt moderate oppositionists. In November 1974 there were held the first significant elections since 1965. The opposition had considerable freedom to campaign, and it marked up large gains, winning most of the contested Senate seats and majorities in seven state assemblies. It was strong enough to block some government programs and require paying some attention to the elected bodies.[62] By January 1975, censors were withdrawn from newspaper premises, never to return. On the other hand, Geisel actually achieved more presidential power than any other Brazilian president since Vargas' Estado Novo,[63] and in 1977 he demonstrated the ambivalence of the regime by turning sharply although briefly back to hard-fisted rule.

In February a councilman in Pôrto Alegre, a stronghold of the opposition, ventured to criticize the absence of liberty and presence of torture in his state; he was deprived of political rights for ten years. In March-April the opposition Brazilian Democratic Movement (MDB) in the Congress thought that the Carter administration's civil rights advocacy permitted it to block changes proposed by the government in the judicial system—changes requiring a two-thirds vote.[64] The oppositionists demanded provisions for habeas corpus and guarantees of the independence of judges. But they overestimated U.S. influence, perhaps because for years they had been decrying the military government as an American creature. Geisel adjourned Congress and enacted the judicial reform on his own. To reduce the likelihood of future insubordination, he also decreed the "April package" to make elections less important and more predictable. The most important changes were the indirect election of state governors and a third of federal senators. In June an opposition leader was allowed to speak freely on radio and television for the first time since 1974. He naturally appealed for freedom and democracy, and almost as naturally was deprived of political rights.[65]

Yet by late 1977 opinion had shifted within the military sufficiently that many of the junior officers, who had been the bulwark of the hard line, were urging free elections, a new constitution, and human rights, as though echoing the Carter administration.[66] In September a leading general, Sýlvio Frota, led a minor insurgency against Geisel and Geisel's choice of successor, Gen. João Baptista Figueiredo. Frota preferred repression to conciliation, and his enforced departure cleared the way for more liberal policies.[67]

The year of change was 1978. Possibly the human rights policy of the Carter administration and its concern for democracy, after the relative indifference of the Nixon and Ford administrations, had its effect; possibly Geisel, as his term neared its end, wanted to leave a better taste and a sounder system behind, while he did not mind restricting the powers of his successor. In June, censorship of the press was practically ended, although it was retained over the theater, cinema, radio, and television. In September, Brazil was beset by strikes and slowdowns, still legally prohibited but tolerated for the first time in many years. In the November elections there was the first formal contest since 1964 for the presidency. The candidacy of the dissident general was only symbolic, but the opposition party polled a majority in legislative and local elections—an overwhelming majority in the more modern sectors of the country, especially São Paulo. The government kept a slim majority in the Senate and Chamber only by gerrymandering and by its hold in the more backward area—ironically those that had least profited from its economic policies. There remained only three military men in the cabinet, compared with the nine of ten years earlier.

Most significantly, the president renounced various special powers, and the charter of dictatorship, Institutional Act Five, was revoked at the end of 1978. The president could no longer suspend Congress, and could declare a state of siege for only five days without approval of Congress. He gave up authority to annul the mandate of elected officials or to deprive citizens of political rights. Habeas corpus was restored, the courts recovered some independence, and death and exile were eliminated as punishment for political crimes.

The Figueiredo administration has continued in the direction of abertura—the more remarkably because Figueiredo, was chief of the Brazilian equivalent of the CIA, the National Information Service, an organization much more politically powerful than the CIA, and was reputedly a rightist hard-liner. From convictions or the influence of the milieu, the new president seemed to change his personality. He shed his dark glasses and gruff, noncommunicative manners, met the press and public, and assumed folksy manners with an affable smile.[68] Castelo Branco had declared loftily, "I do not seek popularity," but Figueiredo became the first military president to act like a popularity-hungry politician. When designated for the presidency, he said, "I'm only taking this job because I have to. I don't think I'm the best one for it."[69]

Before his election, Figueiredo had spoken of "the transitory nature of the mandate [of the revolutionary government] and the purpose of leading Brazil to democracy,"[70] and afterward he promised to make Brazilians democrats even though he might have to put them in jail to convince them. In April censorship was removed from the theater. Strikes became frequent, and the right to strike was recognized—conditionally. In August 1979 political exiles were permitted to return with very few exceptions, and onetime leftists streamed back to Brazil from Europe and the United States, free to resume political activity. Political parties were allowed to organize freely, and several new opposition parties were set up—only the Communists were excluded from electoral politics, although they were otherwise free to organize and agitate. It was assumed that in the future governors and the entire Senate would again be directly elected. When the president was harassed in a riotous meeting, he did not angrily decree reprisals but commented, "This disturbance proves there really is democracy in Brazil."[71]

The government also became more populist in economic policies, as though more concerned with pleasing the masses, less completely focused on economic growth. Wages were raised, in compensation for inflation, relatively more for the least paid.[72] Antônio Delfim Netto, who became Figueiredo's planning minister, in August, under Geisel had favored

checking wages for the sake of growth; in 1979 he seemed more concerned about purchasing power of workers than controlling inflation. The
government extended a helping hand to dwellers in the shantytowns,
offering titles to lots and assistance in home building.[73] Sugar workers in
the Northeast have received new contracts promising the first real
improvement in at least 15 years.[74] As a result of such policies, Figueiredo
earned general approval; by one poll, two-thirds had good or very good
expectations of his government;[75] by another, 57 percent expressed
approval, while only 4 percent strongly disapproved.[76]

It did not appear that Figueiredo or other generals desired to
surrender power to political parties and contending politicians. The
president repeatedly made clear that abertura is to come on his terms and
according to his judgment, not that of his opponents; and he was
unwilling to consider direct election of the president.[77] As of 1980, the
presidency, as head of the military leadership and of the nation, retained
ample powers despite all concessions. The Congress had no control over
the budget, could not question ministers, and possessed very little
initiative. The progovernment party held a majority, and official proposals were automatically enacted unless rejected by Congress within 45
days—which never happened. The Congress looked humbly to the
president for orders and was happy that he received their leaders every
few weeks.[78] There was nothing—except perhaps the temper of the
country—to prevent the president from turning backward any day to
authoritarian rule. The police and security forces could be turned loose at
any time.

It seemed that the generals desired democracy because of the general
sense of values and the need for legitimacy, but they wanted democratic
institutions that would not seriously interfere with their running the
country. To some extent, this means resorting to gimmicks, such as
indirect elections, and permitting a free press as an outlet for dissent while
restricting television, a more effective mass medium. It also means some
appropriation of the value and ideas of democracy. Thus, Figueiredo has
spoken of an undefined "relative democracy" in the military-dominated
government. According to an army commander:

> The democracy we foresee is not necessarily neglectful, tepid, crawling,
> inert, and defenseless, trembling at prefabricated slogans based on
> liberty and human rights. The traffickers of this line forget that liberty
> and rights emanate from the state. The state grants these privileges to
> man and therefore cannot be subordinated to these prerogatives lest it
> fall prey to anarchy.[79]

It has also been possible to give the government credit for much more
democracy than meets the eye. In the view of one writer, "We will not say

[in 1976] that Brazilian democracy is the most brilliant, but we can affirm that it is among the most perfect in the world. . . . Legislative, executive, and judicial powers are independent and mutually harmonious."[80]

But the authoritarian government can hardly be legitimized by calling it relatively or among the most perfectly democratic, and insubstantial concessions nourish the clamor for more solid ones. If the government could build a fence around the country, it could presumably legitimate itself adequately on the basis that it effectively holds power, is well organized to use it, and has fairly rational ways of selection of leadership. But Brazil lives in an environment largely made by the advanced industrial states led by the United States. Close links with the industrial world, particularly the United States, with their emphasis on free choice and individualism as well as democracy, make difficult the institutionalization of authoritarianism.[81] The countries that dominate the world of Brazil and have achieved economic levels to which Brazil aspires are democratic, that is, have free and meaningful elections, civil rights, independent courts, freedom of press and speech, and the accompanying institutions that have come to be accepted as normal in civilized governments. The only real rival of the democratic ideology in the modern world is Marxism-Leninism, which is completely unacceptable to a large majority of influential Brazilians.

Brazil faces the same problem as other authoritarian and semiauthoritarian governments of Latin America. In this region, there are virtually no overtly prodictatorial parties; and dictatorships, even very stiff ones, such as those of the Somozas in Nicaragua and Stroessner in Paraguay, have cloaked themselves in democratic forms. There is no other acceptable legitimation. Few Brazilians, at least among the articulate sectors, seem to doubt that the government ought to be responsible to the people and representative of them. Pride virtually requires this; to accept anything less is to accept inferiority. Why should we not be capable of democracy like the United States? Are we not advanced enough to have a modern government? Hence the desirability of abertura seems to be completely accepted, and it is understood to be irreversible. Especially the richest parts of Brazil, which might have most to lose from populist policies and which have benefited materially most from the present government, are the most democratic and most skeptical of the military-dominated government. Big business may have its reservations, but outwardly it subscribes fully to democratization.[82] Few intellectuals back the regime.

This has large practical consequences. The government must make concessions to secure support, but gratitude is ephemeral, and indifference or hostility returns; thus in 1980 most of the goodwill of 1979 evaporated as democratization seemed to stagnate. The ideology of anti-Communism is worn out as justification for repression or arbitrary action. Third World socialist-anti-imperialist ideology is excluded because of the breadth and depth of bonds with the democratic-capitalist world. But unless the government can justify.itself as answering to some ideal, it faces probably growing indifference if not hostility. It becomes taken for granted that opposition to it is proper and to be supported in strikes or protest movements of any nature. Deputies of the progovernment party (Social Democratic Party), although they obediently vote for government measures, are openly critical, as seems to be dictated by self-respect.

Yet there is no indication that a democratic system in Brazil is likely to be more successful than that of the 1960s. The leaders surviving from pre-1964 politics—Brizola, Arraes, Tancredo Neves, and so forth—present no credible alternative; and little new leadership has arisen. If class differences have been deepened, as seems generally agreed, the prospects are even poorer now than they were 20 years ago. Where the social gulf is so great, it is naive to expect respect for a democratic constitutional order to bridge it and provide a sound foundation for the state of the whole people. Democracy would probably be less manageable now than it was a generation ago because the electorate has been hugely enlarged and the more volatile cities have overwhelmed the more conservative countryside.

Brazilian radicals and conservatives admire U.S. democratic institutions for different and partly conflicting reasons: the former for freedom, populism, and egalitarianism; the latter for orderly process, rule of law and constitutionalism—neither sector perhaps possessing much real understanding of the complex system.[83] Correspondingly, the former reject, the latter accept the U.S. economic presence.

The military-dominated government thus finds itself impelled to surrender power to democratically chosen authorities, although the threat of instability, corruption, and radicalism is obvious; and there is no party that the generals could consider as qualified to run the country as they themselves. They have, after all, shown a certain practical capacity, with a highly qualified and generally dedicated service, technocrats and administrators for whom authoritarian government means public order and an opportunity to do their work; and the government has not gone stale but has shown continuing dynamism and innovativeness. But, in their inability to employ totalitarian methods, or even to organize the country politically in the Mexican fashion, they have come up against the great moral problem of creating faith in their leadership.

The influence of the United States has here operated to push a friendly state in morally desirable but operationally difficult directions. For the most part, this influence has been broad and elemental, but at the same time the U.S. government has, at least since 1977 as before 1969, discreetly and usually quietly encouraged democratization. This is dictated by its own ideology, despite the fact that a Brazil in which the masses were really called upon to decide issues would in all probability turn against the United States, its influence, and its economic stake if not strategic interests.

NOTES

1. Frank D. McCann, Jr., *The Brazilian-American Alliance 1937-1945* (Princeton: Princeton University Press, 1973). p. 247.
2. Data of Roper Public Opinion Research Center.
3. Data of American embassy in Brasília.
4. *Visão*, June 25, 1979, p. 72.
5. Thomas E. Weil et al., *Area Handbook for Brazil* (Washington, D.C.: American University Press, 1975), p. 273.
6. U.S., Congress, House, Committee on International Relations, *Report of Staff Survey Team on U.S. Information and Cultural Program*, March 1979, pp. 13–14.
7. U.S., Congress, House, Committee on Government Operations, *Embassy Operations in Rio de Janeiro*, p. 35.
8. *Estado de São Paulo*, July 1, 1979, p. 21.
9. R. A. Amaral Vieira, *Intervencionismo e autoritarismo no Brasil* (São Paulo: Difel, 1975), p. 200.
10. F. H. Cardoso, "Associated Dependent Development," in *Authoritarian Brazil*, ed. Alfred Stepan (New Haven: Yale University Press, 1973), p. 144.
11. *Estado de São Paulo*, July 1, 1979, p. 22.
12. Richard J. Barnet and Ronald Muller, *Global Reach: The Power of the Multinational Corporations* (New York: Simon and Schuster, 1974), p. 145.
13. Fernando Pedreira, *Brasil político* (São Paulo: Difel, 1975), p. 57.
14. E. Blum, "The Time-Life Caper: Brazil's Yankee Network," *Nation*, May 29, 1967, p. 681.
15. Genival Rabelo, *O capital estrangeiro na imprensa brasileira* (Rio de Janeiro: Civilização Brasileira, 1966), p. 67.
16. Weil, *Handbook*, p. 278.
17. Gabriel C. Galache, *Brasil, processo e integração* (São Paulo: Editora Loyola, 1977), p. 55.
18. Nelson Werneck Sodré, *Síntese de historia da cultura brasileira* (Rio de Janeiro: Editora Civilização Brasileira, 1970), pp. 82–83.
19. Weil et al., *Handbook*, p. 203.
20. As published weekly by *Veja*.
21. Sodré, *Síntese*, p. 123.
22. *Anuario Estatístico do Brasil 1978* (Rio de Janeiro: IBGE, 1978), p. 641.
23. *Statistical Yearbook*, UNESCO 1977, p. 502.
24. Carlos Guilherme Mota, *Ideologia de cultura brasileira* (São Paulo: Atica, 1977), p. 263.
25. *Visão*, December 20, 1976, p. 79.
26. Moniz Bandeira, *Presença dos Estados Unidos no Brasil* (Rio de Janeiro: Editora Civilização Brasileira, 1973), p. 394.
27. Charles Wagley, *An Introduction to Brazil*, rev. ed. (New York: Columbia University Press, 1971), p. 119.

28. Jan K. Black, *United States Penetration of Brazil* (Philadelphia: University of Pennsylvania Press, 1977), pp. 260–61.

29. *Visão*, June 25, 1979, p. 76.

30. Sodré, *Síntese*, pp. 73, 84, 91.

31. *Isto É*, July 27, 1977, pp. 38–39.

32. Claudio de Araujo Lima, *Imperialismo y angustia* (Buenos Aires: Editora Corjoacán, 1962), p. 67.

33. Joseph A. Page, *The Revolution that Never Was: Northeast Brazil 1955–1964* (New York: Grossman, 1972), p. 235.

34. Dom Bonafede, "Blunder in Brazil: Washington Backs the Pooh Bahs," *Nation*, May 26, 1969, p. 664.

35. Augusto Boal, *A deliciosa e sangrenta aventura latina de Jane Spitfire* (Rio de Janeiro: Editora Codecri, 1977), p. 277.

36. Pedreira, *Brasil político*, p. 58.

37. Bonafede, "Blunder in Brazil," p. 665.

38. Robert O. Myhr, "Student Activism and Development," in *Contemporary Brazil: Issues in Economic and Political Development*, ed. Jon H. Rosenbaum (New York: Praeger, 1972), p. 353.

39. *Newsweek*, November 14, 1966, p. 56.

40. Sodré, *Síntese*, pp. 82, 84.

41. *Visão*, January 26, 1976, p. 35.

42. *Wall Street Journal*, April 19, 1971, p. 14.

43. *Jornal do Brasil*, July 12, 1980, p. 9.

44. Sodré, *Síntese*, p. 78.

45. Boal, *A aventura*, p. 8.

46. Sodré, *Síntese*, pp. 114–17.

47. *Visão*, June 25, 1979, p. 72.

48. Roger W. Fontaine, *Brazil and the United States: Toward a Maturing Relationship* (Washington, D.C.: American Enterprise Institute, 1974), pp. 43–46.

49. Data from Roper Public Opinion Research Center.

50. *Isto É*, March 23, 1977, p. 10.

51. Bruce Lamounier, "The U.S. and Brazil in the Mirrors of Time," *Isto É*, July 1976, p. 40.

52. Alfredo Palermo, *Estudo de problemas brasileiras* (São Paulo: Livros Irradiantes, 1971), p. 142.

53. *New York Times*, June 5, 1978, p. A-10; Pedreira, *Brasil político*, p. 19.

54. *Estado de São Paulo*, July 1, 1979, p. 11.

55. *Federalist Papers*.

56. Lawrence S. Graham, *Civil Service Reform in Brazil: Principle versus Practice* (Austin, Tex.: University of Texas Press, 1968), pp. 31, 37, 38.

57. *Isto É*, July 20, 1977, p. 12.

58. *New York Times*, December 13, 1968, p. D-30.

59. *New York Times*, October 8, 1969, p. 16.

60. *New York Times*, March 11, 1970, p. 2.

61. *New York Times*, April 4, 1973, p. 8.

62. Tad Szulc, "Letter from Brasilia," *New Yorker*, March 10, 1975, p. 73.

63. Walder de Goes, *O governo do General Geisel* (Rio de Janeiro: Editora Nova Fronteira, 1978), p. 65.

64. Álvaro Valle, *As novas estructuras políticas brasileiras* (Rio de Janeiro: Nordica, 1977), pp. 112–13.

65. Peter Flynn, *Brazil: A Political Analysis* (Boulder, Colo.: Westview Press, 1978), p. 512.

66. T. Murphy, "Twilight of the Brazilian Military," *Contemporary Review* 234 (January 1979):21.

67. *Isto É*, October 19, 1977, p. 4.

68. *Veja*, July 25, 1979, p. 20.

69. *New York Times*, March 16, 1979, p. A-3.

70. *Veja*, September 10, 1978, p. 30.

71. *Christian Science Monitor*, December 31, 1979, p. 24.

72. *Veja*, September 5, 1979, p. 92.

73. *New York Times*, October 22, 1979, p. 1.

74. *New York Times*, October 13, 1979, p. 8.

75. *Der Spiegel*, August 27, 1979, p. 152.

76. *Veja*, October 3, 1979, p. 21.

77. *Veja*, November 14, 1979, p. 19.

78. *Veja*, May 16, 1979, p. 20.

79. Norman Gall, "The Rise of Brazil," *Commentary* 63 (January 1977): p. 52.

80. Benedicto de Andrade, *Organização política e social do Brasil* (São Paulo: Atlas, 1976), pp. 123-24.

81. As observed by Juan J. Linz, "The Future of an Authoritarian System," in *Authoritarian Brazil*, ed. Alfred Stepan (New Haven: Yale University Press, 1973), pp. 252-53.

82. *Business Week*, November 19, 1979, p. 63.

83. As observed by Pedreira, *Brasil político*, p. 119.

CONCLUSIONS

Perhaps the strongest impression that may emerge from this study of U.S. influence on Brazil is the excessive complexity of the subject. The manifold aspects of interaction between the two great states are beyond our powers to sort out, partly because of the limits of our knowledge— what has the American cultural presence meant to the military hierarchy?—and because of complexity inherent where all factors in Brazilian and U.S. thinking might properly be brought into consideration. There are many actors and many channels, and nowhere is it possible unequivocally to assess actions on one side in terms of desires on the other. It would be difficult to point to any actions of Brazil in recent years taken clearly because of U.S. desires, while the economic and cultural penetration of Brazil may be treated either as an indication or a source of influence.

It has seldom been clear even what U.S. purposes really were, as strategic, economic, political, and ideological interests have sometimes countered, sometimes reinforced one another. The United States has usually paid little attention to Latin America except when trouble seemed to loom, and concerns have risen and fallen. Worry that the Brazilian Northeast might serve as bridgehead for extrahemispheric military aggression no longer seem very relevant, although Pentagon planners doubtless keep it on file. The nightmare of peasant leagues turning the *sertão* into a bigger version of Castro's Sierra Madre has likewise faded; and recent American presidents have not been calling for bulletins on the progress of development programs there, although human misery is approximately what it was in Kennedy's time. The whole problem of economic aid for Brazil has fallen by the way, as Brazil has expanded industrially; the new preoccupation is Brazil's excessive foreign debt.

163

Worry that Brazil may contribute to the spread of nuclear weaponry has not entirely disappeared, but it is mostly forgotten in preoccupation with the Near East and South Asia.

Motives in foreign policy are unclear if not contradictory. This is most obvious in regard to such matters as trade negotiations, in which a parochial interest—to restrict Brazilian export of shoes, for example—clashed with broader interests in Brazilian prosperity and goodwill. Decision makers have usually acted in ignorance of long-term consequences, if not in indifference—understandably, because they are not held responsible for long-term consequences.

American motives are usually expressed idealistically, as in the nuclear controversy, but the suspicion is never distant that idealism covers less exalted purposes, chiefly commercial gain. Ideals clearly become more compelling when reinforced by self-interest, but it may be unfair to insist that the grosser reason is the real one. Thus in the nuclear episode it was doubtless to the commerical advantage of the United States that Brazil should desist from the deal with Germany and buy enriched uranium on American terms, but it is not credible that this dominated Carter's thinking, which differed from that of Ford and Kissinger in idealism, not sensitivity to business interests. Recently the Congress has seemed (as in the case of India) prepared to sacrifice both commerical and strategic considerations to uphold principles of nonproliferation. The issue is basic in any judgment of the morality of U.S. actions in Brazil, or Latin America, or the whole Third World: does the United States really seek to promote a more just and progressive or egalitarian order, as has been often claimed and as many Americans obviously heartily desire, or does it back small, self-seeking privileged classes whose material interests are parallel to those of U.S. investors and who accept U.S. predominance as protection against the cheated masses? Does the United States favor the masses, in accord with democratic tenets, or the classes, with whom Americans most easily associate and do business? Does the United States genuinely stand for populist politics, when these are inevitably more or less hostile to business interests, including American? Or does it prefer dictatorial regimes that are more reliably anti-Communist and probably hospitable to foreign corporations?[1]

In practice, of course, the United States does both, with varying degrees of enthusiasm; and it may contribute to the pendular swings between more democratic and more dictatorial regimes. It holds the conviction that popular government is a good thing, and is inclined to promote it when it is absent, but when Latin American parties become sufficiently democratic to appeal to mass discontents, the United States may become apprehensive and shift emphasis to the maintenance of order. For such reasons, the United States supported the democratic movement in Chilean politics prior to Allende and then supported the movement to remove Allende at the risk of military dictatorship. It likewise favored the establishment of the Brazilian constitutional government in 1946 and the overthrow of that government when it turned radical in 1964. But the uncertainty of relations between intentions and results also clouds judgment of influence. The keen desire of Washington to see the end of the Allende government does not tell us whether it really had much to do with bringing it about; longing to see the sun rise does not raise it.

Both the ways in which the United States may exert influence and the difficulties of a realistic assessment are well illustrated by the most controversial matter ever to arise in U.S.-Brazilian relations, the coup of March 31, 1964. It is hardly to be supposed that the coup would have been impossible without U.S. approval and support—the chief motive of the generals was one with which the United States had nothing to do, the threat to discipline in the armed forces, and there have been many coups in Latin America of which the United States has disapproved. But in many ways the United States, unknowingly for the most part, helped to set the stage. A basic fact of the background was the long-term friendship of the United States and Brazil, since the beginning of Brazilian nationhood, and the importance of the United States as political model, the inspiration of Brazilian republican institutions. As it became evident that the United States was unhappy with the government of President João Goulart, American sentiments helped to legitimize military intervention. More operative was the close relationship that had been established between U.S. and Brazilian armies in the alliance in World War II, the nexus of officer training in the United States, supply of American equipment, and relevant instruction. Especially significant was the establishment of the Escola Superior de Guerra in imitation of the American National War College. This institution was intended to improve the training of higher officers; no one in 1948 could guess that it would become the intellectual center of anti-Communism and pro-U.S. sentiment in the face of a government turning away from the United States.

Economic relations also contributed. The fact that Brazil badly needed credits from American sources or international agencies attuned to American policy reduced the freedom of Brazil to embark on a socialistic-nationalistic course in the early 1960s. So did the fact that the United States took the biggest share of Brazilian coffee and was the leading supplier by a wide margin of Brazilian imports. There was no need for any threat of embargo; as it came to seem that Brazil might face a choice of directions in 1964, it was evidently reckless to go strongly counter to trade patterns. Another factor was the foreign sector of the economy. Foreign capital, about half North American, dominated the most modern and dynamic sectors of Brazilian industry. The effect, however, was ambivalent. On the one hand, a considerable fraction of the Brazilian economic elite was associated with the American system. On the other hand, the foreign presence was a major irritant and best target of the leftists and nationalists.

The atmosphere was propitious for the coup because a majority of Brazilians, an overwhelming majority of the middle classes, accepted the general thesis of the cold war, the evil of Communism, and the American mission of combatting it. The Brazilian press was filled with news from U.S. sources, and one may assume that its attitudes were shaped to some extent by advertisers, multinational or Brazilian. There were many books of U.S. authorship, magazines were filled with materials from the United States, as were radio and television programs, and so forth—all reflecting not the views of the U.S. government but those of the American intellectual community. The situation would have been different if the question of a coup had arisen in 1969 or 1970 when anti-Communism was widely discredited among opinion leaders in the United States and Brazil. At least, the generals might have hesitated longer.

Of course, the U.S. government also tried concretely to determine the political outcome. Brazil had come to count on a fair amount of economic aid; when the United States began holding back on helping the Goulart government, outwardly because of incompetence, while giving aid (in small amounts) to anti-Goulart governors, it was more than a hint that the United States would welcome a change and would be more forthcoming to a less radical government. Less legitimately, the CIA gave some training and financial backing for anti-Communist or anti-Goulart organizations, as though in a preplay for the destabilization of the Allende government. There is no evidence of concrete participation by American embassy officials in the scheming of the generals prior to the coup, but the strong personalities of the American Ambassador Lincoln Gordon and his military attache, Col. Vernon Walters, close friend for many years of Humberto Castelo Branco, army chief of staff and first military president, certainly played their part. It was also significant that after the assassination of President Kennedy the Johnson administration shifted emphasis from support for democracy in Latin America to search for anti-Communist allies. Finally, Washington made it clear, shortly before the coup, that in case of conflict it would be prepared to help the right side. This reduced the risks of failure for the generals, who had been somewhat inhibited by the inflated estimates of the strength of the left.

In all probability, however, the concrete measures were much less important for the success of the coup than the background of relations and attitudes. Those around Goulart were aware of the desires of the State Department and of at least some of the activities of the administration, but they were not impressed. Knowledge and suspicions of foreign intervention exacerbated the nationalists, and Washington could at best encourage or discourage Brazilian groups. No one has seriously contended that the generals were coerced or bribed into taking power. The CIA might help anti-Communist organizations, but it could not have persuaded hundreds of thousands of women to get out pans to drum in a "March with God for Family" unless there had been deep and genuine fear of Communism. It may be noted, moreover, that direct interventionism, of doubtful efficacy in the short run, was costly in the long run, as Brazilian public opinion tended to regard the military government as a creation of the United States and to blame the United States for its faults. It was not much help that the U.S. purpose had not been to put Brazil under military rule, only to get rid of what was believed to be a dangerous movement and return the country to more reliable civilian leaders.

In other controversies since 1967 the U.S. government has had only middling success. In regard to instant coffee and territorial waters, the Brazilians fairly well had their way. In regard to shoes and other exports, the Brazilians were minimally penalized, but they finally yielded by removing most export incentives. Presumably they felt this necessary because the American administration was restricted by Congress. It would seem that Brazil has enjoyed greater bargaining in such controversies because: first, the general atmosphere has called for industrial states to make concessions to developing instead of vice versa; second, Brazil buys more from the United States than it sells; third, the issues have been important for Brazil, secondary for the United States; and fourth, the Brazilian government is more monolithic than the American.

In the nuclear issue, the Carter administration was more exercised, but it failed to assess its lack of leverage and to perceive that it would become a point of honor for Brazil, to a lesser extent for West Germany, not to be coerced. Washington also failed to anticipate that both Brazil and Germany would take a cynical view of its motives. The effect was negative, increased determination of Brazil to proceed; only after the United States backed away and dropped the subject could Brazilian opposition to the nuclear program take shape. The pressure for better observance of human rights was also resented as intrusive but it was more successful because of the legitimacy of its purpose and because it corresponded to the aspirations of very many Brazilians.

It thus seems clear that U.S. leverage on specific issues is very limited, unless this country is prepared to make a much larger economic or political investment in swaying or coercing Brazil than it has made in the past. And while diplomatic leverage is slight, the most effective U.S. influence on Brazil is diffuse and unplanned, the general impact of one society, economy, and culture on another. Brazil is involved with the economic and trading system in which the United States is the leading component, and its economic growth is powered by the multinational corporations, in which the United States has the largest share. Even if the multinationals are distrusted and the world trading is regarded as unfair, they are in effect restraints on Brazilian policies. Cataclysmic forces would be necessary to break radically with them. At the same time, Brazil is culturally and informationally bound to the United States, which plays an even larger role in the world market of ideas than in the world industrial economy.

Economic influence is closely linked to political, and both have shrunk markedly and almost unremittingly since the high tide around 1965. There are many reasons deriving from changes in Brazil, in the United States, and in the world. The mentality of the coup of 1964 and those eager to ally themselves with the United States in an anti-Communist battle could not last long, and the pro-American leadership moved from the center of the scene. The cold war atmosphere eased or changed, and Brazil tended to see itself less as a partner in the East-West struggle, more as a leading power in the North-South confrontation. Brazil shared the growing independence and assertiveness of the rest of Latin America and the Third World.

More broadly, the inequality central to influence has substantially decreased. Although Brazilian per capita GNP is still far inferior to that of the United States, the gap has been narrowed enough that Brazilians have shed some of their inferiority complex and feeling of dependence. The U.S. military and economic aid program has disappeared, and Brazil gets its loans on a commercial basis. Brazil sees itself as more of a power in its own right; having surpassed Argentina industrially, it has a sphere of influence of sorts in South America and can reasonably enjoy visions of becoming one of the world greats within a generation. On the other side of the balance, the U.S. economy has performed relatively poorly; the sad condition of Detroit and the weakening of U.S. clout in Brazil are facets of one big problem.

There is some compensation. If the United States is less of a prominent domineering presence, it is less resented, and as official influence ebbs, unofficial influence is less rejected. It appears that the United States is no longer considered synonymous with foreign corporations; Brazilians flail multinationals in general, spreading the blame over Europeans and Japanese as well as Americans. As there is less fear of U.S. domination, less is heard of the evils of "cultural imperialism." Americanization is cumulative, and it goes forward even though the relative weight of the United States diminishes. However, it tends increasingly to merge into general modernization, as Europe regains some of its former cultural force and Japan enters the scene as a leading technological power. In one extremely important area U.S. influence has remained relatively strong; namely in adherence to the democratic ideology, the demand for government by popular choice, with free elections, effective legislative bodies, civil rights, and all that these imply. Democratic values come not only from the United States, of course; but the United States is the most emphatically democratic of the major powers and it is the preeminent political model. As a result, the military government has never been able—if it really so desired—to legitimize itself as an authoritarian state, corporatist, dictatorial, or simply military; and the difficulty of so doing has only increased in recent years. Even here it is probable, however, that the model is increasingly that of the democratic industrial states in general.

In this situation, the old special relation has lost its force, probably irretrievably. Recent American administrations have recognized this reality (except for the efforts early in the Carter administration to press the nuclear and human rights issues) by adopting a bland, low-profile approach. In this diplomacy, less is better; and controversy has been minimized mostly by not pressing the Brazilians where there are no ready means of pressure. In effect, there is little positive U.S. policy toward Brazil. Differences of views and priorities are accepted calmly; if the Brazilians do not care to join the United States in checking grain shipments to the Soviet Union or boycotting the Olympics, there is nothing to be done or said about it. Diplomacy is reduced to consultations over different matters of mutual interest. Recently the agenda included: double-taxation of citizens, promotion of U.S. exports at a center in São Paulo, Brazilian barriers to the import of U.S. planes, the International Cocoa Agreement, changes in the International Coffee Agreement, U.S. participation in the International Sugar Agreement, consultations on energy problems, cooperation in relations with the Near East and Africa, the North-South dialogue, and Law of Sea negotiations.[2]

Some of these matters lose relevance, and new ones are perpetually arising. It seems probable that U.S. leverage will continue to decline, as the factors tending to diminish it are not likely soon to be reversed. Whether relations between the two countries become more acerbic or more cordial depends upon many unpredictable trends, such as the political tendencies of the two countries. Economic developments will also be determinant: if Brazil fully enters the industrial world, prospects for partnership will be much better than if greater hardships and regression lead to bitterness and extremism, perhaps to a determination to seek improvement in ways hostile to the United States.

Through minor differences, however, it seems likely that relations between the United States and Brazil will continue to be basically cooperative, and the United States will continue to have some mild influence over Brazilian policies and development. Brazil is important to the United States both economically and politically as a leading Latin American and Third World power and, it is hoped, a focus of regional stability. The fundamental security interests of the two powers coincide. For Brazil, the United States is and will probably long continue to be the most important single foreign power and axis of its international relations. There is a background of goodwill on both sides. There has seemed to be an enduring desire in the State Department not to antagonize Brazil; on the other side, there is in Brazil more pro- and less anti-U.S. feeling than in most countries of the world. It is characteristic that in Brasília the American embassy occupies the place of honor and convenience; the Soviet is far down the line. In past years, many students and intellectuals have been angered by U.S. policies in Vietnam, Chile, and Cuba; now they can better denounce the Soviet invasion of Afghanistan. Latin American intellectuals have long been convinced that anything desired by the United States was for purposes of domination; and Brazilians, too have been critical. They will to some extent certainly continue to be so because of the fundamental irritant of inequality in U.S.-Brazilian relations. But as 60 years ago, Brazil is closer to, or less alienated from the United States than is much of Spanish America. There is still some sense of the "customary South American xenophobia with regard to Brazil."[3] As it becomes easier—as seems probable—for Brazilians to feel themselves equal to the United States, relations with Brazil should take on more of the character of relations with mature industrial nations like Canada or Japan, and what seemed a situation of one-sided influence may mature into unburdened mutuality.

NOTES

1. As contended by many writers, such as Jan K. Black, *United States Penetration of Brazil* (Philadelphia: University of Pennsylvania Press, 1977), p. xiii.

2. Speech by Claus W. Ruser, Director of Office of East Coast Affairs, Bureau of Inter-American Affairs, Department of State, before Brazilian-American Chamber of Commerce, March 30, 1979.

3. *Veja*, November 7, 1979, p. 41.

BIBLIOGRAPHY

Arruda, Marcos, Herbet de Souza, and Carlos Afonso. *Multinational Corporations and Brazil*. Toronto: Latin American Research Unit, 1975.

Bandeira, Moniz. *Presença dos Estados Unidos no Brasil*. Rio de Janeiro: Editora Civilização Brasileira, 1973.

Black, Jan K. *United States Penetration of Brazil*. Philadelphia: University of Pennsylvania Press, 1977.

Brown, Peter G., and Douglas MacLean, eds. *Human Rights and U.S. Foreign Policy: Principles and Applications*. Lexington, Mass.: Lexington Books, 1979.

Burns, E. Bradford. *Nationalism in Brazil: An Historical Survey*. New York: Praeger, 1968.

Chilcote, Ronald H. *The Brazilian Communist Party: Conflict and Integration 1922-1972*. New York: Oxford University Press, 1974.

D'Adesky, Serge. "Brazil's Rise to Dominance in Latin America." *Fletcher Forum* 3 (Summer 1979):46-65.

de Goes, Walder. *O governo do General Geisel*. Rio de Janeiro: Editora Nova Fronteira, 1978.

Dulles, John W. F. *Castelo Branco: The Making of a Brazilian President*. College Station, Tex.: Texas A & M University Press, 1978.

————. *Unrest in Brazil*. Austin, Tex.: University of Texas Press, 1970.

Egan, Joseph R., and Shem Arungu-Olende. "Nuclear Power for the Third World." *Technology Review* 82 (March 1980):47-58.

Evans, Peter. *Dependent Development: The Alliance of Multinational, State, and Local Capital in Brazil*. Princeton: Princeton University Press, 1979.

Fiechter, Georges-André. *Le régime modernisateur du Brésil 1964-1972*. Leiden: Sijthoff, 1972.

Flynn, Peter. *Brazil: A Political Analysis*. Boulder, Colo.: Westview Press, 1978.

Fontaine, Roger W. *Brazil and the United States: Toward a Maturing Relationship*. Washington, D.C.: American Enterprise Institute, 1974.

————. "The End of a Beautiful Relationship." *Foreign Policy* 28 (Fall 1977): 166-74.

Frank, André Gunder. *Capitalism and Underdevelopment in Latin America: Historical Studies of Chile and Brazil*. New York: Monthly Review Press, 1967.

Gall, Norman. "Atoms for Brazil, Danger for All," *Foreign Policy* 23, (Summer 1976):44-77.

————. "The Rise of Brazil." *Commentary* 63 (January 1977).

Gugliamelli, Juan E. *Argentina, Brasil y la bomba atómica*. Buenos Aires: Tierra Nueva, 1976.

Gurgel, José Alfredo Amaral. *Segurança e democracia: uma reflexão política*. Rio de Janeiro: Livraria José Olympio, 1975.

Hewlett, Sylvia Ann. *The Cruel Dilemma of Development: Twentieth Century Brazil*. New York: Basic Books, 1980.

Hovey, Harold A. *United States Military Assistance*. New York: Praeger, 1965.

Jaguaribe, Hélio. Brasil: *Crise e alternativas*. Rio de Janeiro: Zahar Editore, 1974.

Kamenka, Eugene, and Alice Erh-Soon Tay, eds. *Human Rights*. New York: St. Martin's Press, 1978.

Keith, Henry H., and Robert A. Hayes. *Perspectives on Armed Politics in Brazil*. Tempe, Ariz.: Arizona State University Press, 1976.

Kommers, Donald B., and Gilbert D. Loescher. *Human Rights and American Foreign Policy*. Notre Dame, Ind.: University of Notre Dame Press, 1979.

McCann, Frank D., Jr. *The Brazilian-American Alliance 1937-1945*. Princeton: Princeton University Press, 1973.

Martins, Carlos Estevam. *Capitalismo do estado e modelo político no Brasil*. Rio de Janeiro: Ediciones de Braal, 1977.

Morris, Michael. *International Politics and the Sea: The Case of Brazil*. Boulder, Colo.: Westview Press, 1979.

Page, Joseph A. *The Revolution That Never Was: Northeast Brazil 1955-1964*. New York: Grossman, 1972.

Parker, Phyllis R. *Brazil and the Quiet Intervention, 1964*. Austin, Tex.: University of Texas Press, 1979.

Pedreira, Fernando. *Brasil político 1964-1975*. São Paulo: Difel, 1975.

Perry, William. *Contemporary Brazilian Foreign Policy*. Beverly Hills, Calif.: Sage Publications, 1976.

Rabelo, Genival. *O capital estrangeiro na imprensa brasileira*. Rio de Janeiro: Editora Civilização Brasileira, 1966.

Robcock, Stefan H. *Brazil: A Study in Development Progress*. Lexington, Mass.: D.C. Heath, 1975.

Roett, Riordan. *The Politics of Foreign Aid in the Brazilian Northeast*. Nashville, Tenn.: Vanderbilt University Press, 1972.

———. ed. *Brazil in the Seventies*. Washington, D.C.: American Enterprise Institute, 1976.

———. *Brazil in the Sixties*. Nashville, Tenn.: Vanderbilt University Press, 1972.

Rojas, Robinson. *Estados Unidos en Brasil*. Santiago: Prensa Latinoamericana, 1965.

Rosenbaum, Jon R., ed. *Contemporary Brazil: Issues in Economic and Political Development*. New York: Praeger, 1972.

Schneider, Ronald M. *Brazil: Foreign Relations of a Future World Power*. Boulder, Colo.: Westview Press, 1977.

———. *The Political System of Brazil: Emergence of a "Modernizing Authoritarian Regime."* New York: Columbia University Press, 1971.

Selcher, Wayne A. *Brazil's Multilateral Relations Between First and Third Worlds*. Boulder, Colo.: Westview Press, 1978.

Skidmore, Thomas. *Politics in Brazil: An Experiment in Democracy 1930-1964*. New York: Oxford University Press, 1967.

Sodré, Nelson Werneck. *Síntese de historia da cultura Brasileira*. Rio de Janeiro: Editora Civilização Brasileira, 1970.

Stepan, Alfred. *The Military in Politics: Changing Patterns in Brazil*. Princeton: Princeton University Press, 1971.

———. ed. *Authoritarian Brazil*. New Haven: Yale University Press, 1973.

Tullis, F. La Mond. *Modernization in Brazil*. Provo, Utah: Brigham Young University Press, 1973.

Tuthill, John W. "Operation Topsy." *Foreign Policy* 8 (Fall 1972):62–85.

Valle, Álvaro, *As novas estructuras políticas brasileiras*. Rio de Janeiro: Nordica, 1977.

Vieira, R. A. Amaral. *Intervencionismo e autoritarismo no Brasil*. São Paulo: Difel, 1975.

von Doellinger, Carlos, and Leonardo C. Calvacanti. *Empresas multinacionais na industria brasileira*. Rio de Janeiro: IPEA/INPES, 1975.

Wagley, Charles. *An Introduction to Brazil*, rev. ed. New York: Columbia University Press, 1971.

Walters, Vernon A. *Silent Missions*. Garden City, N.Y.: Doubleday, 1978.

INDEX

174

ABOUT THE AUTHOR

Robert Wesson is professor of political science at the University of California, Santa Barbara, and senior research fellow of the Hoover Institution, Stanford University.

Dr. Wesson received his B.A. from the University of Arizona, an M.A. from the Fletcher School of Law and Diplomacy, and a Ph.D. from Columbia University. He has spent many years in various countries of Latin America, including Brazil. His publications include *The Imperial Order, Foreign Policy for a New Age, State Systems*, and *Modern Governments: Three Worlds of Politics*.